Advance Praise for
Ghostriders 1976-1995

"I am honored to provide the introduction to William Walter's second deep dive into the combat history of the USAF side-firing gunships.

"My involvement has lasted over four decades. Beginning in the 16th Special Operations Squadron, 8th Tactical Fighter Wing, Ubon, Thailand in 1970 as a Pilot Instructor, Flight Examiner, and Maintenance Officer. Over the years, I have continued to support a weapon system that continues to play a significant role in our National Security and Joint Forces mission.

"The poem 'Invictus' (1875) by William Ernest Henley excerpts: 'Out of the night that covers me; My head is blooded but unbowed. Beyond this place of wrath and tears. Finds and shall find me unafraid. I am the master of my fate. I am the captain of my soul.'

"As you read the history, 1976–1995, I believe you will see the relevance of the above. It is an exacting and personal history of heroism, dedication, and loss.

"Beginning in 1968, the value of the Gunship was firmly established as a viable and deadly weapon of war. This is well documented in William Walter's *Ghostriders 1968–1975*. Employment limitations such as AAA threat, altitude, and day operations were established in deadly combat. Over the years, continued improvement of its unique capabilities often have been disrupted by changes in DOD command structure, targeting by budget cutters and tasking by unknowledgeable mission planners.

"'People are more valuable than hardware' is a SOF tenet. Incredible aircrews, maintainers, armorers, and logisticians have magically endured over virtually every situation thrown at them.

"What is next? I quote Thomas Wolfe's *The Right Stuff*. 'When the showdown comes, and the showdown always comes—not all the wealth in the world, or all the sophisticated weapons we could buy would take the place of those who have the uncritical willingness to face danger. Those who, in short, had the Right Stuff.'

"Read *Ghostriders 1976–1995: "Invictus" Combat History of the AC-130 Spectre Gunship, Iran, El Salvador, Grenada, Panama, Iraq, Bosnia-Herzegovina, Somalia* and salute those with the RIGHT STUFF."

— Major General Robert Patterson,
USAF (Ret), Former Air Force
Component Commander for United
States Special Operations Command.

"During the time span of this book, only twenty AC-130s were in existence. The 16th Special Operations Squadron (SOS) inventoried ten AC-130H on active-duty, while the 711 SOS inventoried ten AC-130A gunships as part of the Air Force Reserve. When aircraft and crews returned from Southeast Asia in 1975, there was no centralized training program, no simulators, and no training coded aircraft. AC-130As were scheduled to retire in 1980 and the AC-130H was to be transferred to the 711 SOS. Suffice to say, the once strong AC-130 program was destined to be shut down forever had it not been for one world-changing event.

"That event occurred on November 4, 1979, when American Hostages were taken in Iran. Though not fully understood at the time, this mission was the figurative Phoenix element for the AC-130 and other Special Operations units. The time period following Operation Eagle Claw proved to be the setting for one of the busiest times in Spectre history. From 1982 to 1995, AC-130s participated in missions in Grenada, El Salvador, Panama, Saudi Arabia, Kuwait, Iraq, Somalia, and Bosnia.

"Throughout all this, no matter what the mission was, Spectre answered the call. Crewmembers froze in Europe and sweated in Africa and the Middle East, regularly flying at 10,000 feet or higher in unpressurized aircraft. Every deployment had a line of volunteers. Crewmen and Maintainers were proud to be part of America's fighting force and even prouder to be Spectres."

— Colonel Jim Connors, USAF (Ret), 16th Special Operations Squadron Commander

Also by William Walter

Ghostriders 1968-1975: "Mors De Caelis"
Combat History of the AC-130 Spectre
Gunship, Vietnam, Laos, Cambodia

GHOSTRIDERS
1976-1995

Wesley,
Best wishes
from one SOF brother
to another!
22 Oct, 2022

WILLIAM WALTER

"INVICTUS" COMBAT HISTORY OF THE AC-130 SPECTRE GUNSHIP,
IRAN, EL SALVADOR, GRENADA, PANAMA, IRAQ, BOSNIA-HERZEGOVINA, SOMALIA

KNOX PRESS

A KNOX PRESS BOOK
An Imprint of Permuted Press
ISBN: 978-1-63758-157-5
ISBN (eBook): 978-1-63758-158-2

Ghostriders 1976-1995:
"Invictus" Combat History of the AC-130 Spectre Gunship, Iran, El Salvador, Grenada, Panama, Iraq, Bosnia-Herzegovina, Somalia

Permuted Press, LLC
New York • Nashville
permutedpress.com

Published in the United States of America
1 2 3 4 5 6 7 8 9 10

After conclusion of the war in Southeast Asia in 1975, the USAF considered the side firing AC-130 Gunship an outdated and unnecessary aircraft to fight the "Cold War." Nevertheless, Spectre vaulted deep into the shadowy world of special operations, providing persistent and lethal fire support in the Joint Special Operations arena.

This book is dedicated to the unsung professionals who operated, maintained, and supported the AC-130 gunship mission from 1976 through 1995.

TABLE OF CONTENTS

AC-130A Gunship 53-3129 was the first production C-130A built and was one of the first four C-130As modified into AC-130 configuration in 1968. (Credit: USAF photo)

THE AC-130 FLEET, 1976–1995[1]

Tail #	Name	Model	Status/Unit of Assignment
53-3129	*The First Lady*	AC-130A	USAFR, 711 SOS
54-1623	*Ghost Rider*	AC-130A	USAFR, 711 SOS
54-1626	*Vulcan Express*[2]	Gunship II	USAF, ASD
54-1628	*The Exterminator*	AC-130A	USAFR, 711 SOS
54-1630	*Azrael, Angel of Death*[3]	AC-130A	USAFR, 711 SOS
55-0011	*Night Stalker*	AC-130A	USAFR, 711 SOS
55-0014	*Jaws of Death*[4]	AC-130A	USAFR, 711 SOS
55-0029	*Midnight Express*[5]	AC-130A	USAFR, 711 SOS
55-0046	*Proud Warrior*[6]	AC-130A	USAFR, 711 SOS
56-0469	*Grim Reaper*	AC-130A	USAFR, 711 SOS
56-0509	*Raid Kills Em Dead*[7]	AC-130A	USAFR, 711 SOS
69-6567	*Ghostrider*	AC-130H	USAF, 16 SOS
69-6568	*Night Stalker*	AC-130H	USAF, 16 SOS

---

1 Other names were known to have been used but names listed are the last known record.

2 Also called *Big Spooky* and *Super Spooky*

3 Was *Mors De Caelis* until Pave Pronto modification

4 Retired as *Jaws of Death*

5 Retired as *Midnight Express*

6 Retired as *Proud Warrior*

7 Retired as *Ultimate End*

69-6569	*Excalibur*[8]	AC-130H	USAF, 16 SOS
69-6570	*Bad Company*[9]	AC-130H	USAF, 16 SOS
69-6572	*Grave Digger*	AC-130H	USAF, 16 SOS
69-6573	*Heavy Metal*	AC-130H	USAF, 16 SOS
69-6574	*Iron Maiden*	AC-130H	USAF, 16 SOS
69-6575	*Wicked Wanda*	AC-130H	USAF, 16 SOS
69-6576	*Hell Raiser*[10]	AC-130H	USAF, 16 SOS
69-6577	*Death Angel*	AC-130H	USAF, 16 SOS

8 Was also *Fatal Attraction* after SOFI modification

9 Was also *Widow Maker, The Hussy* after SOFI modification

10 Was also *Predator* after SOFI modification

PREFACE

Beginning in the early 1960s, the number of U.S. ground forces steadily increased in Vietnam. Numerous U.S. Army Special Forces camps were situated in South Vietnam to protect the citizens of South Vietnam from attack by North Vietnamese insurgents. These small SF camps protected hamlets and villages that came under constant attack by communist Viet Cong guerrillas. Though most attacks were conducted by small teams, large attacks of one thousand or more had occurred whereas SF camps were overrun and defenders killed. It was evident U.S. Army Special Forces desperately needed persistent, lethal Close Air Support (CAS) to defend against Viet Cong human wave attacks, especially at night.

Unfortunately, a capabilities gap existed since the majority of USAF fighter aircraft were designed to fight a third world war scenario against the Soviet Union. The USAF discovered fighters capable of supersonic speed with short mission duration (because of fuel burn rates) proved difficult to employ in a slow speed, long time on target role. Once USAF leadership (Air Staff) recognized the capabilities gap, World

War-II era propeller driven fighter/bomber aircraft were pressed into service in Vietnam. These aircraft were more appropriate for the CAS role since they were slow and could remain over target for long periods. Though these aircraft were primarily day only, use of illumination flares provided a rudimentary night capability.

Recognizing the issues at hand, Aeronautical Systems Division (ASD) Engineers at Wright Patterson Air Force Base (AFB), Ohio brainstormed ideas to quickly improve CAS capabilities in Vietnam. Acknowledging the fundamental capabilities of an effective CAS aircraft are persistence, lethality, and survivability, the challenge to find a solution via conventional means was difficult. Recognizing the dilemma, engineers believed the "pylon turn" was a logical concept. This tactic required the pilot to fly a circular orbit over a fixed point on the ground. In effect, the pilot would fly a constant left-banked turn for extended periods to ensure constant, uninterrupted sight of the target or ground force. Firepower would be provided by multiple guns and a large amount of ammunition and fuel to remain on station for long periods of time. With all engineering tenets and constraints considered, converting a cargo aircraft into a gunship was considered the best option. Though ASD Engineers initially met resistance at Air Staff, by 1964, ASD received a small budget to proceed. Initial experiments were conducted on a C-131 transport, first using a camera, then a gun. The experiment demonstrated enough promise to move the experiment into a project phase.

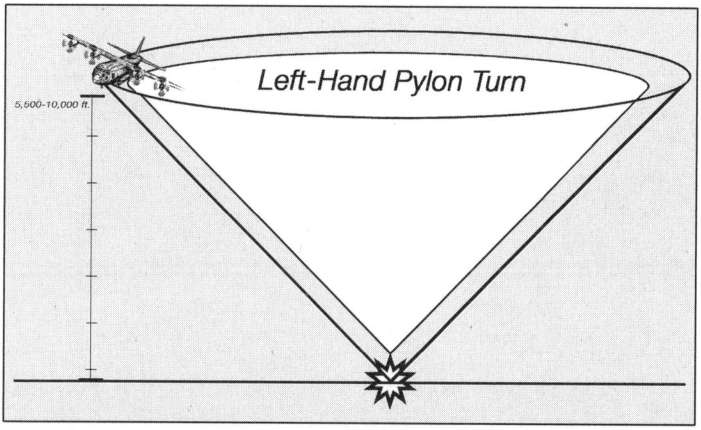

The basic pylon turn concept requires the pilot to maintain a constant left-hand bank, encircling a target. Once aligned and at the proper airspeed and bank angle, the ballistic targeting solution remains relatively constant, enabling constant fire on the target for as long as needed. The firing solution, referred to as on-nominal geometry, was the critical aspect of gunship effectiveness proven by all models of side firing gunships during the Vietnam War. (Credit: Sarah Walter, Dennis Bivens)

In 1967, The ASD Gunship Program Office set forth an effort to upgrade proven AC-47D capabilities with a larger and more powerful aircraft, and the C-130 was favored for conversion. Details of the initial AC-130 program can be found in *Ghostriders*, 1968–1975, *Mors De Caelis*; however, the Vietnam era AC-130 gunship remained unchanged as of 1976, where this story begins.

PROLOGUE

When the US military withdrew from Vietnam in 1975, the Department of Defense (DoD) dramatically changed national defense priorities. Though the small fleet of AC-130 gunships of the 16th Special Operations Squadron (SOS) "*Spectre*" destroyed over ten thousand trucks on the Ho Chi Minh Trail and saved scores of soldiers lives during Close Air Support (CAS) missions, Air Staff felt the AC-130 was no longer needed. Instead, they focused on "Cold War" capabilities to fight a third world war scenario against the Union of Soviet Socialist Republics (USSR). Accordingly, Air Staff placed priority on supersonic capable fighters and large subsonic bombers designed to deliver nuclear payloads from high altitude, over long distances. As a result, Special Operations Forces (SOF) from all military branches were either cut back or in some cases, eliminated. By the beginning of 1976, it was clear that the AC-130's days were numbered and for the next three years, the gunship program languished. By the fall of 1979, the AC-130H fleet was slated to be transferred to the Air Force Reserve and the AC-130A was scheduled to retire to the Boneyard at Davis Monthan, AFB Arizona.

On November 4, 1979, the US Embassy in Tehran, Iran was overtaken by Revolutionaries who held US citizens hostage. Soon afterward, 16 SOS commander, Lt Col Florin White received a phone call that altered the course of gunship history.

The AC-130 was a key participant in Operation Eagle Claw and in the following years, supported Special Operations ground and naval forces, almost exclusively, but USAF funding and support was limited. After the United States Special Operations Command (USSOCOM) was established in 1987 the AC-130 program received high-level support. From that point forward, the AC-130 gunship became USSOCOM's heavy firepower, dedicated to supporting USSOCOM surface forces. As with all USSOCOM "*Quiet Professional*" mandates, much of the AC-130 mission was classified. Now, decades later, most information from 1976–1995 has been declassified and approved for public release.

The AC-130 gunship is a stubborn beast. Either by design or by chance, the side firing gunship's unique capabilities remain in high demand today. The *Spectre* legacy extends to this day with new aircraft and aircrews who continue to put the right effect in the right place at the right time in support of fellow American warriors.

PAVE PRONTO CONFIGURATION

AC-130A	Crew
Optical Gun Sight	Pilot/Aircraft Commander (AC)
20mm M61 gun (x2)	Copilot (CP)
7.62mm MXU-470 gun (x2)	Fire-control Officer (FCO)
40mm /M2A1 (mod) gun (x2)	Flight Engineer (FE)
AN/APQ-133 Side-Looking Beacon Tracking radar	Navigator (NAV)
APQ-136 Forward-Looking radar	Navigator/Sensor Operator (IR and Radar)
AN/ARN-92 LORAN Navigation Set	Navigator/Sensor Operator (LLLTV)
AKY-9 Fire-control System Computer	Navigator/Electronic Warfare Officer (EWO)
LTN-51 Inertial navigation & targeting system	Illuminator Operator (IO)
AXQ-10 LLLTV	Aerial Gunner (x5) (AG)
2 KW Steerable Illuminator	
LAU-74 Flare dispenser	
AN/AAD-6/7 Forward Looking Infrared set	
AN/ASD-5 Black Crow sensor	
ALQ-87 Electronic Warfare pods	

Ceramic armor plating
Inert polyurethane foam-filled fuel tanks
Doppler Navigation radar
ID-48 Steering indicator
AGMTIP Moving-target indicator
WR-201 Video Bomb-Damage-Assessment-recorder
KY-20A Laser Target Designator
TRIM-7 active ECM
AN/APR-25/26 RHAW
Laser 8451-840000-1

PAVE SPECTRE CONFIGURATION

AC-130H	Crew
Optical Gun Sight	Pilot/Aircraft Commander (AC)
20mm M61 gun (x2)	Copilot (CP)
7.62mm MXU-470 gun (x2)	Fire-control Officer (FCO)
40mm M2A1 (mod) gun	Flight Engineer (FE)
105mm M137 gun	Navigator (NAV)
AN/APQ-150 Beacon Tracking Radar	Navigator/Sensor Operator (IR and Radar)

APN-59 Forward Looking Radar	Navigator/Sensor Operator (LLLTV)
ASN-90 -Inertial Navigation System	Navigator/Electronic Warfare Officer (EWO)
ASN-91 Fire-control Computer	Illuminator Operator (IO)
AXQ-10 LLLTV Sensor	Aerial Gunner (AG) (x5)
2 KW Steerable Illuminator	
LAU-74 Flare Dispenser	
AN/AAD-7 Forward Looking Infrared Set	
AN/ASD-5 Black Crow Sensor	
AN/ALQ-87 Electronic countermeasure pods	
Ceramic Armor Plating	
Inert polyurethane filled fuel tanks	
Nav System S431-1	
Direction-Finding Homing avionics	
FM Radio transceiver	
Pave Mace	
TRIM- 7 and AN/APR-25/26 Warning Receiver	
Laser 8451-84000-1	

AC-130A/H BASIC CREW DUTIES

Aircraft Commander (AC): Has the overall responsibility for coordinating the mission. Flying from the left seat of the cockpit, the AC attains firing geometry, balances the gunsight, controls aircraft bank, fires the guns, and has the ultimate responsibility for putting munitions on target.

Copilot (CP): Assumes the duties and responsibilities of pilot as necessary. The copilot controls aircraft speed, verbally directs aircrew checklists, handles outside communications with escorts, and controls the aircraft altitude should the autopilot fail.

Navigator (NAV): Has the responsibility for en route navigation, aircraft positioning in the target area and aircraft traffic separation. The NAV confirms target location and pre-established no-fire areas.

Fire Control Officer (FCO): Monitors the fire-control display and coordinates crew effort in detecting, validating, and engaging targets. The FCO is also responsible for computing and compensating for ballistic wind and gun/sensor alignment errors.

Flight Engineer (FE): Operates systems controls and observes engine instruments, systems indicators, and control devices and reports abnormal conditions to the pilot. The FE also monitors and controls the gun control panel as directed by the pilot and coordinates between the pilot and gunners.

Lead Gunner/Aerial Gunner (AG): Gunners man three positions in the aircraft. Forward and aft gunners operate, repair malfunctions, reload and remove spent casings from all gun systems as required. The Lead Gunner is responsible for coordinating and leading gun crew efforts. One gunner performs duties as the right scanner to alert the crew of AAA fire and airborne traffic. The right scanner directs defensive maneuvers as required.

Infrared Sensor Operator (IR): Has the responsibility for operating and monitoring the infrared system to search, locate and track targets. When selected as the primary sensor operator, the IR provides guidance to the fire-control system and can fire 40mm and 105mm guns in the automatic trainable mode with consent of the pilot. The IR also assesses battle damage inflicted on the target.

Low-light-level-television Sensor Operator (TV): Coordinates with other sensor operators, navigator, and FCO, acquiring, tracking and maintaining proper target orientation. The TV can fire 40mm and 105mm guns in the automatic trainable mode with consent of the pilot and assists in the assessment of battle damage inflicted on the target.

Electronic Warfare Officer (EWO): Operates the Black Crow sensor to locate hostile targets, and beacon tracking radar to track friendly forces. The EWO operates all ECM equipment, advises the crew of threats and directs appropriate countermeasures.

Illuminator Operator (IO): Performs aft scanner duties advising the crew of ground fire and other airborne traffic and directs defensive maneuvers and performs the duties of loadmaster as required.

A typical AC-130 crew circa 1993. (Credit: Johnny Saunderson)

Crewmen were equipped with survival/security equipment to meet individual mission demands. Basic equipment included:

1. Survival vest
2. Basic first Aid Kit
3. Compass and map of working area
4. Survival radio w/extra battery
5. Tourniquet
6. MK-13 signal flares
7. Gyrojet launcher and flares
8. Signal Mirror
9. Water purification tablets
10. Model 15 revolver or M9 pistol and/or GUU-5P carbine and a basic load of ammunition
11. Parachute
12. Ballistic helmet and/or communications headset
13. Survival knife

SITUATION REPORT: 1976–1980

When the 16th Special Operations Squadron (SOS) and its AC-130H gunships were transferred to Hurlburt Field, Fl, personnel literally stepped into the building vacated by the 415th Special Operations Training Squadron (SOTS). The two gunships (69-6567 and 69-6568) temporarily assigned to the 8th SOS were transferred to the 16 SOS. The main squadron building contained the command section, administration, mission control center, main briefing room and life support equipment section. All other functions, including crew position specific offices were located in a series of dilapidated double-wide temporary buildings across the parking lot from the main building. Total active duty AC-130H inventory assigned to Tactical Air Command (TAC) was ten. The Air Force Reserve's 919 Special Operations Group and 711 SOS at Duke Field, FL were assigned the ten remaining AC-130A gunships. Since a formal AC-130 training school no longer existed, both squadrons took responsibility for their own in-house training programs.

Though the AC-130 program was on a figurative chopping block, by happenstance, five AC-130s were included in a larger USAF plan to modify the C-130 fleet with Universal

Aerial Refueling Receptacle Slipway Installation (UARRSI) receptacles. This modification was truly a capabilities multiplier that enabled world-wide range without the need to land to refuel. Once modified, augmented crews were able to fly indefinitely as long as there were no mechanical issues and food and water were available. This system was put to test quickly when AC-130 crews were routinely tasked to use their night sensors to find people all up and down the east coast who were either lost in the woods or at sea. Tragically, most missions failed to discover survivors, but nevertheless the AC-130 was the most capable USAF aircraft for the task at hand.[11]

Meanwhile, in Central America, the governments of Nicaragua and El Salvador were in the midst of civil war with communist guerilla forces. Nicaragua was the first to fall in 1979, coinciding with the overthrow of President Anastasio Somoza.[12] On July 8, two AC-130H gunships and seventy-nine personnel deployed from Hurlburt Field to Howard AFB, Panama to support a Noncombatant Evacuation Operation (NEO) of the US Embassy in Managua, Nicaragua. Within a week, the situation resolved politically and crews returned to Hurlburt Field.

---

11 Herbert Kissling, *An Air Commando and Special operations Chronology, 1961-1991* (Hurlburt, FL: First Special Operations Wing, Air Force Special Operations Command, United States Air Force, 1991), 145, 147.

12 Ibid, 165.

CHAPTER ONE

OPERATIONS RICE BOWL, EAGLE CLAW, AND HONEY BADGER, 1979-1980

AC-130H 69-6570 flying a formation training mission near Guam, 1980. (Credit: Author)

Iran is the second largest country in the Middle East and home to one of the oldest civilizations on earth. During the first half of the 20th century, Iran and America shared a positive relationship until the early days of World War-II. During this time, Iran declared neutrality but allowed Nazi Germany to manage and operate the Iranian Railroad system. Iran's Monarch, Reza Shah Pahlavi, defied British warnings to disperse the Nazis, who were blocking allied shipments of weapons through Iran to the Soviet Union. The situation resulted in an allied invasion of Iran and rapid collapse of the Iranian military. As a result, Reza Shah Pahlavi was forced to abdicate his throne in September of 1941, and was replaced by his twenty-one-year-old son, Crown Prince Mohammad Reza Pahlavi.[1]

During his early years as Shah (King), of Iran, Mohammad focused his attention on royal ceremonies with little interest in Parliamentary affairs. He developed a love of flying and reputation for being a womanizer and egotist. Eventually, he began interfering in Iranian parliamentary procedures, especially when elements of self-interest were involved.

The Shah's rich lifestyle can be traced back to 1908 when Britain discovered large oil deposits in Iran. Though the British organized, built, and maintained a world-class petroleum operation, working conditions and wages for Iranian workers were atrocious. Though royalties paid to Iran via the Anglo-Iranian Oil Company (AIOC) made the Shah rich, they were miniscule in comparison with British profits.

In 1948, National Front of Iran leader Mohammad Mosaddegh established the National Iranian Oil Company (NIOC) to nationalize Iran's petroleum industry and force the British out of Iran. The move created political turmoil resulting in assassination of Prime Minister Haj Ali Razmara. In 1951, Parliament successfully nationalized Iran's petroleum

1 *Gholam Reza Afkhami, The life and times of the Shah (Berkeley, CA: University of California Press, 2009), 79.*

industry and the Shah appointed Mohammad Mosaddegh as Prime Minister.

British and American governments defied Parliament's edict, electing to remove their employees from Iran and boycott purchase of Iranian oil. In short order, the British-built Abadan Refinery was closed. Oil prices on the global market were hyper-inflated, resulting in a dramatic reduction of revenue. Since petroleum operations were a major source of national income, Iran's economy began to decline dramatically for the working and middle class, but the ruling class and wealthy elites continued to live a life of luxury. Politicians were in a quandary and there was no easy fix to the situation as it dwelled in international courts for several years. During this time, Mosaddegh gained popularity while the Shah's stranglehold on Iranian politics began to slip. Incrementally, Mosaddegh took steps to limit the Shah's interference in parliamentary affairs, especially his control of the military. In turn, the Shah perceived Mosaddegh as a threat to his dynasty while British and American governments thought Mosaddegh was a communist who would ally with the USSR if given the chance. A three-way struggle for control of Iran's oil industry ensued and it appeared Mosaddegh was winning, much to the chagrin of the Shah and western governments.

In 1953, the Central Intelligence Agency (CIA) and British Secret Intelligence Service (MI6) devised *Operation Ajax*: a coup d'état to overthrow Prime Minister Mosaddegh.[2] To

2 James Risen, "Secrets of History: The C.I.A. in Iran," *The New York Times* (The New York Times Company, 2000).

facilitate their plan, the CIA conducted large-scale propaganda campaigns in print media and staged riots and political activism with paid protesters to discredit Mosaddegh and give everyday Iranians the impression he was corrupt and inept. Nevertheless, Mosaddegh remained popular with everyday Iranians, even after the Shah issued an edict to forcefully remove Mosaddegh from office. When Mosaddegh detected the CIA/MI6 plot, *Operation Ajax* failed. In the wake of the failed coup d'état, the Shah fled to Europe until Mosaddegh was arrested. When the Shah returned to Iran, he appointed western-friendly General Fazlollah Zahedi as Prime Minister. Though some Iranians involved in the failed coup were summarily executed, Mosaddegh was arrested, tried, and eventually sentenced to life in internal exile.

The Mosaddegh coup d'état solidified his image as a nationalist with the working and middle class while the Shah was viewed as a figurehead monarch and elitist with no regard for everyday Iranians. Fearful his enemies would eventually overthrow his dynasty, the Shah established secret police force (SAVAK) to identify his enemies and keep them under control by violence, imprisonment, torture, and execution.

Seeking to pull Iran out of poverty and win the support of the working and middle classes, Shah and Prime Minister Zahedi began negotiations with a consortium of countries willing to invest in Iran's petroleum industry. Eventually an agreement was reached whereas the consortium and Iran would split profits at about the 50/50 rate. The new deal pulled Iran out of poverty and profits from the oil industry soared. With newly-found wealth, the Shah began an infrastructure program he named "the great civilization." For the next decade, life for the Iranian working and middle class improved greatly. By the early 1960s, Iran rivaled western countries in most societal aspects. Unfortunately, the Shah's record of shady secret deals, underhanded profiteering, and human rights abuses was ignored by western powers solely because he supported western efforts to block Soviet expansion in the Middle East.

In 1963, the Shah launched a program called the White Revolution: a massive overhaul of the Iranian socioeconomic system. Though the program touted lofty western-like goals, it caused unintended consequences since it strayed far away from traditional values of religion and Persian culture. Religious clerics in particular condemned the Shah as a western puppet who traded traditional Persian culture for a morally sinful western culture based on money and power. One vocal cleric in particular, Ruhollah Khomeini, directly challenged the Shah on numerous occasions. Khomeini identified with the common Iranian citizen, something the Shah couldn't do. Eventually, the Shah feared Khomeini's popularity was a threat to his monarchy. After several arrests in 1964, Khomeini was exiled from Iran. Though a large swath of the Iranian population viewed Khomeini as their charismatic and intellectual leader, the Shah thought Khomeini's influence was culled from society. Nevertheless, Khomeini remained a popular figure in Iranian life as writings and recordings of his philosophies were smuggled back into Iran for distribution.[3]

---

3 Abbas Milani, *The Shah* (New York, NY: Palgrave Macmillan, 2011), 291.

During the early 1970s, Iran, as a member of the Organization of the Petroleum Exporting Countries (OPEC), was financially impacted by a worldwide oil embargo and the goals of the Shah's White Revolution began to fade. Though the working and middle class suffered, the Shah continued to live a life of luxury. At the same time, the Shah made sure his royal family, loyal politicians and his military leaders were well taken care of. The situation was further negatively impacted by hyperinflation of worldwide oil prices that essentially divided Iranian society into class warfare between the haves and have nots.

In 1974, the Shah was diagnosed with cancer, but kept his condition secret, traveling out of Iran for treatments.[4] Since the Shah insisted his hand would control all government decisions, the Iranian Parliament and military began to unravel as he attempted to rule in absentia. For the next few years, his deteriorating condition resulted in strange, erratic behavior and delusions at a time when Iran's worldwide oil industry was in decline. By 1977, the Shah entered a period of paranoia, indecision, and distrust of foreign powers. In reality, western governments supported the Shah; though, through his indecision and poor management of oil production, Iran's economy was on the verge of collapse.

Unhappy with the Shah's policies and mismanagement of the country, Iranian citizens staged public protests at great risk. When people gathered, the Shah's Army quickly dispersed the groups with overt threats of violence. In an

---

4 Marvin Zonis, *Majestic Failure: The Fall of the Shah* (Chicago, IL: University of Chicago Press, 1991), 160.

attempt to squelch public gatherings, the Shah declared martial law, threatening to kill all protesters who opposed him.

On September 8, 1978, during an incident known today as Black Friday, thousands of Iranians gathered in downtown Tehran for a religious demonstration in direct opposition to declaration of martial law. When citizens refused to disperse, the Iranian Army opened fire on the crowd, killing and wounding hundreds of unarmed civilians. As a result, the Shah lost nearly all public support and Iranian military leadership began to fragment.[5]

By October 1978, large public demonstrations filled the streets of Tehran with protesters calling for the overthrow of the Shah. Though his monarchy was dissolving at a rapid pace, the Shah left Iran on January 16, 1979 for cancer treatments, hoping the situation would settle down before he returned.

In the Shah's absence, Ruhollah Khomeini returned to Iran from exile in France. Khomeini's charismatic speeches and lectures condemning the Shah soared in popularity while splinter groups battled for control of the government.

While the British Broadcasting Company (BBC) flooded the airwaves with television news reports of events surrounding the Embassy, US Press Attaché Barry Rosen tended to his duties and it seemed every day the protests became larger and louder.[6] On February 14, the Marxist group "Organization of Iranian People's Fedai Guerillas" stormed the US Embassy, taking several hostages.

---

5 Abbas Milani, *The Persian Sphinx: Amir Abbas Hoveyda and the Riddle of the Iranian Revolution* (Washington, DC: Mage Publishers, 2001), 292–293.

6 Mr. Barry Rosen, phone interview with Author, Feb 2019.

Through the actions of US Ambassador William Sullivan and Iranian Foreign Minister Ebrahim Yazdi, the Embassy was returned to US control after three hours, but US Marine Kenneth Kraus was kidnapped and removed from Embassy grounds. Since Kraus had fired his weapon at the advancing guerrillas, the Marxist group accused him of murder, tried him in a "Kangaroo court" and sentenced him to death. After six days, President Jimmy Carter and Ambassador Sullivan secured Kraus's release and he was quickly flown out of Iran.

By the end of February, Ruhollah Khomeini assumed control of the Iranian Parliament and Iranian Army leadership declared neutrality. At the same time, US military aircraft flew thousands of Americans out of Iran. Eventually the only Americans remaining were Ambassador Sullivan, a small staff, and a contingent of US Marine guards. While Khomeini declared the US government as "the Great Satan," he condemned the US Embassy compound as a "den of CIA spies."

On April 1, 1979, Iran's Parliament was replaced by an Islamic Republic and Ruhollah Khomeini was installed as Grand Ayatollah. From that point on, Mohammad Reza was a man without a country, seeking temporary residence in any country willing to let him in.

While Ayatollah Khomeini publicly demanded Mohammad Reza be returned to Iran for trial, he first bounced through Egypt, Morocco, the Bahamas, then settled in Mexico for medical treatment. In October 1979, President Jimmy Carter allowed Mohammad Reza to enter the US under an assumed name for cancer treatment at hospitals in New York and Texas. When Iranian Intelligence discovered his whereabouts, Ayatollah Khomeini demanded President Carter return Mohammad Reza to Iran to stand trial for crimes committed during his reign, but Carter refused.

Tolerating protests and turmoil became routine for the remaining US Embassy staff. Groups of university students assembled outside the gates of the Embassy to chant "Death to America" and similar unsavory threats. Most protests seemed to be tailor-made for international news media, complete with English language slogans condemning the American government. Some of the more enterprising revolutionaries burned American flags and effigies of Uncle Sam and President Carter.

On November 4, 1979, with anti-American sentiment at its peak, university students calling themselves "Muslim Student Followers of the Imam's Line" stormed the twenty-seven acre US Embassy compound in Tehran. In short order, they took sixty-three Americans hostage within Embassy grounds and three more in the Foreign Ministry building about a mile and a half from the Embassy. In response, the Carter Administration demanded immediate release of the hostages, then froze eleven billion dollars' worth of Iranian assets held in US financial institutions. From that point on, Khomeini sided with the students who refused to release the hostages. Likewise, Carter refused to release Iranian assets, resulting in a stalemate. The Carter administration proposed diplomatic solutions, but all were rejected by Khomeini, who allowed the students to retain all sixty-six hostages. During the tense days following, the BBC was granted scripted interviews with English speaking Revolutionaries to air their demands which included threats to begin killing hostages if their demands were not met. At the same time, some hostages suspected of being CIA agents were being subjected to psychological torture and mock executions.

On November 6, 1979, President Carter's National Security Advisor Dr. Zbigniew Brzezinski tasked Secretary of Defense Harold Brown and the Joint Chiefs of Staff to begin planning military options. Unfortunately, the Department of Defense was caught off guard and unprepared to deal with such a contingency. The once strong joint Special Operations community had been decimated since the end of combat operations in Vietnam and there was no Unified Command Structure. The last remaining remnant of Special Operations capabilities had been reduced to an undermanned Pentagon Joint Staff Operations Directorate (J-3) known as the Special Operations Division (SOD).

Nevertheless, Chairman of the Joint Chiefs of Staff—Gen David Jones—ordered the USS Navy Kitty Hawk Carrier Battle Group to the Gulf of Oman and assigned the SOD Commander, US Army Colonel Jerry King, the responsibility to devise and plan military options including maritime blockades, air strikes, and a rescue operation.

Col King then summoned commanders of special operations elements from the US Army, Navy, and Air Force to report to the Pentagon to lay out the basic framework for military options. The planning task was purposely named

Operation Rice Bowl as a cover & deception tactic to mask any connection to Iran. Cleverly, the name *Rice Bowl* implied a connection to the October 26, 1979 assassination of South Korean president Park Chung-Hee, but there was absolutely no connection at all.

After receiving an initial briefing and orders from Col King, each element broke into Top Secret, compartmentalized Operational Planning Groups (OPG) to define potential courses of action. The USAF element, commanded by Maj Gen Robert Taylor, directed 1st Special Operations Wing (SOW) commander Col Richard "Dick" Dunwoody to prepare an AC-130 strike plan on the main source of Iran's income, the Abadan oil refinery about thirty-five miles inland from the Persian Gulf. The AC-130 was considered the optimum aircraft since it could strike the cracking towers of the refinery with precision, at night with low collateral damage potential to temporarily shut down the refinery, while not destroying it. Furthermore, since the Iranian Army and Air Force had no real nighttime capability, planners sought aircraft capable of night operations, so the AC-130 was considered the most capable aircraft for the task.

Once the AC-130 was selected, Col Dunwoody phoned his Director of Operations, Col Tom Wicker at Hurlburt Field. Without divulging a reason, he ordered AC-130 mission planner Capt Wayne Thom to the Pentagon. Capt Thom was directed to travel on verbal orders via self-funded commercial air travel while dressed in civilian clothes.[7] Though

7 During the 1970s, all military funded travel mandated wear of a military uniform. Traveling in civilian clothing was not permitted.

Thom found the order unusual, he got on the next available commercial flight from Okaloosa Air Terminal without question. Accordingly, the following morning, Thom reported to Lt Col Richard Gadd at the Pentagon. For most of the day, he was treated like a leper until his security clearance was validated. When presented with the proposed mission, Thom conducted a threat assessment, calculated routes and fuel requirements, then laid out a basic mission profile. Normally, this level of effort was conducted by three or four AC-130 planners, but, for security reasons, he was the sole AC-130 crewman working the entire mission plan.

> "My task was to plan a strike mission of two Gunships to Abadan, Iran on the Shatt al-Arab (a river which separates Iran from Iraq). We were to take off from Diego Garcia. I worked for 4 or 5 days with hardly any sleep. Every time I thought I had everything figured out, someone would change something. I did get to work with the tanker guys to coordinate A/R tracks. They were great! We were to fly out of Diego Garcia, refuel about 500 miles out then refuel again just before arrival over the Persian Gulf."
> **Lt Col (Ret.) Wayne Thom**

It was three thousand miles from Diego Garcia Island to Abadan; a ten plus hour flight one-way. The strike itself was planned for thirty minutes total time. The egress route to be taken after the strike was even more perilous than ingress. After the last aerial refueling, there wouldn't be enough fuel to reach the coast of India, so landing on a remote island was necessary. This was a big problem since there was no guarantee an AC-130 could get fuel there, or take off afterward. No doubt Capt Thom was challenged when planning for these contingencies.

While OPG planners at the Pentagon burned the midnight oil, the Chairman's policy of limiting numbers of OPG personnel because of operational security reasons took a toll. All planning groups were understaffed, especially the rescue planning cell. Realizing this limiting factor, Maj Gen Taylor queried his staff for names of Colonels with Pacific Area Special Operations expertise to augment the JTF commanders' staff. Maj Lee Hess suggested Col Jim Kyle, then stationed in New Mexico. Years before, Maj Hess worked with Col Kyle on the PACAF Headquarters Special Operations Staff and was confident he was a good fit for the task at hand. Col Kyle not only had a reputation for leading from the front but had significant special operations experience in Vietnam, Laos, and Cambodia as an AC-130 pilot, 16th SOS Operations Officer, and 7th Air Force Special Operations staff officer. With Maj Gen Taylor's approval, Maj Hess called Col Kyle at his duty station, relaying instructions to report to the Pentagon immediately with no questions asked. The next day, for security reasons, Col Kyle traveled on verbal orders, purchased his own airline tickets, and traveled in civilian clothes just like Capt Thom did a few days earlier.

When Col Kyle arrived at Pentagon JCS/SOD, he was surprised to see several familiar faces, including 1 SOW Commander Col Richard "Dick" Dunwoody and his

Operations Officer Col Tom Wicker. Though it was obvious something big was going on, conversations were kept at the social level for classification (need to know) reasons. Later that day, Col Kyle reported to US Army Major General (MG) James Vaught and was assigned as his deputy. The next day, Col Kyle discovered Col Dunwoody had left in haste with no explanation.

When Col Dunwoody returned to Hurlburt, he was the only one on station "read in" on the Abadan mission. His challenge was to deploy four AC-130s, crews, maintainers, and support personnel halfway around the world without anyone figuring out the goal of the mission. Thus, furthering the Operation *Rice Bowl* mantra, the training location he selected was Andersen AFB, Guam.

Since the Iran hostage situation was the biggest news story at the time, people world-wide were watchful for clues pertaining to the Carter administration's response. This was a challenge since AC-130s drew unwanted attention when landing on transition airfields. To maintain OPSEC, Col Dunwoody believed the only way to mask the AC-130 deployment was to fly to Guam nonstop. Fortunately, the first five AC-130H gunships had already been modified with the Universal Aerial Refueling Receptacle Slipway Installation (UARRSI). Since the capability was new, only a handful of pilots were qualified for aerial refueling operations, but instructor pilots were confident they could train and upgrade unqualified pilots while en route to Guam.

Flying nonstop over a distance of about eight thousand miles was a tall order, but crews were confident they would make the thirty hour flight as long as engine oil levels remained within safe limits. To guard against single-point failure, the bulk of each crew consisted of extra crewmen who would rotate positions between flying and rest for the duration of the mission. Flight Surgeon Lt Col William Postles would fly on one of the aircraft to monitor crewmen who were issued "go pills" to remain alert. To lessen logistic and physical burdens, tactical crewmen were to deploy to Guam via commercial air, dressed in civilian clothes.

On November 13, under travel orders indicating purpose as Tac Air Operations, Col Dunwoody led the first two ship formation of AC-130s towards Guam. The following day, Lt Col John "Pappy" Gallagher led the second two ship formation westward. Since the AC-130 could not pressurize, the entire journey was flown at ten thousand ft. Mean Sea Level (MSL). Because of the low altitude, fuel burn rates were higher, performance was sluggish, and aerial refueling was difficult.

> "Hanging on the boom for 30 minutes and taking on 60,000 pounds of fuel is very difficult and requires serious concentration by the pilot. Every pilot was soaking wet from perspiration after each event, especially when flying near clouds which was a common occurrence at 10,000 feet." **Col (Ret.) Donn Kegel**

After 29.5 hours average flight time, four AC-130H gunships were on station at Andersen AFB, Guam. The deployment established a world record nonstop C-130 flight.

1979 World Record C-130 Flight Crews

	Crew 1 (69-6570)	Crew 2 (69-6576)	Crew 3 (69-6575)	Crew 4 (69-6569)
Pilot	Maj Michael Couvillon	Capt James Lawrence	Maj Robert Kovarik	Maj Darrell Giffin
Pilot	Col Richard Dunwoody	Capt Mike McClellan	Capt Donn Kegel	Capt Herman Youngblood
Pilot	Capt Clark Lee	Lt Mark Wildermuth	Capt McNair	Maj Carl Woodall
Nav	Capt James Braswell	Maj Carl Houston	Capt Jack Dickinson	Capt Marion Hamilton
Nav	Maj John Thomas	Capt Carlos Garcia	Capt Bruce Rasmussen	Capt Dennis Broussard
FE	SSgt Earl Parchment	MSgt John Schugmann	CMSgt Don Beardsley	TSgt Rodney Arviso
FE	MSgt Jerald Appleby	TSgt Eugene Carter	TSgt Lewis Adkins	TSgt Fred Beach
IO	SSgt Roy Duncan	TSgt Michael Hosenbackez	MSgt Anthony Denoi	SMSgt Arthur Humphrey
IO	SSgt Victor Hinderer	TSgt Bill Patterson	MSgt Richard Hall	SSgt Lawrence Weber
Staff	Lt Col William Postles			Lt Col John Gallagher

Though the entire trans-Pacific crossing occurred without a security compromise, the arrival of AC-130s on Guam created a stir. A few days after arrival, the Andersen Air Force Base paper ran the headline "Strike Force Lands on Guam." It was presumed the reference was related to trouble in Korea, but nevertheless, OPSEC concerns prompted some enterprising maintainers to make their AC-130s appear as if they were WC-130 Weather Aircraft by painting large US roundel insignias on the gunships. Since the bumps, humps and guns of the AC-130 made it impossible blend in with the WC-130s, the roundel was painted over with cans of blue spray paint, which gave an even stranger appearance.

Once flying operations began, crews went to work quickly to develop partial-orbit and low-level strafing tactics because of the ROEs levied for the Abadan mission. These tactics were needed to prevent crossing into Iraqi airspace, which was right across the *Shatt al-Arab* River, bordering the Abadan refinery. Unfortunately, crews discovered partial-orbit tactics were difficult and low-level strafing ineffective.

> "The Joint Chiefs of Staff had initially approved plans for a punitive airstrike by the AC-130. These targets would require some special tactics that were refined during our deployment to Guam. These new tactics included low level air refueling and firing the 20mm cannons at low levels in a strafing like pattern. The practice

> strafing runs never proved to be effective." **Col (Ret.) John "Pappy" Gallagher.**

Meanwhile at the Pentagon, MG Vaught realized Col Dunwoody deployed to Guam and he no longer had an Air Force SOF commander available at the Pentagon to take charge of his conceptual rescue plan. Forthwith, Col Kyle was assigned as Air Deputy Senior Planner, then "read in" to Joint Task Force (JTF) 1-79 a task force so classified MG Vaught denied its existence to all other OPGs. With the exception of two JCS Generals and President Carter, less than twenty planners in J-3 SOD were involved.

> "JTF-1-79 had a single purpose and mission—prepare a plan and train a force to rescue the American citizens illegally held in Iran, and prepare to execute it 'ON ORDER'" (Lenahan 1998, 39).

To maintain air-tight OPSEC, JTF-1-79 was masked from the prying eyes of US Secretary of State Cyrus Vance and his staff who were vehemently opposed to any military action. Part of MG Vaught's OPSEC regimen included a list of "no speak" words that could not be spoken by anyone outside of a secure vault. To ensue absolute secrecy, some planners used substitute words exclusively, even in the vault, to ensure OPSEC.[8]

---

8 Though some would later claim OPSEC mandates were overzealous, one small leak could have been detected by Soviet or Iranian intelligence, who were watching US actions closely.

Through the month of November, MG Vaught was presented with a litany of plans to insert a rescue force, but few had merit. Meanwhile, OPGs continued to develop emergency strike plans ranging from B-52 carpet bombing to AC-130 precision strikes. Though it was known President Carter would not authorize strikes unless Iranian Revolutionaries began killing hostages, considerable effort was expended developing strike concepts that went absolutely nowhere.

While Army Special Forces and USAF SOF air planners struggled to develop a workable rescue plan, AC-130 crews were training for the Abadan mission, completely out of sight of MG Vaught. The first mention of the AC-130 within the JTF-1-79 planning cell came from Maj Gen Taylor, who sought Col Kyle's advice on AC-130 capabilities. Though the General's intent was unclear as to the target location, he wanted to know if an AC-130 was accurate enough to fire over the top of protective revetments into hardened aircraft shelters located at Khatami Air Base in Iran. The overall intent of his proposed mission was to ricochet, skip, or project high speed shell fragments into the shelters to damage or destroy F-14s parked within. This concept, dubbed "Golden BB," was considered valid by Col Kyle based on his experience as an AC-130A pilot ten years earlier. To ensure a more current position, he called 16 SOS Operations Officer Lt Col John "Pappy" Gallagher in Guam to discuss AC-130H capabilities. After a conversation via secure phone, they agreed the concept was sound, but felt proof was required before validating the capability. In a few days, TSgt Bill

Patterson in the 16 SOS Tactics Office at Hurlburt Field was tasked to set up a live-fire test on Eglin Reservation. Though Patterson was not advised why the test was being conducted, he was accustomed to reacting to unusual tactics development requests and didn't ask questions. Within a week, a makeshift revetment wall was built in front of a concrete aircraft shelter on Eglin's Range C-52. During the following days, three live fire tests were conducted resulting in success and one well shredded surplus F-84 fighter.

While numerous compartmentalized plans for air strikes from other OPGs continued to be presented to the JCS, MG Vaught's JTF 1-79 planning cell focused solely on a clandestine rescue. The rescue he envisioned would follow the lines of Operation *Ivory Coast* (the Son Tay, POW rescue mission), conducted in November of 1970. During that mission, USAF and US Army special operations forces successfully infiltrated North Vietnam via HH-3 Jolly Green and HH-53 Super Jolly helicopters supported by MC-130 Combat Talons, A-1E Skyraiders, F-4 Phantoms and F-105 Wild Weasels. The infiltration and exfiltration succeeded as planned, but, unfortunately, the camp was deserted.

Historically, there were operational parallels relating to challenges of *Ivory Coast* and JTF-1-79, but in reality, they were vastly different sets of circumstances. Distance from operating base to target during Ivory Coast was about five hundred miles, whereas distance for JTF-1-79 exceeded one thousand miles. Although the distance to Tehran could be reduced somewhat by operating from Turkey, Saudi Arabia, or Bahrain, diplomatic and operational security concerns negated use of those locations. Likewise, staging an Aircraft Carrier Battle Group in the Persian Gulf was considered risky since the group had limited maneuver room and was vulnerable to attack. Furthermore, naval vessels could become trapped if the Gulf of Hormuz was mined.[9]

There was no easy route to Tehran. Infiltration from Turkey via surface vehicles was ruled out due to excessive risk and loss of element of surprise. Infiltration via fixed-wing aircraft was possible, but air-drop of the rescue force in the middle of a large urban center was rife with risk of jump-related casualties and widely scattered rescue forces. There was also a significant challenge of extracting air-dropped forces and hostages, once secured. It was evident that air-land of the rescue force on the nearest airfield would expose the operation as soon as it began, losing the element of surprise. Furthermore, the rescue force would then have to fight their way to the Embassy and Foreign Ministry, secure the hostages, and then fight their way through angry mobs and Iranian militants to get back to an extraction airfield. Obviously, the concept was a no-go from the start, and, as one of the Army Special Forces planners quipped, "the only difference between this mission and the Alamo is they didn't need to fight their way into the Alamo."

Considering all options presented, the only viable concept was clandestine infiltration and exfiltration via helicopter. Unfortunately, the closest possible launch point for

---

9 Rod Lenahan, *Crippled Eagle: A historical Perspective of U.S. Special Operations 1976-1996* (Charleston, SC: Narwhal Press, 1998), 32.

a helicopter was from an Aircraft Carrier off the southern shore of Iran, about 1,000 miles from Tehran. Since the airspeed of even the fastest helicopter is about 160 knots (~185 mph), it would take at least five hours to fly to Tehran. Furthermore, the distance to the city exceeded the unrefueled range of all inventoried helicopters, so they would need to either land for refueling or require tanker support if aerial refueling capable.

Though not well known in the Army, Air Force staff officers were aware the premier Combat Search and Rescue force was Military Airlift Command's Aerospace Rescue and Recovery Service (ARRS). This storied organization had vast combat experience in Southeast Asia and were trained and equipped for night operations. Their primary helicopter was the Sikorsky HH-53, which was equipped with aerial refueling capability to extend range without the need to land for refueling.

Significant discussion and opinions were battered back and forth between the JTF-1-79 planning staff concerning selection of the most capable helicopter force, but OPSEC concerns surpassed capability limitations. Because of the distance involved, launching helicopters from an Aircraft Carrier presented a major security concern. There were no doubts USAF HH-53 helicopters aboard a Navy Aircraft carrier would create unwanted attention. Adding to the complicated situation, Russian intelligence collection aircraft were known to be surveilling the USS Nimitz Carrier Battle Group while cruising in the Gulf of Oman. This was a serious OPSEC issue since the Russians would certainly advise

Iran if they detected a rescue mission was in the works. Even if the HH-53s were flown onto the USS Nimitz at night for security reasons, the HH-53s would need to stay on the deck in plain view since they did not have folding rotors and would not fit on the ship's elevators. These OPSEC concerns narrowed selection to Navy RH-53D minesweepers which would not likely attract attention on the USS Nimitz.

From a performance perspective, the RH-53D was an acceptable choice. It was equipped with large fuel tanks and aerial refueling and could lift more weight than other helicopters of that series. The primary limiting factor was speed; it could cruise no faster than 150 knots. Even if aerial refueling tactics were used, it is a difficult and demanding task for any crew to travel 1,000 miles in one period of darkness. Furthermore, some planners believed aerial refueling at the usual 1,000 ft. AGL altitude may expose the formation to Iranian early-warning radar, thus compromising the mission.

Because of these factors, mission planners focused their efforts on low-level infiltration (two hundred ft. AGL or below) and establishment of a Forward Area Refueling Point (FARP) somewhere in Iran. This decision resulted in removal of the aerial refueling probes and Engine Air Particle Separators (EAPS) for weight savings and increased power. Considering these factors and the ground commander's insistence of pre-mission reconnaissance of the Embassy and Stadium, the mission was split into two nights.[10]

10 Col (Ret.) Jim Kyle, phone interview with Author, Sep, 2014.

Once the RH-53D decision was final, planners first determined six would be required. In late November, six RH-53Ds from the Navy's Helicopter Minesweeping Squadron HM-16 at Norfolk, VA, were flown via C-5 Galaxy to Diego Garcia Island in the Indian Ocean. A few weeks later, two more were added for a total of eight at the staging site.

As mission planning continued, JTF 1-79 planners surmised OPSEC regarding helicopter positioning was adequate, but staging fixed wing aircraft without exposing the operation an OPSEC issue. Bases selected to support fixed wing operations were remote desert locations in Wadi Kena, Egypt, and Masirah, Oman. These sites were covertly prepared several months prior to the planned mission by flying MC-130, C-130, AWACS, and KC-135 aircraft in and out under the guise of a routine training exercise. Consistent with MG Vaught's absolute OPSEC policy, only a few JTF-1-79 planners flew into the remote sites alongside aircrews who were not aware they were actually staging equipment and supplies for the rescue force.

While individual OPGs churned out plan after plan for military options ranging from strike to rescue, the State Department continued to pursue diplomatic courses of action. Their efforts were unsuccessful, but on November 19, Khomeini released thirteen women and African-American hostages on their own accord. The release was viewed as a "divide and conquer" propaganda effort designed to demonstrate solidarity with minority groups within the US while stimulating social unrest. Nevertheless, revolutionaries retained fifty-three Americans, including two women and one man who were thought to be CIA operatives. Meanwhile, Iranian financial accounts held in American banks were frozen.

On November 22, Col Kyle met with MG Vaught to discuss Maj Gen Taylor's "Golden BB" plan for AC-130 strikes on Khatami Air Base. During their meeting, the subject of fire support for the rescue force was brought up. MG Vaught knew it was impossible to arm Army Special Mission Unit assaulters with enough CS gas or weaponry to defend themselves from hundreds of angry Iranians. Without fire support from the air, the rescue force and hostages could be trapped, injured, or killed with no possibility of escape. There was no doubt that once the element of surprise was breached, mobs of Iranians would surround the Embassy and the Iranian Army would mobilize in response. Furthermore, a ZSU-23-4 *Shilka* AAA gun was known to be stationed at a military outpost near the Embassy. If it were to be used against the rescue force or RH-53Ds, its four 23mm guns could wreak havoc on the helicopters and blow right through Embassy walls, decimating the rescue force and hostages. While it was possible for Navy carrier-based fighter aircraft to take out the *Shilka*, F-14s had no night capability or equipment to identify or track friendly forces. Fighter ordnance was either too big or inaccurate for Close Air Support (CAS) in urban terrain. Faced with a probable "show stopper," MG Vaught sought a suitable capability to provide fire support for Army Special Forces assaulters.

The next morning, Col Kyle met with MG Vaught and suggested he consider employing the AC-130 for fire support and overwatch for JTF-1-79. Since the AC-130 could remain on station for extended periods, had night vision sensors, and low collateral damage potential, it seemed like the ideal fire support system for the rescue force. From that point on, the "Golden BB" plan was dropped and AC-130s were committed to the rescue operation.

> "He considered this for a moment, then said, 'Okay, go ahead. But only the primary planners. I'll tell the Chairman.'" **Col (Ret.) Jim Kyle**

Col Kyle immediately contacted 16 SOS squadron commander Lt Col Florin White and operations officer Lt Col John "Pappy" Gallagher. A few days later, Col Kyle escorted them along with 16 SOS planner MSgt Don Boudreaux into a secure vault for a JTF-1-79 "read-in." Up until this point, nobody in the AC-130 community knew a rescue was being planned. Sitting inside the vault were two men, both with out of regulation haircuts, dressed in civilian attire. Though their appearance was casual, both men were US Army Majors assigned to a heretofore unknown Army Special Mission Unit Commanded by Col Charlie "Chargin' Charlie" Beckwith. The unit was America's clandestine anti-terrorist force—so classified the US Army denied its existence. Everything about the unit was nonconventional, including tactics, weapons, and mandatory wear of civilian clothing. Furthermore, soldiers assigned to this unit were exempt from strict Army grooming standards as a cover & deception tactic to blend in with the civilian population.

> "Following an Iran situation report, I explained the AC-130s primary mission was to provide close air support for the Army Special Forces assault on the Embassy. I stressed the crucial aspect of pre-strike and post-strike in-flight refueling to enable the long-distance route to and from the target area. The Intelligence assessment of the AAA threats in the Tehran area were ineffective against gunships at night, employing the element of surprise. This was a particularly challenging task because of the complexity of the urban area surrounding the Embassy compound. I directed the planning team to develop a method to quickly pinpoint good guys from bad guys so gunships could commence firing rapidly on designated hostile areas without endangering assaulters or hostages. I recommended the 40mm gun and Misch Metal HEI as the primary type ammunition for use to minimize the chances of collateral damage. I then left to allow Army Special Forces and 16 SOS planners to develop details of operations." **Col (Ret.) Jim Kyle**

AC-130s from the 16 SOS were then added to the Top-Secret list of JTF-1-79 mission units including the following:

- US Army Special Mission Unit
- 1/75 Ranger Battalion (C/1/75)
- USAF Combat Control Team "Brand X", assigned to Charleston AFB, SC.
- MC-130 Combat Talons assigned to the 8 SOS, Hurlburt Field, FL.
- MC-130 Combat Talons assigned to the 7 SOS, Rhein Main, Germany.
- MC-130 Combat Talons assigned to 1 SOS, Kadena AB, Okinawa Japan.
- EC-130 aircraft stationed at Keesler AFB, MS.
- RH-53D Helicopters assigned US Navy HM-16, Norfolk, VA.
- C-141B Starlifters assigned to Charleston AFB, SC.
- KC-135 Refueling Tankers assigned to Grissom AFB, IN.
- Harvest Eagle Fuel system and technicians assigned to MacDill, AFB, FL
- Central Intelligence Agency Special Activities Division
- Joint Communications Support Element, MacDill, AFB, FL

Though the AC-130 mission had changed, the ongoing training and tactics development deployment in Guam continued. As with the first mission assignment, AC-130 crews were required to penetrate Iranian airspace at low-level altitude to retain the element of surprise and prevent detection by radar. For this reason, crews trained to fly segmented routes in formation, while avoiding populated areas while maintaining strict radio silence. Not until they reached their working areas would they climb to altitude and establish a firing orbit.[11] There were caveats, however. As opposed to the lightly defended Abadan complex, the city of Tehran was equipped with an Integrated Air Defense System, Radar AAA guns, and US-made fighter jets.

Mission Planning Factors: The Iranian military was assessed to be capable during daylight operations but had no significant nighttime capability. This analysis drove the requirement for any US military operation into the hours of darkness.

Rules of Engagement: Minimal use of force was directed. Lethal force was to be used only as a last resort of self-defense.

Integrated Air Defense System IADS: Iran operated a US-designed IADS prior the beginning of the revolution but much of it fell into disrepair during the turmoil and economic collapse during the Shah's last days. The IADS capability was deemed marginal since all the US support contractors who operated and maintained the systems had already left the country.

Fighter-Interceptor aircraft: While it was known there were US-supplied F-4 and F-14 fighters, their operational status was unknown. For planning purposes, systems were presumed to be fully capable even if only in small num-

11 Phone interview with Col (Ret.) John "Pappy" Gallagher, Nov 21, 2013.

bers. Khatami Air Base was distant, but two F-4s were known to be on alert at Mehrabad Airport in Tehran. To counter airborne threats during the rescue, one AC-130 crew was assigned the responsibility to orbit the airport and fire on the F-4s when and if they started engines.

<u>Missile Systems:</u> Of particular concern were I-Hawk tracking radars which were not detectable by the AC-130's AN/ALR-69 Radar Warning Receiver. The problem could be mitigated somewhat by local purchase of commercial "Fuzz Buster" radar detectors mounted in the cockpits of mission aircraft.

<u>AAA:</u> Iranian 23mm *Shilka* AAA guns could be a threat at altitudes below nine thousand ft. AGL. Planned AC-130 altitude was nine thousand ft.; therefore, the threat to the AC-130 was determined to be moderate. The *Shilka*, however, was equipped with a tracking and acquisition radar, so it was considered a viable nighttime threat for low-flying aircraft, especially helicopters.

<u>Communications:</u> To enable communications security, cutting-edge Satellite Communications (SATCOM) radios were installed on AC-130s, complete with escape hatch mounted antennas that could be quickly installed and removed when not needed. To maintain positive tracking of Army Special Mission Unit Assaulters, Tactical Electromagnetic Impulse Generator (TEMIG) beacons and SS-109 transponders were employed to the maximum extent possible to maintain situation awareness and the locations of friendly forces.

TRAINING

Considering the rapid shift in AC-130 mission tasking and MG Vaught's absolute OPSEC mandate, AC-130 crews remained in Guam. MC-130 pilots from the 1 SOS, Kadena AB, Japan were sent to Guam to train AC-130 pilots for low-level, blacked-out flying while using AN/PVS-5 Night Vision Goggles (NVG). In practice, gunship pilots found PVS-5s marginally useful for low level operations and unacceptable for take-off or landing operations. Instead, PVS-5s were used by Flight Engineers, Right Scanners and Illuminator Operators to scan for light sources, including other aircraft, and to "talk on" the LLLTV sensor operator onto potential targets via the gunship's Gated Laser Intensifier for Night Television (GLINT).

Meanwhile, AC-130 crews from Hurlburt were sent to Yuma, Arizona and Indian Springs, Nevada for exercises touted as being routine joint readiness training. The scope of AC-130 training challenges were monumental, but crews primarily focused on critical aspects of fire support with emphasis on persistence, secure communications, and situation awareness. Since fire support requests were likely to be in close proximity to friendly forces or hostages, precise targeting was required.

> "Early training with the Army Special Mission Unit was troublesome as there were only limited AC-130 assets to train with ... we were able to use one 16th SOS stay-behind crew led by Maj Mike Couvillon to develop realistic training sce-

> narios including live-fire demos. Hurlburt based Combat Controller Sgt Rex Wollman provided range safety. Also restrictive was the remaining AC-130s at Hurlburt were not in-flight refuelable so we were unable to work in the SAC tanker options. That aside, we worked out basic details of how Gunships would be deployed, ingress/egress to target and in general terms provide fire support for Army Special Forces Assaulters/Marines at the Tehran embassy."
> **Col (Ret.) Jim Kyle**

Leading the fire support element for the Army Special Mission Unit was Major Lewis "Bucky" Burruss, a combat-experienced Mobile Strike Force (MIKE Force) Special Forces Officer and Forward Air Guide during the Vietnam War. Since close-in targeting in the vicinity of the Embassy and Foreign Ministry was likely, Major Burruss, SGM Forrest Foreman, and Major Mike Couvillon developed a map grid system pinpointing targets and zones to better coordinate fire support. At the same time, Army Special Forces Assistant Intelligence Officer, CPT Wade Ishimoto, identified potential Iranian Army threat weapon locations.

Mission success hinged on navigation and timing constraints to maintain the element of surprise. It was critical for the AC-130 to arrive over target at the same time the assault began. The entire mission was expected to take no more than forty-five minutes. All this time, AC-130 crews would remain overhead monitoring the situation real-time and firing only to keep Iranians separated from the rescue force, helicopters, and hostages. Once the operation began, one AC-130 would shadow the rescue element while maintaining direct radio contact with Major Burruss. Sensor operators would continually scan the area surrounding the Embassy searching for mobs and military elements approaching the compound, firing only upon direction of Major Burruss.

If Burruss requested fire support, Rules Of Engagement (ROE) handed down from the Carter Administration were strict. The Carter administration considered the mission a rescue, not a battle, so lethal force was prohibited unless used as a last resort for self-defense. President Carter specifically requested use of CS Riot Agent (tear gas), but there were physical limitations that could not be overcome. From an AC-130 perspective, use of 105mm CS projectiles was unrealistic since the thirty-two-pound steel projectile presented ricochet and fragmentation hazards and a TNT bursting charge. If application of CS was the only option, AC-130 crews would need to fire a near-constant barrage to counter wind effect and rapid dispersal of gas. Realizing an effective CS capability was not achievable by the AC-130, the concept of aerial delivery of CS was dropped. The rescue element, however, could employ CS grenades from short range, but Colonel Beckwith also considered CS ineffective and more of a problem for his assaulters than the Iranians.

Though it was clear use of CS gas was an issue, use was mandated by President Carter. While debating the quandary, other less lethal options were considered. Planners settled on use of 40mm HEI Misch Metal fired by the AC-130. This round was originally developed to start trucks on fire on the Ho Chi Minh Trail in Laos and Cambodia. Though it exploded with a loud bang, flash, and shower of sparks, its lethality was low in comparison with other AC-130 ordnance. Because of its high visual and audible signature and low lethality, it was clearly the best available capability for personnel suppression. In the end, the planning team cleverly devised a tactic where Major Burruss would carry a single CS grenade to the objective. If Assaulters needed fire support, Burruss would mark the target position with the CS grenade, then the AC-130 crew would fire 40mm Misch Metal at the grenade. Both felt the solution met the commander's intent and would be more likely to disperse angry mobs than CS gas alone.

> "The CS requirement/solution was actual. If the compound was attacked by a mob, I was going to throw it and call Pappy and tell him to hit the puff of smoke with some 40mm Misch." **Lieutenant Colonel (Ret.) Lewis "Bucky" Burruss**[12]

Once the hostages were secured, Assaulters would either climb over or breach the walls of the Embassy compound with explosive charges, then evacuate to the nearby Aryamehr soccer stadium for extraction.[13] Once onboard the helicopters, all former hostages would be flown to an

---

12 Email from LTC (Ret.) Lewis Burruss, Nov 2013.

13 The stadium was renamed "Azadi" (Persian for "freedom") at some point after the Iranian Revolution.

abandoned Air Base at Manzariyeh about sixty miles southwest of Tehran to be exfiltrated out of the country via C-141 and/or MC-130.

If the airfield was unable to be secured, a back up plan included exfiltration by vehicle convoy to the Turkish border with an AC-130 escort. For this reason, AC-130 and Army Special Mission Unit planners developed night convoy escort procedures using AN/PVS-5 NVGs. The tactic employed the AC-130's Gated Laser Illuminator for Night Television (GLINT) which was used to illuminate the roadway in front of a blacked out convoy as well as search for roadblocks or ambush sites. The first sign of trouble ahead would result in either a change of route or direct engagement by the AC-130.

AC-130 MISSION RESPONSIBILITIES

Gunship crews were to take off from Wadi Kena on night two then fly over Saudi Arabia and the Persian Gulf about thirteen hundred miles nonstop to their assigned operating areas.

> "The employment of Gunships at the time of the assault of the Embassy was to be one overhead the Embassy, one at Mehrabad Airport. The third gun supports the airfield seizure at Manzariyeh Airfield. Post attack, two guns escort helos to Manzariyeh with Assaulters and former hostages aboard. Eventually, all three Guns cover the C-141 exfil of the rescue force

and the fourth gun would be directed to targets by MG Vaught's Command Center." **Col (Ret.) James Kyle.**

AC-130 MISSION ASSIGNMENTS

Operation *Eagle Claw* Mission Assignments			
Crew	Aircraft	Working Area	Aircraft Commander
1	69-6569	Embassy Compound	Lt Col John "Pappy" Gallagher
2	69-6570	Mehrabad Airport	Capt Herman "Bubber" Youngblood
3	69-6567	Manzariyeh Airfield	Capt Donn Kegel
4	69-6575	Airborne Spare (as directed)	Capt James Lawrence

In January of 1980, eight RH-53D helicopters were flown to the USS Kitty Hawk as it passed Diego Garcia en route to the Gulf of Oman. Once it arrived on station, all RH-53Ds were flown to the USS Nimitz and quickly stowed below deck. Since such an increase in RH-53Ds could be construed as being unusual, JTF-1-79 planners intentionally exaggerated message traffic concerning increased mining of the Persian Gulf to establish a solid cover story.

By the middle of March, the JTF-1-79 mission plan was briefed to the JCS. With summer approaching, the hours of darkness were growing shorter to the point the route to Desert Two could not be completed before sunrise. Planners were aware if the mission did not launch before May, they would have to wait until Fall for acceptable conditions to return. National Security Advisor Dr. Zbigniew Brzeziński and a few fervent supporters of the plan were convinced JTF-1-79 had a satisfactory chance of success. The time crunch was a nagging problem and though the Chairman of the Joint Chiefs estimated probability of success could be as high as 60–70 percent, mission planners surmised probability of success was much lower due to operational risk and inadequate training.[14]

Col Beckwith and Col Kyle had reasons to be concerned since training was conducted on segments of the mission only and no full-scale rehearsal had been attempted. Though the AC-130/Army Special Mission Unit lash-up went well, other aspects of the mission, especially helicopter navigation and refueling operations were less capable than expected. Nevertheless, main operating locations were selected and at least some level of Advance Echelon (ADVON) inspections and preparations had occurred. The primary base of operations selected was a remote Egyptian military base near Wadi Kena, listed as Operating Location Alpha (OLA). Other Operating locations included:

- US Naval Base, Diego Garcia
- The USS Nimitz (helicopter launch point in the Indian Ocean).
- Operating Location Bravo (OLB) in Masirah, Oman.

14 Email from CPT (Ret.) Wade Ishimoto, Nov 2013.

- Desert One (remote refueling strip in Iran for the RH-53D helicopters).
- Desert Two ("hide site") in the mountains near Tehran.

On April 11, Chairman of the Joint Chiefs of Staff General David Jones gave his final briefing to the National Security Council, then on April 16, with current Human Intelligence (HUMINT) confirming the exact location and condition of the hostages, he briefed President Carter. Desperate to end the situation, President Carter approved JTF-1-79 under the code name Operation *Eagle Claw*. His order surprised many since the overwhelming consensus of mission commanders and Intelligence officers was the joint team was not yet adequately trained. Nevertheless, President Carter's order was final and the mission was a "go." When Secretary of State Cyrus Vance was advised of the decision, he resigned in protest.[15]

GENERAL MISSION PLAN DATES & TIMELINE

Feb–Mar:	MC-130s from the 7 SOS deploy to Wadi Kena, Egypt to establish operations under the cover story of a military exercise, then depart before the rescue force arrives.
Early Apr:	CIA Twin Otter crew infiltrates Iran with Combat Controller Maj John Carney to a remote airstrip code named "Desert One" to emplace remote-controlled landing lights and ensure desert surface will support C-130 and RH-53D operations.

15 Lenahan, *Crippled Eagle*, 109.

Mid Apr:	All USAF mission aircraft and support personnel, Army Special Mission Unit assaulters, USAF Combat Controllers and C/1/75 Rangers deploy to Wadi Kena, Egypt.
April 22	MC-130s, Army SF unit and a Ranger security element depart Wadi Kena for Masirah, Oman.
April 24	MC-130 and EC-130s launch from Oman and fly to Desert-1. RH-53Ds depart the USS Nimitz for Desert-1 for refueling. MC-130s and EC-130s depart Desert one and return to Oman. RH-53Ds transport Army SF to a hide site in the mountains near Tehran. Army SF links up with a covert ADVON team and are transported to a hide site. They remain concealed during daylight preparing for missions. Three MC-130 crews depart Masirah for Wadi Kena via C-130 support aircraft. C-141s land at Dhahran Saudi Arabia, pre-positioned for night two.
April 25–26	Col Beckwith and covert ADVON members perform clandestine recon of the Embassy and Foreign Ministry to ensure no "surprises" are evident. MC-130s load Ranger airfield seizure team onboard then take off for Tehran. AC-130s launch from Wadi Kena, in-flight refuel over Saudi Arabia and fly directly to Tehran.

	Covert ADVON team delivers Army SF Unit assaulters to Embassy and Foreign Ministry building via truck. AC-130s arrive over the Embassy, Mehrabad airport, and Manzariyeh at the same time Army SF begins rescue operation. MC-130s deploy a 100 man Ranger airfield seizure element on Manzariyeh airfield. Rangers secure Manzariyeh airfield, CCT controls air traffic. C-141 Starlifters land on Manzariyeh airfield. Hostages are secured and extracted from the Embassy grounds then transferred to the nearby Aryamehr soccer stadium for extract by RH-53. Helicopters fly everyone to Manzariyeh airfield where they board C-141s and MC-130s. All aircraft depart Manzariyeh airfield with hostages, Army SF Assaulters, Rangers and the Covert ADVON team. AC-130s destroy helicopters and all aircraft depart Iranian airspace.
	AC-130s disperse

OPERATION EAGLE CLAW MISSION EXECUTION:

With approval to proceed, MG Vaught directed covert insertion of a four man Army Special Mission Unit ADVON team posing as businessmen into Tehran via commercial air. This team, led by Dick Meadows, would acquire vehicles and prepare for the arrival of the rescue force.[16] On April 18, AC-130 tactical crewmen and support specialists began to deploy to Operating Location Alpha via C-141 and C-5 under routine travel orders listed as *Exercise Flintlock 80* in Germany. Though nobody believed they were actually going to Germany, the official cover story ensured a sanitized departure. In the following days, two ship AC-130 formations departed Hurlburt, destined for Egypt. For security reasons, aircraft were assigned fictitious call signs and pilots' names to disassociate the formations as being AC-130s. Both formations set out for a twenty-four hour nonstop flight directly to Wadi Kena, Egypt. Everything proceeded normally until the KC-135 tanker Capt James "Jim" Lawrence's aircraft was receiving fuel from was struck by lightning.

> "During one night refueling north of Bermuda... the KC-135 tanker was struck by lightning. A fireball passed across the KC-135, came down the refueling boom, across the top of our aircraft, and rolled off our left wingtip. I was temporarily blinded, but could do nothing but hit

16 Known as Major Meadows, he had retired from the Army at that rank, but was a Department of the Army Civilian (GS-13) at the time.

> the boom disconnect button, reduce power and drop back to gather my wits. ...the flight engineer and navigator did a check of all things electrical and decided there were no electrical problems apparent" **Lt Col (Ret.) James Lawrence.**[17]

As planned, the arrival of JTF-1-79 at Wadi Kena seemed as if it were a continuation of the ongoing exercise, so Egyptians thought nothing of it. Crews quickly found the location hot, dusty, and populated with large biting flies. All aircrews and Harvest Eagle fuel specialists were housed in one shelter, sleeping on standard issue military cots arranged in multiple rows. Rangers were bunked in an identical shelter next to the aircrews. The Army Special Mission Unit and Combat Control Team were bunked in another shelter near the end of the runway. The main command post was next to the aircrew shelter. All mission aircraft were parked near the aircrew shelter while crews prepared for a long night mission to Iran.

Two days before the start of the mission, MG Vaught called all gunship aircrews into the command post for a formal briefing. Standing on a table, he divulged the true nature of JTF-1-79 and stressed the importance of AC-130 fire support to the Army Special Mission Unit. He clearly stated AC-130s were to remain on station, regardless of fuel status until the entire rescue force had taken off from the extraction airfield. If there was a delay in departure, he

17 James Lawrence, *Airman's Odyssey* (Marietta, GA: Deeds Publishing, 2013), 164.

required at least one AC-130 to remain overhead, even if fuel condition was below what was required for exfiltration from Iran. If this were to happen, that crew was to remain overhead until fuel minimums, then land on Manzariyeh airfield, destroy their aircraft, then board the C-141 for extraction. Immediately after passing that order he said, "don't worry, Jimmy will buy you a new gunship." Since KC-135 tanker support was available over Saudi Arabia, there was little chance the situation would deteriorate to that point and most considered MG Vaught's comments as overemphasized bravado to make a point. Furthermore, mindful of OPSEC, he insisted in a complete post-mission black out of the identities and units involved in the mission. Aside from the cover story of *Exercise Flintlock 80*, he directed all four crews to take a long route home, preferably with a stop in Bermuda for a few days, while the news media focused on the hostages. Crews were urged to delay flying back to Hurlburt to give the impression they were returning from the exercise in Germany. Shortly after their meeting with MG Vaught, AC-130 crewmen were escorted to the Army Special Mission Unit shelter for a face-to-face meeting with Major Burruss to review details of the plan on a CIA-built three-dimensional model of downtown Tehran. Walking into the shelter, crewmen noticed upwards of one hundred Army Special Mission Unit soldiers dressed in blue jeans, t-shirts and widely varied civilian attire. For most, this was their first exposure to "the casual soldiers with long hair."

On April 22, as AC-130 crews at Wadi Kena prepared their aircraft for the mission, MC-130, EC-130 crews and Harvest Eagle fuels specialists departed Wadi Kena for Operating Location Bravo (OL-B).[18] The following day, Army Special Mission Unit Assaulters, USAF Combat Controllers, the US Army Ranger roadblock team and direct support specialists flew to OL-B via C-141. After all personnel were in place, they readied to depart for the first refueling point inside Iran, code named *Desert One*.

Army Special Mission Unit soldiers preparing to depart Wadi Kena. A mission ready AC-130H can be seen in the background. (Credit: DoD photo)

On the night of April 24, while AC-130 crews and maintainers were preparing for their mission, serious trouble

18 Col James H. Kyle, USAF (Ret.) and John R. Eidson, *The Guts to Try: the Untold Story of the Iran Hostage Rescue Mission by the on-Scene Desert Commander* (New York, NY: Orion Books, 1990), 181, 213.

occurred at *Desert One*. While MC-130s and EC-130s were establishing the FARP, a bus carrying Iranian passengers and a fuel tanker truck approached the site. CPT Ishimoto's roadblock team stopped the bus, filled with several dozen surprised Iranian civilians. While securing the bus, a vehicle approached and refused to stop. Ranger Robert Rubio fired an M72 Light Anti-Tank Weapon into the vehicle, halting it and causing its driver to flee. Unfortunately, the vehicle turned out to be a petroleum tanker truck carrying several thousand gallons of gasoline that erupted into a large fire, lighting the entire area. Meanwhile, EC-130s remained in place with engines running waiting for the helicopters to arrive.

The journey of the RH-53Ds was fractured and slow because of system failures and large suspended dust clouds known as "Haboobs" that resulted in zero-visibility conditions. The RH-53s limped in one by one to refuel. Prior to the helicopter's arrival, Col Kyle was advised via SATCOM from the command center that two of the eight helicopters launched had aborted but the crews were safe. Additionally, Beckwith came charging up to advise him that one of the helicopters that had just arrived had a problem and the pilot shut the engines down. Kyle ran to the disabled helicopter, jumped aboard to get a status report from the pilot. He was told one of the Marine Crew Chiefs discovered a hydraulic pump overheat situation and the helicopter was unsafe to fly in that condition. Colonels Kyle and Beckwith boarded the helicopter to debate options with the helicopter flight leader. After a heated discussion it was determined the hydraulic issue could not be repaired at Desert One. Ultimately, after an hour and a half on the ground, Col Beckwith was faced with a devastating fact; without six flyable helicopters, the mission could not be completed. Col Beckwith made a decision to abort and Col Kyle transmitted a SATCOM report to MG Vaught explaining the situation. MG Vaught relayed the message to President Carter, who concurred with the decision to abort. MG Vaught then directed the captured Iranian bus passengers to be released and ordered the RH-53Ds to return to the *USS Nimitz*.

In the process of departing, an RH-53D crashed into EC-130 (call sign Republic 4). The Loadmasters, Radio Operator, and more than forty Army Special Mission Unit Assaulters onboard Republic 4 managed to escape the burning EC-130; however, the cockpit crew of five perished. RH-53D casualties were three, with only the pilot and copilot surviving the crash. Unable to affect the situation or retrieve the bodies of their fallen comrades, the remaining elements of the rescue force hastily withdrew, plowing through a sand berm on takeoff roll. One MC-130 crew experienced engine damage, ultimately shutting it down before exiting Iranian airspace. The rescue force returned to Oman, then Wadi Kena, before setting out for CONUS a day later.

After Operation *Eagle Claw* aborted, AC-130 mission participants returned to Hurlburt just as subtly as they left. No mass debriefing was conducted; however, all were ordered to sign an SF-Form 312 Nondisclosure Agreement (NDA). For many years, few people outside the Special

Operations Community were aware of the planned involvement of AC-130 gunships in the rescue plan.

OPERATION HONEY BADGER

Almost immediately following the disaster at Desert One, efforts to develop a second rescue plan began.

> "Operation Honey Badger was established by Carter personally to do two things;
>
> 1. In extremis rescue of the hostages should they be clearly endangered—notice to be ten days prior to execution.
> 2. Development of a real, robust, permanent force for future ops of this nature. Beirut, Baader-Meinhof, Brigada Rosso etc. all were the background to the failed mission and subsequent negative publicity. Dugway, White Sands, Bliss and YPG were all major training areas. Issue was altitude and distance with OPSEC as a major determinate." Colonel (Ret.) Keith Nightingale

In July 1980, a Joint Army and Air Force mission code named Operation *Honey Badger* began. This full-scale mission rehearsal included nearly all the mission participants from *Eagle Claw* plus USAF HH-53C/Pave Low and the US Army Task Force 158 helicopter fleet.[19]

---

19 Task Force 158 was renamed named Task Force 160, later 160th Special Operations Aviation Group, and finally 160th Special Operations Aviation Regiment.

The *Honey Badger* plan was larger and more elaborate than what had been assembled for Operation *Eagle Claw*. For several weeks, AC-130, MC-130, TF-158 crews, Army Special Forces and Rangers trained on the White Sands Missile Range, New Mexico. Primary AC-130H operations were based out of Condron Army Airfield, while mission participants were billeted at a barracks compound about fifteen miles from the airfield.

Because of the unique nature of the mission and classification of the *Honey Badger* element, peacetime operational safety restrictions were essentially thrown out the window to allow crews to develop mission-specific tactics. Highly orchestrated airfield seizure tactics were invented, eventually leading to a full-scale, blacked-out nighttime airfield seizure of Reese AFB. Identification Friend or Foe (IFF) was accomplished with the GLINT via a small piece of reflective tape on all ground force personnel. Reflections shined like a beacon when illuminated by the GLINT but were not visible without night vision equipment. GLINT illumination was also useful to spotlight Landing Zones (LZ) and for directing fire support for ground forces, but the GLINT exacerbated PVS-5 depth perception issues in both regards. From that point on, the GLINT was used judiciously, and only under circumstances where it would not hinder MC-130 or Helicopter crews on final approach. Another method of IFF used to track helicopters and ground forces were TEMIG beacons.

On July 29, 1979, the Shah of Iran died in Egypt, but Khomeini allowed the Muslim Student Followers of the

Imam's Line to retain the hostages. At the same time, secret negotiations between both countries continued.

By the fall of 1980, *Honey Badger* was extensively rehearsed and ready to go, but Iranians scattered the hostages in multiple prisons throughout Iran, rendering rescue of all hostages during a single mission impossible.

On December 15, 1980, JTF-1-79 was formally dissolved and responsibility for planning and execution of any future rescue was passed to a newly established Joint Special Mission Unit at Fort Bragg, NC.

By mid-January 1981, the Carter administration and Ayatollah Khomeini had reached a diplomatic agreement via an Algerian intermediary (the Algiers Accords) to release all hostages. Nevertheless, as an apparent affront to President Carter, Khomeini waited until President Reagan was inaugurated on January 20, 1981 to release all 52 hostages.

MISSION DEBRIEF

Operation *Eagle Claw* was a complicated mission with many moving parts. Army Special Forces and C/1/75 Rangers were well trained for the task. MC-130 and EC-130 crews and Harvest Eagle fuel specialists performed magnificently under difficult circumstances. Aside from the long-distance routes to and from their target areas, the demands on AC-130 crews were CAS centric and well rehearsed. The RH-53D helicopter contingent was adequately trained, but their task was vastly different from their usual mission. Though Marine and Navy crews put forth a Herculean effort, several crew men's willingness to complete the mission was questioned by Colonels Beckwith and Kyle. Another important factor contributing to the abort was the lack of full-scale dress rehearsal with all personnel and aircraft involved. Unfortunately, an accumulation of unforeseen negative circumstances contributed to multiple personnel and mechanical issues, ultimately resulting in mission abort. Had the mission progressed as planned into night two, AC-130 sensor capabilities and firepower would have certainly dispersed Iranian mobs advancing on the rescue force. How those effects would have played into the larger scheme however, will never be known.

In the months following the aborted mission, Admiral James Holloway led a commission to analyze JTF-1-79 failures. Though details of the findings were debated for many years, the experience was an important factor in stimulating reforms in special operations organizational structure. There is no doubt the Office of Assistant Secretary of Defense for Special Operations/Low Intensity Conflict (ASD SO/LIC) and a Joint Special Operations capability were formed as a direct result of Operation *Eagle Claw*.

> "Vitally important were the lessons learned as a result of Eagle Claw, especially the quantum leap in tactics and associated unique hardware capabilities for night Special Operations. SOF forces today are far better prepared to support contingencies worldwide ... Any place - Any time - Anywhere." **Col (Ret.) Jim Kyle**

Considering the post-Vietnam reduction of SOF, the complexity of the task, level of effort, and acceptance of risk, Operation *Eagle Claw* has gone down in US military history as one of the most successful military failures of the 20th Century. There is no doubt the Phoenix-like rise of all modern SOF capabilities can be traced back to that one night on April 24, 1980.

SITUATION REPORT: 1981–1986

Crews participated in numerous on-station and off-station training exercises during this period. TDY locations included Alaska for *Exercise Brim Frost* and Korea for *Exercise Team Spirit*. When not deployed, daily operations of the 16 SOS and 711 SOS could be considered mundane since most flying training missions were straightforward four hour local missions to Eglin ranges A-77 or A-78 and dry fire missions over the local area. Gunships lit Bob Hope's entrance to Choctawhatchee High School football stadium with their 2KW spotlight during annual fundraisers for the Theresa Village and Bob Hope Village Widows home. Periodically, crews would be sent out on Search And Rescue (SAR) missions. Sometimes crews would find poachers on the Eglin Reservation during training missions and turn them into authorities. Underlying all other tasking was the priority to maintain two AC-130H aircraft on call for SOF mission tasking; therefore, 16 SOS crews traveled to Ft Bragg frequently to train and develop tactics to support Joint training with Army Special Operations Forces.

In 1983, all USAF special operations aircraft, including AC-130H gunships, were transferred from Tactical Air Command to Military Airlift Command. There were multiple reasons for the transfer of special operations from Tactical Air Command to Military Airlift Command (MAC). Military Airlift Command was almost entirely made up of multi-engine cargo aircraft, and TAC was dominated by single and dual engine fighters and the pilots who flew them.

Aside from the perception, AC-130s found a better home in the Military Airlift Command. MAC's 23rd Air Force focused specifically on Special Operations and was ultimately headquartered at Hurlburt Field. On the operational side, MAC had a completely different culture than TAC, which took some getting used to. Though the standards and administrative procedures of Military Airlift Command were not fully compatible with special operations, maintenance support and funding were much better. Just about forty miles northeast of Hurlburt Field, Air Force Reserve Command continued to operate the AC-130A at Duke Field. Likewise, the 711 SOS supported the gunship mission during exercises and operations, but lack of aerial refueling capability limited mission tasking.

CHAPTER TWO

OPERATIONS *BIELD KIRK, BLUE FLAME,* AND *BLINKING LIGHT,* EL SALVADOR, 1983–1990

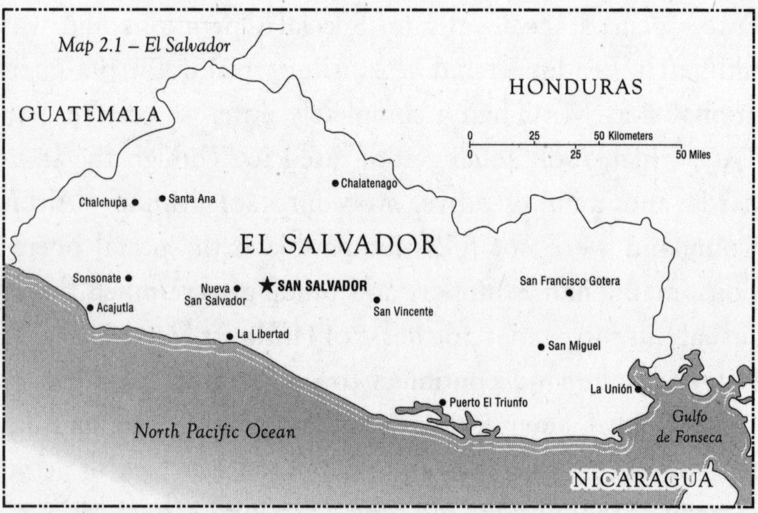

Map of El Salvador (Credit: Carl Mauro II)

US military strategy in the late 1970s focused almost exclusively on a World War Three scenario in Europe, between the USSR and NATO allies. The bulk of US military spending was dedicated towards what was referred to as The Cold War, a threat on threat stalemate between the east and west.

At the time, Cuba was the only communist nation near the Continental United States (CONUS) and little attention was given to Central and South America.

In the summer of 1979, Nicaragua fell to communist rule. In the fall of 1979, a full-scale civil war broke out in El Salvador between the right-wing Revolutionary Government Junta (JRG) and the left-wing Farabundo Martí National Liberation Front (FMLN). The Carter Administration supported the JRG with military aid hoping the situation would stabilize with time and effort.

By 1980, the JRG had morphed into a full-fledged military government that ruled by force, intimidation, and murder. In February of 1980, Archbishop Oscar Romero wrote a letter to President Carter requesting cessation of military aid since the JRG was killing scores of Salvadoran citizens who opposed military rule. About a month later, Archbishop Romero was assassinated while celebrating Mass. A week later at his funeral, forty-two mourners were killed by Salvadoran Army snipers. In December of 1980, members of the Salvadoran National Guard were suspected of raping and killing three American nuns and a missionary. In response, military aid was cut off but was re-established six weeks later.

During 1981 and 1982, El Salvadoran Army and FMLN tactics became increasingly violent, resulting in murders by death squads and large-scale massacres of those suspected of supporting the FMLN. In 1982, the FMLN began calling for a peace settlement while elections were being held. In the end, the voting process was stymied by threat of violence, attacks, and boycotts, rendering results invalid.

With the situation unravelling in El Salvador and the potential for a communist takeover, the Joint Chiefs of Staff (JCS) found intelligence provided by the El Salvadoran Army to be unreliable and untrustworthy. Determined to acquire accurate and timely intelligence information, US Army Special Forces were deployed to monitor El Salvadoran counter insurgency operations. At the same time, the AC-130H was selected to surveille and record movements of the El Salvadoran Army and FMLN guerrillas during the hours of darkness. Though the Sensitive Reconnaissance Operations (SRO) mission was far removed from typical gunship tasking, the AC-130 could surveille areas for hours at a time, and its nighttime sensor and video recording capabilities were rare commodities in the DoD.

On February 27, 1983, Chairman Joint Chiefs, GEN John Vessey, directed the classified reconnaissance effort Operation *Bield Kirk* to begin. To maintain operational security, AC-130 personnel deployed under routine travel orders indicating destination as "Anyplace within Central America." The deployment cover story was listed as Unit support of 193rd Infantry Brigade, but there was no interaction with them whatsoever. On February 28, an Advance Echelon (ADVON) team activated 1st Special Operations Wing (SOW) Detachment 1 (DET-1) at Howard Air Force Base, Panama.

In early March, four AC-130H gunships, five crews, and support personnel departed Hurlburt Field for Howard AFB. Supporting the gunships were two KC-135 tankers, crews, and support personnel from Grissom AFB, Indiana.

Upon arrival, officers were billeted in the Visiting Officers Quarters (VOQ) near the Officer's Club. Enlisted crewmen were billeted in family housing units near the Navy's Farfan housing area. There were security concerns regarding crews billeted in base housing; however, since neighbors had seen overflow from billeting happen previously, there were no questions asked or accusations made by base housing residents. AC-130 maintainers stayed in barracks on Howard, near their aircraft.

Gunship maintainers worked around the clock to prepare each gunship for mission tasking. Since arming of peacetime SRO aircraft was not permitted, number two 20mm gun was removed entirely and number one gun had its barrels removed. The 40mm gun barrel was removed and the 105mm blast diffuser was removed and the muzzle closed off with tape. The unarmed mandate extended to personal defense weapons also. Crews were not allowed to carry their customary self-defense Smith & Wesson Model 15 .38 caliber revolvers. The only weapon aircrews were allowed to carry was a survival knife.

Initially, the El Salvadoran Army was not advised of the AC-130 mission. Instead, deception and sanitation procedures included removal of all insignia and unit patches and use of a cover story of being a crewman on a cargo aircraft delivering humanitarian supplies. The sole identification allowed to be carried on a mission was the standard AF black leather aircrew name tag, Geneva Convention ID card and dog tags, and small personal survival kits as long as it met security sanitization requirements. The only other item allowed to be taken was an Escape & Evasion (E&E) kit furnished by the Intelligence office which would be signed out before the mission and turned in after completion.

Typical mission profiles were repetitive. Before takeoff, during mission planning, crews were given prioritized surveillance targets and routes between targets. Because of the distance involved, mission length was ten plus hours. Their course traveled northwest off the west coast of Panama, Costa Rica, Nicaragua and Honduras for nearly three hours. Once near the coast of El Salvador, the gunship would rendezvous with a KC-135 (rarely a KC-10) tanker using standard en route overtaking (known as Gin Bear procedures) which was accomplished with minimum lighting and radio silence. During the operation, the only communication an AC-130 crew had with the tanker was through the refueling boom when connected. Once fully fueled, the KC-135 turned towards Howard AFB and the AC-130 continued towards El Salvador. Gunship crews then turned off all exterior lighting and blacked out the interior lights as much as possible.

Before crossing into El Salvadoran airspace, crews were required to check in with two US mission monitors. The first was a Command and Control Communications (C3) ship stationed off the coast, call sign Jittery Prop. The second was a mountaintop US radar site code named Carrot Top. Once all prerequisites had been met, crews went "feet dry" near the river outlet at La Union or near the Rio Lempa and the Playa de Icacal at altitudes ranging from six thousand–eight thousand feet AGL. It was not uncommon for crews to be re-tasked in-flight depending on the ground situation being reported, but most missions occurred as planned. Typically, crews were tasked to search and video record an average of six–ten locations per mission. However, during high activity periods, upwards of twenty locations were tasked.

Though the AC-130 operated above the threat range of small arms, they would occasionally draw small arms tracer fire that fell off before reaching altitude. One of the initial crews did draw suspected 20mm AAA fire from an El Salvadoran Army gun site, but no damage occurred.

After about four hours in the country, with adequate fuel remaining to return to Howard AFB, crews exited El Salvador for a three hour return flight. It was difficult for some to stay awake on the return leg of the mission at 0400–0500 in the morning. The light emitted from the navigator's equipment usually kept him awake, but the pilots and flight engineer were in the dark and the aircraft was on autopilot. More than once did the navigator call for a heading change at a way point only to discover the pilots and flight engineer fast asleep, strapped into their seats.

> "The missions were long, with some 'dawn patrols' that landed after sunup the next morning. After a particularly long mission, we were getting radar vectors to Howard AFB. The co-pilot was flying and was heading to the final approach course. I saw we were approaching final but the copilot did not start the turn onto final. I asked twice if he was going to turn but got no response. I looked over and saw the copi-

lot, chin resting on his chest, sound asleep. I was not surprised since we had not yet adapted to a full night schedule. He bought the first round of 'bravos' that morning." **Lt Col (Ret.) Tom Waylett,** Aircraft Commander

The gunship crew would typically land at Howard AFB as the sun began to rise, debrief their findings and submit video tapes to intelligence analysts for review and study. Initially, two missions were flown every night, but eventually the tasking was reduced to one mission per night. There were, however, critical time periods where the unit would surge and provide additional aircraft and crews to fly the mission. These periods normally coincided with events such as elections or holidays.

Mission tasking was high during the first two weeks of the operation. It was dark by the time AC-130s skirted the coast of Nicaragua while over international waters. During this portion of the mission, crew members reported they were being shadowed by small aircraft. Intelligence analysts believed crews were seeing things and the stars were playing tricks on them, but crews were certain there was something following them. The small aircraft appeared to be behind the gunship, just after coming off the tanker and prior to going "feet dry" into El Salvador.[1] The aircraft appeared to be Lear Jets, but they stayed just far enough away to make positive identification difficult. About three weeks into the mission, the lead-in story on ABC News showed an AC-130

1 Feet dry is a common aviation term indicating overfly from a body of water across a coastline.

taking off from Howard Air Force Base with a story that followed headlining a story that AC-130 Gunships were flying missions over El Salvador. Obviously, the origin of the shadows was exposed, but US Officials denied AC-130 activity in El Salvador.

After the story broke, locals started watching the Howard flight line closely. For weeks, reporters with binoculars could see AC-130s come and go. They'd see fresh aircraft come in from Hurlburt and witness gun barrels being removed and dream up wild reasons for it. One news article accused AC-130 crews of "firing so much the barrels had to be changed after every mission," a claim crews found particularly amusing since they didn't carry ammunition and their guns were deactivated.

Though OPSEC was compromised, the mission continued unabated while the El Salvadoran Army thought the AC-130 was focusing their attention solely on the FMLN, but, in fact, both sides were being watched. During the following months, crews and maintainers developed a regular forty-five day rotation from Hurlburt to Panama.[2] Missions continued, activity was observed, videotaped and reported to Intelligence on every flight. However, weather was sometimes a factor.

In August 1983 the United States and Honduras began a large-scale military exercise code named Big Pine. US Army, Air Force, and Navy participated, sending two Aircraft Carrier Battle Groups to operate off the coast of

---

2 As the mission progressed into the second year, rotations were reduced to thirty days, then fourteen days.

Honduras. Since the *Bield Kirk* mission was classified as Special Category (SPECAT), Aircraft Carrier sailors were not aware of nightly AC-130 missions which would pass almost directly overhead. Similarly, AC-130 crews were unaware of the position of the Battle Group.

> "On one mission, just after coming off the tanker, the scanners reported bogeys approaching the aircraft. In a flurry of traffic calls, the scanners informed me that there were F-14 fighters off of each wing. As I was talking to the Nav about getting a hold of the Navy to have them call off their dogs, the IO called to tell me to 'hold what you got' because there was an F-14 pilot looking at him through the bubble. He was in close trail and the IO thought if we made any move, we'd have a midair. That got the adrenaline flowing!" **Lt Col (Ret.) Tom Waylett,** Aircraft Commander

On August 8, 1984, a joint State Department and US SOUTHCOM news briefing on Intelligence Information on External Support of the Guerrillas in El Salvador took place.[3] The original briefing was classified and prepared for members of the Congress. Ambassador Thomas R. Pickering, at the urging of Congressional members, worked with the DoD to declassify 95 percent of the briefing material.

---

3 Thomas R. Pickering and Paul F. Gorman, "News Briefing on Intelligence Information on External Support of the Guerrillas in El Salvador," (Washington, DC: Released by the Department of State and the Department of Defense, August 1984).

At the press conference, Ambassador Pickering and the Commander-in-Chief of US SOUTHCOM, General Paul F. Gorman, told the world about external FMLN support coming from Nicaragua via land and sea to support the guerrillas. During the course of this briefing, AC-130 activities were publicly disclosed including video of arms transfers from ships into large ocean-capable canoes (called cayucas). Furthermore, AC-130 video recorded overland movement of arms shipments within El Salvador and from Honduras by pack animals.

When the AC-130 *Bield Kirk* connection was revealed, the mission continued under the code name *Blue Flame*. There were no mysteries anymore, so guerillas sought cover whenever the gunship was heard approaching overhead. Concealment from the gunship in open terrain was futile since hotspots were easy to detect on the Infrared sensor. During high-moon illumination conditions, personnel were easy to spot with both LLLTV and IR sensors. Once individuals were spotted, gunship crews reported activity to *Jittery Prop* or *Carrot Top* who would advise the Salvadoran Army. This lash-up worked effectively especially with the US-trained ARCE Battalion and the Salvadoran-trained, anti-terrorist, Ponce Battalion. FMLN guerrillas were aware that being spotted by the AC-130 would certainly be followed by an attack by the El Salvadoran Army.

Towards 1986, *Blue Flame* missions continued while guerrillas became more proficient at avoiding detection. Essentially, anytime an AC-130 was overhead, guerillas remained hidden and tactically insignificant.

Year-round weather conditions limited intelligence collection efforts. During the dry season, the countryside was absolutely covered with agricultural burns and ever present livestock. Gunship sensors were state-of-the-art, but it was still difficult to distinguish between a group of humans or a group of cattle moving through tall grass and jungle. Crews recorded everything they saw and routinely reported cattle sightings. Intelligence analysts questioned whether some of the targets were cattle and called reports inconclusive. Gunship crews were confident they were sighting cattle since there is no mistaking a 1,000-pound steer for a 150-pound man. Since all video tapes were sent to the JCS at the Pentagon for review, gunship crews were chastised for identifying most unidentifiable hot spots as cattle. From that point on, AC-130 crews were prohibited from using any and all descriptions of cattle. Instead, the acceptable term mandated was "hot spot larger than human," which was used for the remainder of the operation.

By 1986, the fact AC-130s were flying missions over El Salvador became common knowledge and there were organized protests at the Hurlburt Field front gate. Over time, the operation name was changed to *Blinking Light* but the mission remained the same. At one point in 1986, under the code name of Operation *Nine Iron*, two aircraft were tasked to strike two targets in El Salvador. Crews, supported by KC-135 tankers flew nonstop from Hurlburt Field, across Honduras and into El Salvador. About six hours into the mission, both crews orbited their assigned targets with guns armed, ready to fire. After orbiting for almost an hour waiting for clearance to fire, both crews were ordered to abort their missions and return to Hurlburt Field. After almost 14 hours airborne, crews landed uneventfully on Hurlburt, appearing as they had just completed a routine training mission.

On June 17, 1986, a KC-135A took off from Howard AFB on what was then the standard profile. After completing their mission and return to Howard AFB, they were informed the KC-135 that refueled them crashed on landing with no survivors.[4]

AC-130H gunship crews continued flying nightly missions to El Salvador until October 15, 1987 when *Blinking Light* missions were scaled back to focus on security of US facilities and personnel stationed in Panama. By 1987, USSOCOM was established, and in 1988, the 23rd Air Force reported directly to USSOCOM. Both commands technically owned the AC-130 fleet and Gunships were in high demand for special operations tasking. The JCS, however, maintained a stranglehold on the small fleet for *Blinking Light* tasking. In light of the change in AC-130 command structure, 23rd Air Force Commander Maj Gen Robert Patterson and 16 SOS Commander Lt Col Howard Chambers grew increasingly concerned that gunship crew readiness was negatively affected by the *Blinking Light* mission. Furthermore, AC-130 missions at Howard AFB were split between *Blinking Light*

4 Aircrew members lost in the 305th Air Refueling Wing, Grissom AFB, KC-135A crash, tail number 63-7983, crew R-135, were: Capt Thomas McDerby, 29, Aircraft Commander, 1 Lt John Bristow, 25, Copilot 1 Lt Wayne K.S. Ching, 25, Navigator, SSgt Quinn Dewitt, 31, Boom Operator.

and *Prayer Book* tasking in direct support of Panama Canal security because of deteriorating relations with Panamanian dictator Manuel Noriega. Since AC-130A gunships were not equipped with aerial refueling capabilities, they could not perform the *Blinking Light* mission from Panama. Instead, AC-130A gunships were deployed to Palmerola, Honduras from August to September 1988 to evaluate potential to move the operation there. Unfortunately, the deployment discovered multiple operational, infrastructure, and support problems which deemed operations unfeasible. The result was to maintain *Blinking Light* operations at Howard AFB. From there, the 16 SOS would "dual-hat" missions between *Blinking Light* and *Prayer Book*, while AC-130A gunships would fly *Prayer Book* missions exclusively. This arrangement continued until the operation officially ended.

PROJECT PEACE ASP AND PEACE EMERALD

In 1984, coinciding with AC-130 operations in El Salvador, the US Department of State initiated Project *Peace Asp* to equip the El Salvadoran Air Force with AC-47 gunships. Crew members from the 16 SOS participated in flight testing at Eglin AFB to develop and field the system. Two AC-47s and crews were sent to El Salvador in 1985 to train the initial cadre of Fuerza Aérea Salvadoreña (El Salvador Air Force). The aircraft were similar to the original AC-47 *Spooky* gunship, but instead of being armed with mechanically complex MXU-470-gun modules, they were armed with .50 caliber machine guns. Aside from easier operation, the .50 caliber round was capable of much higher operational altitudes which was important in El Salvador's mountainous terrain. After successful fielding of AC-47, in 1988 an identical program was established for Columbia code named project *Peace Emerald.*

MISSION DEBRIEF

The AC-130 mission commitment to the mission in El Salvador ran continuously for nearly seven years. National Command Authorities were satisfied with the intelligence collected by AC-130 crews, even though it was difficult to differentiate guerrilla activity from normal day-to-day activities of farmers and ranchers. The psychological effect of constant AC-130 missions caused many FMLN Guerillas to either scramble or hide when hearing the sound of the gunship approaching. Gunship crews found the missions long, tedious, and sometimes boring. At the time, it was the longest continuous mission to date ever accomplished by the 16 SOS and was considered both good and bad for the squadron.

On the good side, direct JCS tasking ensured the AC-130 would not be retired, regardless of the desires of TAC or MAC. Another positive element was the upgrade of the communications suite to include modern, secure satellite communications. On the negative side, the squadron of ten aircraft was spread thin from 1983–1989 while supporting missions in El Salvador, Grenada, Panama, exercises in Korea, Alaska and elsewhere. Attempts to fortify AC-130 operations in

Central America with Air Force Reserve AC-130A aircraft were problematic since none were equipped with aerial refueling capabilities, but at least some AC-130A missions were conducted from Honduras.

Overall, the mission in El Salvador proved the validity of situation awareness, psychological effect, and sensor capability of the AC-130. It also proved the adaptability of AC-130 crews in the SRO realm, who successfully completed their mission without firing a shot.

CHAPTER THREE

OPERATION *URGENT FURY*, OCTOBER–NOVEMBER 1983

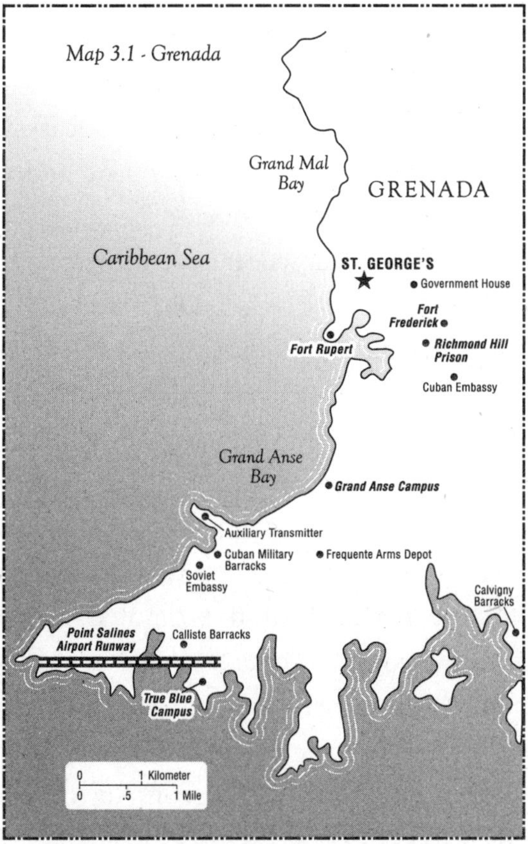

Map of Grenada, 1983 (Credit: Carl Mauro II)

Grenada is an island of the Windward chain, located about fifteen hundred miles southeast of Key West, FL. During the early 1980s, the nation's population was approximately ninety-one thousand and its principal economy was based on nutmeg cultivation, international trade, and tourism. St. George's University and College of Medicine, in which many international students were enrolled, was also a significant source of revenue.

In 1973, Grenadian lawyer Maurice Bishop formed the New Jewel Movement (NJM) party. The NJM was popular with Grenadians as Bishop courted favor with the oppressed population via the Grenadian radio broadcasting system. The station broadcast local popular music and news programs promoting a Marxist theme.

In 1974 Grenada gained independence from Britain. The first Prime Minister of Grenada, Sir Eric Gairy, ruled by brute force. To maintain absolute control, Gairy formed a secret police element called the "Mongoose Gang" to jail, torture, or murder anyone challenging his authority.

In 1979, Bishop's People's Revolutionary Army (PRA) overthrew Gairy, dismantled his cabinet, appointed himself Prime Minister, and suspended Grenada's Constitution. With newfound power, Bishop promoted Marxist ideology, but did not consider himself a Communist. Bishop's Deputy Prime Minister Bernard Coard however, was willing to transform Grenada into a strict Marxist military state, a position shared with General Hudson Austin, commander of the People's Revolutionary Army (PRA).

From that point on, Bishop was recognized as the savior of Grenada, but tremendous effort was needed to improve Grenada's economy. Bishop pledged to improve the island's economy knowing the island's beautiful coastline and relaxed lifestyle attracted tourists from Europe and North America. Increasing tourism was a problem however, since the island's only airport (*Pearls*) was small, remote, and only capable of handling commuter type aircraft.

Efforts to build a new airport on the southern tip of the island known as *Point Salines Estate* began in the 1970s with Canadian-developed plans and British and US contractors. The project moved slowly until Bishop secured loans from Cuba and numerous Middle Eastern and South American countries. Bishop accepted foreign aid from any country offering it, including Fidel Castro, who considered Bishop a son. Beginning in 1979, Castro provided Bishop's NJM economic assistance including medical personnel, teachers, and an improved radio broadcasting system. Castro also pledged millions of dollars to finish construction of the Point Salines airport project.

In December of 1979, Cuban Construction workers arrived in Grenada and Cuban influence and funding greatly affected Bishop's willingness to cooperate with Castro. While Bishop's relations with Cuba improved, relations with the United States declined. The Reagan Administration watched closely as Grenada slid more towards a hard-line Marxist government, but retained a wait-and-see attitude. After Bishop announced a promise to allow Soviet and

Cuban military aircraft to land on Point Salines airport, US National Command Authorities took notice.

Concerned with the militarization of Grenada, US military forces conducted *Exercise Ocean Venture* in August of 1981.[1] The exercise included a mock invasion of an island near Puerto Rico assigned the fictional name "Amber and the Amberdines." The exercise spooked Bishop, who felt the US was preparing to invade Grenada. In response, Bishop requested increased military aid from Cuba and other communist states.

By 1983, Grenada was heavily armed with warehouses full of Eastern Bloc weapons, armored vehicles, and encampments of Cuban military advisors. By that time, most Grenadians thought Cuban presence on the island had less to do with increasing tourist trade and more to do with military occupation of their country.

On October 13, 1983, long-standing friction between Bishop and Coard resulted in Coard demanding Bishop stand down. When Bishop refused, Coard ordered General Austin to place him under house arrest and incarcerate his staff at *Fort Rupert* located on the southwestern coast of the island. Coard then placed Britain's Governor-General of Grenada, Sir Paul Scoon, his wife, and staff under house arrest in the Governor-General's mansion.

News of Bishop's arrest concerned Grenadians who demanded his immediate release, but Coard refused. Then, on October 19, a large group of supporters gathered at

---

1 Two AC-130H gunships participated in Exercise Ocean Venture.

Bishop's residence, overpowered PRA guards, and secured his release. Emboldened by his rescuers, Bishop led a group march to Fort Rupert to rescue his staff. Within a short time, as they marched towards Fort Rupert, PRA militants opened fire, killing or wounding more than one hundred people. In the melee, Bishop and seven others were captured, taken to the center drill court of Fort Rupert, then executed. In light of Bishop's execution, Gen Austin brushed Coard aside and declared himself head of the Revolutionary Military Council (RMC) and the nation's new head of government. Austin then ordered a 24 hour curfew and issued orders for PRA soldiers to shoot violators on sight.[2]

The murder of Bishop and his staff caught both US and Cuban governments off guard. The Reagan administration watched as Grenada fell to communist rule and felt other countries in the Caribbean and South America were next in line. The Organization of Eastern Caribbean States (OECS) was also concerned a communist threat to their countries was at hand. The Prime Minister of Barbados, Tom Adams, flew to Grenada to meet with Gen Austin, but his influence was rejected as he refused to stand down the Revolutionary Military Council. When Sir Paul Scoon met with Prime Minister Adams, he urged him to convince the Organization of Eastern Caribbean States and western powers to depose the RMC and restore order in Grenada.

US National Command Authorities (NCA) were alarmed, but the coup d'état in itself was not considered jus-

---

2 Lee E. Russell and M. Albert Mendez, *Grenada, 1983: Men at Arms Series* (London: Osprey Publishing, 1985), 5.

tification for US military action. There were, however, a large number of US citizens known to be enrolled in St. George's University School of Medicine. Since clandestine intelligence sources indicated students were confined to their dormitories and surrounded by armed militants, military intervention was an option if Americans were not allowed to leave the island. Because of limited intelligence information, NCA feared the students might have already been taken hostage, but, in reality, they were isolated from PRA violence. Dr. Robert Jordan, an American faculty member at St. George's Medical School, observed the situation with great interest.

> "There were a few little boys with big guns just across the street in the Carifta cottages area in Grand Anse and lots of Cuban workers and a few PRA next to our True Blue campus. They never ventured on our campuses (except in a few planned meetings with our Vice Chancellor, Geoffrey Bourne and always in a small group with AKs kept in their cars). In reality we could move about rather easily during the curfew, especially at night." **Dr. Robert Jordan**

Diplomatic Caveats: If Coard allowed the US State Department to peacefully evacuate American citizens, Diplomats promised there would be no military action. When Coard refused to allow American Diplomats to land on Grenada, talk to American students, or allow them to leave the island, mental alarms were activated in the

White House. At the time, the Iran hostage situation was still fresh in everyone's mind and the Reagan Administration feared a repeat of that lengthy and painful ordeal. Believing US citizens were being detained against their will, a Special Situation Group (SSG) of senior policy makers began making plans for military action. Shortly after the SSG met, they recommended the *USS Independence* Aircraft Carrier Battle Group en route to Beirut, Lebanon be diverted to Grenada.

Mission Objectives: The primary mission was to protect and rescue Americans on Grenada, including all students enrolled in St. George's University. Secondary objectives were to restore order, promote a democratic government and remove Cuban and Soviet influence on the island.[3]

MISSION PLANNING FACTORS

There were major planning problems for naval, ground, and air forces. With little to no intelligence available, several courses of action (COA) were considered.

Thursday, Oct. 20 NCA directed CINCLANT (supported CINC) to start planning. CINCLANT developed six COAs. (1) Permissive with com-

3 Daniel P. Bolger, *Special Operations and the Grenada Campaign* (Ft. Belvoir, VA: Defense Technical Information Center, 1988).

> mercial air. (2) Permissive with MAC within 30 hours. (3) Non-permissive using USMC and Independence Battle Group. (4) using Ahuas Tara forces, and Indy. (5) 82nd Airborne Battalion with airdrop/air-land and Indy (6) Show of Force. **Maj Gen (Ret.) Robert Patterson,** Vice Commander, 21st Air Force (MAC)

After significant deliberation and spotty information on PRA intent and force strength, Chairman Joint Chiefs, GEN Vessey, determined the best course of action was a surprise attack with overwhelming force.[4] Normally, a Non-Combatant Evacuation Operation (NEO) was within the capabilities of the *USS Independence* Battle Group's 22nd Marine Amphibious Unit (MAU), but this mission exceeded its capability. With hundreds of medical students and US citizens to evacuate, a larger force was needed, so the JCS tasked MG Richard Scholtes, commander of a Joint Special Mission Unit to develop a rescue plan independent of CINCLANT's plan.

> "The plan requirement to invade Grenada was initially given separately and independently to LANT (its AO) and a Joint Special Mission Unit. Neither were aware of the other at the time of assignment. Both had independent/unique plans

4 Richard H. Cole, *Operation Urgent Fury, The Planning and Execution of Joint Operations in Grenada, 12 October-2 November 1983,* DTIC (Washington, DC: Joint History Office of the Chairman of the Joint Chiefs of Staff, 1997). https://apps.dtic.mil/sti/citations/ADA332041.

> - LANT using solely Marines and naval assets. This was well before Beirut and just before Reagan made his speech on Grenada." **Colonel (Ret.) Keith Nightingale,** Commander Task Force 2-505/82d Airborne

The JCS tasked US Commander in Chief, Atlantic (USCINCLANT) Admiral (ADM) Wesley McDonald to oversee the operation, aptly named Operation *Urgent Fury*. ADM McDonald charged Vice Admiral (VADM) Joseph Metcalf III, commander of the U.S. Second Fleet, as overall commander of Combined Joint Task Force (CJTF) 120. VADM Metcalf was directed to lead the operation from the Amphibious Assault Ship *USS Guam*, which would act as the command center for the operation.

Though the JCS touted command and control of *Urgent Fury* as joint, mission planning could only be described as disjointed. The Navy ruled the operation and coordination between services was nearly non-existent. Furthermore, tasked Courses Of Action (COA) changed hourly and CINCLANT did not issue any deployment orders, timelines, or details. Mission planners at Norfolk overwhelmed the demand for secure voice phones and had to resort to using off base pay phones to coordinate plans.[5]

By the third day of mission planning, ambitious and complex mission plans were continually fractured by TF-120 leadership. About two days before H-Hour, GEN Vessey determined VADM Metcalf was overwhelmed and unfamil-

5 Maj Gen (Ret.) Robert Patterson. phone interview with Author, June, 2017.

iar with US Army capabilities and tactics, so he tapped MG Norman Schwarzkopf, commander of the 24th Infantry Division at Ft Stewart GA, as advisor to VADM Metcalf. MG Schwarzkopf was flown to Barbados then transported to the USS Guam on October 24 while four Task Forces made final preparations for a military operation.

TASK FORCE-123

Led by MG Richard Scholtes, this TF included Army and Navy Special Operations units, Task Force 160 (TF-160) *Night Stalker* helicopters, eleven USAF C-130s from the 317th Tactical Airlift Wing (TAW), five MC-130s and three AC-130 *Spectre* gunships from Hurlburt's 1st Special Operations Wing (1 SOW). One EC-130 *Coronet Solo* aircraft from the 193rd Special Operations Wing, Harrisburg, PA was assigned to perform radio broadcasting and psychological operations duties. Support aircraft included KC-10 and KC-135 refueling tankers, U-2 and SR-71 Reconnaissance aircraft, C-141 *Starlifters* and C-5 *Galaxy's* to transport troops and equipment to Barbados, and ultimately Grenada.

TF-123 was charged with a multitude of H-Hour responsibilities including seizure of *Point Salines* airport, elimination of PRA and Cuban resistance, seizure of the Radio Free Grenada transmitter station, rescue of Sir Paul Scoon, and rescue of political prisoners believed to be held in *Richmond Hill Prison*. Further tasking included assaulting the PRA headquarters at *Fort Rupert* after the *Point*

Salines airport was secure. Furthermore, 1/75 Rangers were responsible for rescue of US medical students known to be on True Blue campus, near the southeastern end of *Point Salines* airport's runway.

Unlike Naval Task Forces equipped to perform self-contained operations from the sea, the TF-123 airfield seizure element was ground-based with a large logistic footprint. With about one thousand operations and support personnel, aircraft and support equipment, operational security concerns squelched any idea of pre-positioning the element near Grenada. Instead, aircraft were required to depart from CONUS bases in a timed sequence to arrive over target exactly at H-Hour. The only elements of TF-123 able to be staged near Grenada were Task Force 160 helicopters and US Army and Navy Special Operations assaulters. These elements were to be clandestinely pre-positioned several hours before H-Hour on Barbados, about 160 miles from Grenada, then inserted by TF-160 UH-60 helicopters at H-Hour.

Since AC-130 crews were required to fly directly from Hurlburt Field, FL (about two thousand miles), to Grenada, significant aerial refueling tanker support was required. To mitigate fatigue, primary crew positions were augmented with additional crew members to split the workload. The overall plan required AC-130s to arrive at the same time as the airfield seizure element. Similarly, C-130 Special Operations Low Level (SOLL) and MC-130 Combat Talons crews faced physiological challenges flying in from Hunter Army Airfield, GA.

Since mission planning was compressed with a short timeline, little information was available to coordinate operations. Intelligence and imagery were sparse, and standardized US maps did not exist. The only available maps of Grenada were published in England and graduated on a 1:25,000 scale. Another problem was the twenty-seven by twenty-nine inch "wallpaper-esque" size of the north and south halves of the map covering the island. The maps preceded airport construction, so *Point Salines* airport was crudely penciled in on the southern map. Furthermore, a printing error resulted in the grid markings between the upper and lower maps being exactly one kilometer off. Though it was difficult, planners worked the best they could to solve these issues.

Leading the Phase-1 airfield seizure element was 1/75 Ranger Battalion commander Lieutenant Colonel Wesley Taylor. His Rangers, supported by USAF combat controllers and Tactical Air Control Party (TACP) elements, would parachute onto *Point Salines* to prepare the airport for airland operations. The physics of airborne operations can be unpredictable, especially on a small drop zone running parallel to the open ocean. Knowing this, Taylor requested the Phase-1 element drop at an unusually low altitude of three hundred feet to limit potential for a water landing and decrease exposure to small arms fire.[6] Leading the

6 According to Col (Ret.) James Roper, LTC Taylor first selected a 300 foot drop altitude, but compromised with MC-130 mission planners because of 400 foot terrain north of the runway, ultimately selecting a 500 foot drop altitude.

2/75 Ranger Battalion was LTC Ralph Hagler. Several 2/75 Platoons would air-drop following 1/75 with the remainder air-landing after the airfield was secure. Both commanders realized potential dangers associated with the air-drop but after they analyzed the situation, they settled on a drop altitude of five hundred ft.

Once on the airfield, the Phase-1 element would establish a Tactical Operations Center (TOC) to direct all aspects of the airfield seizure, including landing of the Phase-2 element and follow-on forces. In concert with airfield seizure tactics developed in the early 1980s, gunship crews would remain on station for a minimum of four hours to provide heavy fire support for airfield seizure elements. Though strict Rules of Engagement (ROE) and UHF and FM fire support nets were developed, a communications-out Suppression of Enemy Air Defenses (SEAD) plan was established to allow AC-130 crews to quickly engage any active AAA gun sites that may pop up during the initial Phase-1 airdrop.[7]

> "Lieutenant Colonel Taylor directed me that due to the restrictive fire support measures placed on us by higher, and due to the risk of collateral damage, fire missions from all fire support assets were to be routed through the 1/75th Fire Support Element to be personally approved by him. This was written in our fire support annex of the 1/75th Operations Order. The Fire Support Teams were instructed that only if they were

7 Memo from Col (Ret.) James Roper to Author,. Jun 2014

> under fire and unable to make comms with the Fire Support Element, were they allowed to task the Fire Support Assets (Gunships)." **Lieutenant Colonel (Ret.) Henry Eisenbarth**[8]

Once the airport was secure, USAF combat controllers would coordinate air traffic for the Phase-2 element equipped with gun jeeps and heavy weapons. The Rangers would then fan out, push PRA resistance away from the airport, rescue medical students at *True Blue Campus*, then return to *Point Salines airport* for departure.

The entire mission was expected to last less than 24 hours. When complete, all three AC-130s were to recover at Roosevelt Roads Naval Base in Puerto Rico, about a two hour flight from Grenada.

> Task Force-121 Included one Brigade, a Division Jump Command post, and support elements of the 82nd Airborne Division. This large task force would deploy to reinforce TF-123 after Point Salines airport was secured.[9]

> Task Force-124: Included the *USS Independence* Aircraft Carrier Battle Group, equipped with A-7 *Corsair* attack aircraft and a platoon assigned to SEAL Team 4 to survey the northeastern coastline for potential of an amphibious assault.

8 Email from LTC (Ret.) Henry Eisenbarth, to Author, Nov 2014.

9 A second brigade was later added to the TF-121 force structure after the Commanding General deemed them necessary to mission accomplishment.

Also included was a Marine Amphibious Unit (MAU), tasked to seize the town of Grenville and Pearls airport. The MAU was equipped with M60 Tanks, AAV7 "amtracks," and CH-46 and CH-53 helicopters.

Task Force-126: This TF was charged with the responsibility of over watch and intercept of all unidentified aircraft approaching Grenada and to prevent interference from Cuban aircraft. TF-126 operated F-15 fighters, RC-135 and E-3A AWACS aircraft from Roosevelt Roads, Puerto Rico.

The Caribbean Peacekeeping Force: About three hundred soldiers and policemen from neighboring countries were assembled by the *Organization of Eastern Caribbean States*. Their efforts were largely symbolic and not coordinated with TF-120.

Command, Control and Communications (C3): TF-123 C3 would be led by MG Scholtes (call sign *Viking*). The Air Component Commander (ACC) for unconventional warfare air forces was Col Bruce Fister. Command and control of the operation would be conducted from a USAF EC-130 Airborne Battlefield Command and Control Center (ABCCC) aircraft. Coordination between mission aircraft and ABCCC would occur via encrypted MX-850 SATCOM radios.

The Grenadian/Cuban Skill set: The strength of the PRA was estimated to be two lightly-armed battalions of about five hundred men each, commanded by approximately eighty East German-trained officers. Of these, it was estimated about half would stand and fight and the other half would flee at the first sign of combat. Alongside an estimated one thousand–twelve hundred PRA Soldiers, there were between four hundred and six hundred Cuban Army reservists and thirty–sixty active duty Cuban soldiers and advisers on the island. Most of the Cubans lived near the runway at *Point Salines*, an area known as "Little Havana" and the *Calivigny Barracks* on the southeastern part of the island.

Identification Friend or Foe (IFF): Ranger Fire Support Teams (FiST), USAF Tactical Air Control Party NCOs and Ranger Forward Observer Teams (FO) would coordinate Close Air Support (CAS) requests to TOC-1 and TOC-2 on open frequencies via UHF PRC-66 and FM PRC-77 radios.[10] Since the fire support network was planned to be conducted on open frequencies, TEMIG beacons and a challenge-response authentication procedures and target identification protocols were standard operations for AC-130 crews, TACP and Rangers.

10 Memo from LTC (Ret.) Henry Eisenbarth, to Author, Nov 2014.

Anti-Aircraft Artillery (AAA): An unknown number 12.7mm and 23mm AAA guns were in the PRA inventory.

Armored Vehicles and aircraft: The PRA were equipped with eight BTR-60 and two BRDM armored vehicles. Antiquated cargo aircraft were known to be on the island, but no fighter or interceptor aircraft were known to exist.

Man Portable Air Defense Systems (MANPADS): There were no known MANPADS in Grenada.

Vehicles, Small Arms, Mortars, RPGs: The PRA was equipped with Eastern Bloc mortars and small arms, including AK-47, SKS, PKM, and RPG-7. They were also equipped with commercial type construction vehicles, heavy equipment and two lightly armed patrol boats.

Photo Intelligence: Aerial photo reconnaissance efforts were conducted, but small, scattered thunderstorms near the island resulted in spotty information. Pearls Airport on the northern part of the island was void of military activity and AAA weapons but did contain several trucks and one AN-2 Colt aircraft. Several AAA guns and military vehicles were suspected at Frequente Military Camp and four AAA guns covered with tarps were suspected at Fort Rupert. Since Point Salines had not yet opened, trucks, construction equipment, and steel drums sat near the runway. Reconnaissance photographs failed to show any AAA guns on Point Salines Airport.

Photo reconnaissance of Point Salines airport was partially obscured by clouds. (Credit: DoD photo)

"We thought AAA was stored in warehouses, but had no confirmation and it didn't factor heavily into the planning. We looked carefully at our 3-day old satellite photos and found no evidence of AAA." **Lt Gen (Ret.) Bruce Fister**

<u>Rules of Engagement (ROE):</u> The operation was envisioned as a rescue, not an offensive combat operation. Minimal disruption to the

> local economy was desired. JCS directed minimal use of force to limit risk to American and Grenadian citizens.

THE START OF OPERATION *URGENT FURY*

After all diplomatic efforts were exhausted, military intervention was inevitable. During the evening of October 21–22, Prime Minister Eugenia Charles of Dominica, acting chair of the *Organization of Eastern Caribbean States*, formally asked the United States to intervene in Grenada.[11] At about the same time, Radio Free Grenada broadcast a mobilization order to the PRA warning them to expect a military attack.[12] Shortly thereafter, PRA soldiers and Cuban construction workers began to break out weapons, anticipating an imminent attack. At the same time, Fidel Castro sent several high-ranking military officers to Grenada, presumably to convince Gen Austin and the RMC to relinquish control of Grenada. The officers delivered Castro's message that Cubans were not to assist the PRA in the fight for Grenada, but were expected to defend Cuba's honor and fight to the last man.

> "Havana's official news media reported that Cuba's 'glorious combatants' were at this

11 Richard W. Stewart, *Operation Urgent Fury: The Invasion of Grenada, October 1983* (Dept. of the Army Center of Military History Publication, 2008), 10. https://history.army.mil/html/books/grenada/index.html.

12 History of the Second Air Division, 1 July 1983-31 December 1983, (all extracts are unclassified), 125.

> moment themselves for the homeland, wrapped in the Cuban flag." (*The Miami Herald*, Oct 24, 2013)

On October 23, ADM McDonald directed airdrop insertion of a SEAL reconnaissance element supported by USAF Combat Controllers into the ocean off the coast of *Point Salines* Airport. Though the weather was bad and seas were rough, the air drop proceeded as planned. When sixteen SEALS and two Boston Whalers entered the water, one boat and four SEALs disappeared under a large wave and did not resurface.[13] Small boats from the *USS Clifton Sprague* were used to recover some of the SEALs while others swam to the ship. While the crew of the *Sprague* continued to search for the missing SEALs, the reconnaissance mission proceeded with a single boat, but the team couldn't get close to the airport because a searchlight-equipped PRA boat was patrolling the coastline. To avoid a mission compromise, the team returned to the *Sprague*, unable to complete their mission.[14]

The next day, a meeting was held at Commander In Chief United States Atlantic (USCINCLANT) headquarters to discuss the current state of mission planning. Considering the failure of the reconnaissance mission and the need for better intelligence, MGEN Scholtes asked ADM McDonald to delay the operation 24 hours, but his request was denied

---

13 Col (Ret.) John Carney, *No Room for Error : the Covert Operations of America's Special Tactics Units from Iran to Afghanistan*. New York, NY: Ballantine Books, 2002, 130.

14 Ibid, 132.

because of State Department political pressure. The same day, in direct contradiction with MG Scholtes desires for a 0200 H-Hour, the mission start time first set by ADM McDonald at 0400, slid to 0500 by order of VADM Metcalf. Since 0500 was only about a half hour before dawn, even a short delay could unmask the airfield seizure element, increasing potential for detection and mission failure. Though Special Operations mission planners considered a 0500 H-Hour risky, they were powerless to change it.

> "Before Dick Scholtes went to the last CINCLANT meeting, he asked me what we should have as H-Hour and I told him 0200."
> **Lt Gen (Ret.) Bruce Fister**

By the morning of October 24, Hurlburt Field was a flurry of activity as maintainers prepared three primary and one spare AC-130H gunship for a mission to Grenada. All aircraft were loaded with 3,000 rounds of 20mm HEI, 256 rounds of 40mm HEI and a mix of 100 rounds of 105mm HE and WP. Extra cans of 20mm and 40mm ammunition cans were added to each aircraft, tied down in the aisle way against the left main wheel well bulkhead. All three aircraft weighed 170,000–175,000 pounds which is the maximum allowable Emergency War Plans (EWP) takeoff weight in the published C-130 Technical Order.[15] Crews were assigned tactical call signs Lima 56, 57, and 58.

---

15 Email from Maj (Ret.) Mike Couvillon to Author, Sep 2014.

At 1830 CST, *Wicked Wanda*, commanded by Maj Mike Couvillon, departed Hurlburt Field for Grenada to perform a reconnaissance of Point Salines. About an hour later, *Night Stalker*, commanded by Lt Col David Sims, and *Heavy Metal*, commanded by Maj Clement Twiford took off. Both aircraft headed to Eglin ranges to tweak their guns. Lima 58 discovered the firing solenoid of their 105mm gun was defective, so MSgt Ron Broyles rigged one of his shoe laces to the guns firing pawl to enable manual firing by gunners via verbal commands of the pilot. Maj Twiford knew accuracy would suffer by manual fire, but the gun could be used as long as friendly forces were not near a target. In any case, there were three other usable guns and that crew would not make it to Grenada on time if they landed for repairs. About the time Lima 58 departed for Grenada, *Night Stalker* experienced a #4 engine fire, declared an In-Flight Emergency (IFE) and began dumping fuel. After the aircraft achieved a safe weight, Lt Col Sims landed his gunship on Hurlburt, transferred to *Iron Maiden*, and took off for Grenada.

Operation *Urgent Fury* Initial AC-130 Crews		
Call Sign	Aircraft	Aircraft Commander
Lima 56	69-6575 "*Wicked Wanda*"	Maj Michael Couvillon
Lima 57*	69-6574 "*Iron Maiden*"	Lt Col David Sims
Lima 58	69-6573 "*Heavy Metal*"	Maj Clement Twiford

A short time later, the sixteen aircraft Phase-1 and Phase-2 airfield seizure formation departed Hunter Army Airfield, GA via MC-130/C-130. They would fly nonstop to

* Capt Robert Hockman assumed the role of Aircraft Commander on D+3 when Lt Col Sims was transferred into a command position.

Grenada, supported by KC-135 refueling tankers. It would take nearly eight hours for the formation to arrive at their hold points about seventy miles west of Grenada.

While the airfield seizure package flew towards Grenada, SEALs made a second attempt to reconnoiter *Point Salines*. Unfortunately, the effort failed when the engines on their boats swamped and could not be started. Now the only current intelligence of Point Salines would come from Lima 56 when they arrived over *Point Salines*.

At about 0330 local Grenada time, after about an eight-hour flight and two heavyweight aerial refuelings, Lima 56 arrived off the coast of the island at an altitude of nine thousand feet. To prevent visual acquisition, the crew turned off all exterior lighting, then headed directly for *Point Salines* airport. Rain showers and scattered clouds hindered the reconnaissance effort, but after Maj Couvillon rolled into orbit, sensor operators MSgt Luther "Bud" Reece and SSgt Bob Anderson determined the runway was blocked with vehicles, debris and barriers. Lima 56 notified Col Fister via secure SATCOM radio and MG Scholtes directed the Phase I element to reconfigure for airdrop. This change caused a major disruption in the mission timeline as Rangers hurriedly reconfigured.

About the same time Lima 56 began searching Point Salines airport, three C-5's approached *Grantley Adams International* airport, Barbados, loaded with Army Special Forces, TF-160 *Night Stalker* helicopters, and Navy Special Operations elements. Onboard one aircraft was Brig Gen Robert Patterson, Vice Commander of 21st Air Force and

Commander of Airlift Forces (COMALF) and his staff who would set up an airlift command and control center at the airport.

> "I was apprehensive about our reception on landing. Could not have been more wrong. We were met by Barbados PM, Mr. Tom Adams, US Ambassador to Barbados, Mr. Millard Bish, US Ambassador to Grenada, Mr. Tom Gillespie, BGen Lewis, the Commander Barbados Defense Force and a Marine one star. The airport had just opened a new terminal and we were offered the old one. As a first step in their wonderful support they restored telephone service to the building in three or four hours." **Maj Gen (Ret.) Robert Patterson**[16]

While *Night Stalker* crews and support personnel unloaded and assembled their helicopters, Army and Navy Special Operations personnel prepared for their missions. By 0430, time was running short and the helicopters were still being prepared for flight.

At about the same time, the Phase 1 airfield seizure formation was preparing for air-drop, Lima 56 had completed reconnaissance of Point Salines, descended to six thousand ft., and was orbiting at its hold point over Fort Juedy.

About 0450, with moderate rain, thunder and cloud cover over the island, the Phase-1 airfield seizure forma-

16 Maj Gen Patterson was an AC-130 Aircraft Commander in the early 1970s at Ubon RTAFB.

tion was inbound to *Point Salines*, while the USMC 22nd MAU began their helicopter-borne assault on Grenville and *Pearls Airport*.[17]

When the Phase-1 element was about twenty miles from *Point Salines*, the lead aircraft's navigation system malfunctioned. Unable to guide the rest of the formation to the drop zone, the drop was aborted and all aircraft returned to their hold points to re-sequence the formation. This event pushed the airdrop to 0530 (near-daylight).

About 0525, a three aircraft drop formation headed for *Point Salines*, in a single file, spaced thirty seconds apart, five hundred feet above the sea. Commanding the lead aircraft (call sign Foxtrot 35) was Lt Col James Hobson. Though the sun began to illuminate the horizon and the weather was marginal, all was proceeding well until about two miles from the runway when a searchlight locked onto Hobson's aircraft. Undeterred, he maintained course and airspeed while loadmasters and jumpers readied themselves for an immediate drop. Just past 0530, Foxtrot 35 entered the drop zone and troops began to rapidly exit from both paratroop doors. About halfway across the drop zone, large caliber tracers streaked towards Foxtrot 35. Surprised with the volume of close-range AAA fire, both trailing aircraft broke out of formation before reaching the drop zone. Foxtrot 35, however, could not perform a defensive maneuver since jumpers were still exiting the aircraft. Instead, Lt Col Hobson maintained course, heading and altitude until

17 Email from Historian GySgt Joe Muccia, to Author, Oct 2014.

the last jumper cleared the aircraft, then banked hard right and descended to about one hundred feet altitude over the sea to escape PRA guns.

The sound of gunfire alarmed Grenadians on the southern tip of the island and Radio Free Grenada began broadcasting a call to arms to fight the Americans.

> At 05:30 hours on October 25, 1983 listeners to Radio Free Grenada (RFG) heard a male voice and a female voice hysterically announcing the assault. The two announcers at RFG read from a prepared script over and over. Songs played were by Peter Tosh and Swallow and Shortshirt, tunes like "Stand Up Grenada" and Bob Marley's "Stand Up For Your Rights."
>
> FEMALE VOICE . . . You should report to your militia bases immediately . . . Why? . . . Because we are under attack . . .
>
> MALE VOICE . . . Defend our homeland! We shall win! We shall beat them back! We shall bury them in the sea! They have to get a beating!
>
> FEMALE VOICE . . . At 5:30 this morning, foreign troops began landing in our country! Our armed forces are engaging them in fierce battle . . . All doctors, nurses, medics, report to the hospital immediately.

> MALE VOICE . . . We shall beat them back . . . Militia come out now! Together with the People's Revolutionary Army, we will save our country . . .
>
> FEMALE VOICE . . . The Revolutionary Military Council is calling on all friendly countries to condemn this act of aggression, and immediately come to Grenada's aid.[18]

Since the airfield seizure operation was truncated by unexpected AAA fire, Foxtrot 35 had dropped Taylor's lightly armed Headquarters Company (TOC-1), one platoon of Rangers, one Combat Controller, and USAF Air Liaison Officer (ALO) Maj James Roper (call sign Delta 75). While the HQ Company and support personnel scrambled for cover on the open airfield, additional attempts to drop the assault force were driven off by heavy 12.7mm and 23mm AAA located on the airfield and on a ridgeline northeast of the runway. Unable to drop the assault force, the Phase-1 element departed for a hold point over the ocean.

> 0532 hrs.:
>
> Foxtrot-35. "Drop complete. Took fire, #2 broke off."
>
> Foxtrot-36 to Viking. "Need help to get in."
>
> Foxtrot-37. "We need the gunships."

---

18 Ann Elizabeth Wilder, "The Grenada Revolution," The Grenada Revolution Online, 2001, https://www.thegrenadarevolutiononline.com.

> Foxtrot-33 "We took 23mm fire."
>
> 0537 hrs.:
>
> Lima-58. "On station. Call AAA by clock position."

From an altitude of 5,500 ft. overhead the drop zone, Lima 58 illuminator operators SSgt Bill Jennings and MSgt Warren Allen alerted their crew of AAA tracer fire directed at Foxtrot 35. Though contact with Alpha Company, 1st Ranger Battalion, 75th Ranger Regiment (A/1/75) had not yet been made, MG Scholtes directed Lima 58 to begin engaging the AAA sites.

At about the same time, Maj Roper was receiving small arms fire but was unable to contact Lima 58. Likewise, Battalion Fire Support Officer (BNFSO) CPT Henry "Ike" Eisenbarth discovered all three radios he intended to use to coordinate AC-130 fire support were damaged on impact and inoperable. He also suffered a broken ankle when he slammed onto the runway.

> "The hills 300 meters north of the runway came alive with AAA fire. I counted eight sources of heavy red tracer (.50 caliber) and estimated 80–100 sources of green tracer (AK-47). One 23mm gun was active from behind the hills. The fire was directed at the aircraft and jumpers, and several rounds zinged close overhead as I sprawled in the grass" **Col (Ret.) James Roper**[19]

19 1983 Official Urgent Fury after action report provided to Author by Col (Ret.) James Roper, 2014.

Cleared to suppress the PRA gun sites, Lima 58 sensor operator TSgt Jerry Andersen systematically followed a string of tracers back to point of origin to find a four-barreled 12.7mm gun near the middle of the airfield. Without hesitation, Maj Twiford opened fire with 20mm HEI, silencing the gun and starting a fire on a nearby building. Next, the crew located and engaged four 23mm gun sites on high terrain near the east end of the runway, not far from St. George's University True Blue campus.

> "We located the AAA pieçes that caused the MC-130 to break off the airdrop. There were four ZU-23/2's located between the east end of the runway and the medical students school. We fired on them with 20MM. After the first burst hit, it was like stepping on a fire ant mound, gunners started coming out of a little shack near the AAA pieces manning the other guns." **CMSgt (Ret.) Jerry Andersen,** Lima 58 sensor operator.[20]

While Maj Twiford's crew engaged the 23mm guns, the HQ Company was taking fire from 12.7mm guns near midfield and north of the runway. When Delta 75 made radio contact with Lima 58, he directed guns near the airfield to be engaged first. Within about five minutes, both gun sites were silenced. Meanwhile, the HQ Company dodged small arms fire as they quickly made their way off the open airfield towards cover.

20 Email from CMSgt (Ret.) Jerry Andersen, to Author, Oct 2014.

Caught in the middle of the action were students and faculty of St. Georges Medical College, some of which were dangerously close to combat activity when fighting began. Dr. Robert Jordan lived in a house about three hundred meters north of the Point Salines control tower. He witnessed not only the airdrop but had a "front-row seat" view of the duel between Lima 58 and PRA gunners.

> "I will never, ever forget the sight and sound of the *Spectre* circling at 5:30 AM on 25th with antiaircraft bursts around you and behind you and the beautiful sound of your guns responding to and silencing the nearby PRA AA guns. Man, those guys ran by us so fast, dropping their uniforms as they did." **Dr. Robert Jordan**

While Lima 58 located and fired on AAA positions one by one, Foxtrot 36 made several more approaches to the drop zone but was driven off again and again by AAA fire. Lima 58 sensor operators found AAA guns fairly easy since poorly trained PRA crews fired excessively, exposing their positions by both muzzle flash and tracer fire.

Lima 58's AAA suppression effort was going well until their 105mm gun misfired. Quickly adapting to the situation, Maj Twiford switched to the 40mm gun while gunner SSgt Jim Habas worked his emergency procedures checklist. After two more attempts to fire, Maj Twiford rolled out of orbit to jettison the misfired round into the sea. All the while, a PRA gun site continually engaged them with inaccurate 23mm fire.

From his holding orbit over Ft Jeudy, Maj Couvillon heard radio traffic concerning Maj Twiford's gun problem. Realizing the urgent situation, he rolled out of holding orbit, flew to Point Salines and located the gun firing at Lima 58 by following a line of tracers back to the gun site. After Maj Couvillon fired several bursts of 20mm HEI, it was effectively silenced.[21]

> "...I quickly fired a 5-second burst, followed by a short pause, then a 3-second burst. I could see the target then rounds from the first burst exploding on and all around the target, then rounds from the second burst hit. The 23mm stopped firing at us...he's done!" **Maj (Ret.) Michael Couvillon**[22]

While Lima 56 was engaging gun sites, Lima 58's lead gunner, MSgt Ron Broyles, determined their 105mm gun's percussion mechanism was defective. By then, the AAA gun sites were silent, but a long line of PRA soldiers situated to the northeast in a ditch running parallel to the runway were firing at Rangers on the open airfield. Maj Roper identified the area of concern, sensor operators located the positions, then Lima 58 opened fire with 20mm and 40mm. Twiford's crew systematically walked fire from one target to the next. As Lima 58 fired on numerous PRA positions, they

---

21 Michael Couvillon, *Grenada Grinder: The complete Story of AC-130H Spectre Gunships in Operation Urgent Fury,* (Marrietta, GA: Deeds Publishing, 2011), 69.

22 Ibid.

were unaware American medical students and faculty were nearby, holed up houses merely three-hundred meters north of the airport control tower. One of the closest to a PRA gun site was medical student Hank Collins, who was awakened at 0530 by the sounds of AAA guns. At first, he thought the sounds of Lima 58's fire were also PRA guns, but it didn't take long to figure out the sounds and flashes were incoming, not outgoing. Peering out a window, he watched position after position come under attack by Lima 58, with each successive attack walking closer to his house. By that time, both Lima 56 and Lima 58 were engaging targets with five to ten rounds of 40mm Misch Metal before moving to the next. With each engagement, loud explosions and the sight of bright flashes and showers of burning metal caused PRA soldiers to abandon their positions, run over the ridgeline and disappear into the jungle. When one of the AC-130s engaged the PRA position close to Hank Collins' house, the sonic crack of projectiles passing overhead and the sound of impacts and explosions were almost simultaneous.[23]

> "Then from across the street, an anti-aircraft gun started firing, very sharp loud rounds in groups of 4–5 that would be echoed shortly after by the rounds exploding in midair above. There then came what I only later realized was *Spectre* firing at the AAA and troops across the street. It was like being in a fishbowl in the midst of a terrific cataclysmic battle." **Dr. Hank Collins**

23 Oct 25, 1983 audio recording made by Dr. Hank Collins given to Author in 2017.

About thirty-eight minutes into the operation, AAA threats were eliminated, prompting MG Scholtes to order the Phase-1 effort to resume. Shortly thereafter, Ranger, TACP, and CCT elements began to drop onto Point Salines under sporadic small arms fire. Once on the airfield, Rangers commandeered heavy equipment to clear the runway while Lima 58 and Lima 56 continued to search for and fire on PRA positions on the ridgeline.

While Lima 58 and Lima 56 were engaging PRA positions near *Point Salines*, Army and Navy Special Operations personnel boarded a flight of *Night Stalker* helicopters at *Grantley Adams* Airport, Barbados.[24] Their missions included rescue of political prisoners at *Richmond Hill Prison*, rescue of Sir Paul Scoon, and to take *Radio Free Grenada* off the air. Because of a time change mix-up, the helicopter formation did not cross the Grenadian coastline until well after sunrise, making the formation easy targets for PRA gunners. As the helicopter formation headed their objectives, PRA soldiers were on full alert.

Unfortunately, the Army Special Forces element didn't know what to expect at *Richmond Hill* prison. On approach, they were met with heavy PRA fire from 23mm gun emplacements on high ground at *Fort Frederick*, located on a ridgeline less than five hundred meters from the prison. After making two approaches, every helicopter was hit multiple times by small arms and AAA fire, and the formation broke away from the prison. *Night Stalker* pilot CPT Keith

---

24 A time zone mix up resulted in them taking off late, pushing their arrival over Grenada into daylight.

Lucas was killed by gunfire and co-pilot CW2 Paul Price tried to keep the helicopter airborne. Tragically, hydraulic failure caused CW2 Price to lose control of the helicopter which crash landed and overturned in the jungle. The rest of the shot-up formation managed to land on the deck of the Destroyer *USS Moosebrugger* or on the western end of *Point Salines* airport. Meanwhile, as the downed helicopter burned, survivors moved away from the crash site. Those able to fight established hasty defensive positions while Army Special Forces troop commander, CPT Jeff Beatty broadcast a "Mayday" alert over Guard frequency via survival radio.

The helicopter insertion of the Navy element at the Governor-General's mansion met similar resistance. Upon arrival, the first helicopter in Captain Robert Gormly's SEAL element began to fast-rope onto the compound to establish a security perimeter and clear an area for the second helicopter to land.[25] While the helicopter hovered, PRA forces opened fire with small arms, hitting it multiple times, wounding its pilot. Forced to withdraw because of battle damage and injuries, the *Night Stalker* crew landed on the *USS Guam*. With the one helicopter out of action, the second UH-60 inserted a SEAL platoon onto the tennis courts behind the Governor-General's mansion. The platoon then entered the Governor-General's mansion without resistance.

Once inside the mansion, SEALs secured Sir Paul Scoon and his wife and staff, but a short time later, PRA troops

25 The helicopter needed to land to insert three State Department employees who could not fast-rope.

surrounded the mansion. At that point, the SEALs realized they forgot their SATCOM radio on the UH-60.[26] With no communications with the outside world other than their low powered intra-team radios, they were unable to contact any command and control agency. Now surrounded by PRA soldiers and unable to call for help, the SEALs prepared for a long fight, armed only with the limited weapons and ammunition they had available.

By 0730, Lima 56 was low on fuel and departed for the KC-10 refueling track. Seven minutes later, Rangers cleared the runway and Foxtrot 40, commanded by Lt Col David Miles, landed on *Point Salines* to deliver the Army Special Forces command element. Additional C-130s landed, loaded with gun jeeps, AH-6 and Hughes 500 "Little Bird" helicopters. While Army SF set up their command post near western end of the runway, TF-160 support crews quickly assembled the Little Birds. Simultaneously, *Night Stalker* UH-60 crews flew Army Special Forces soldiers to CPT Lucas's crash site to tend to the wounded. Since the helicopters were unable to land in the dense jungle surrounding the crash site, soldiers jumped out from treetop level, using trees and vegetation to break their fall. During this time, a second helicopter inserted rescuers near the water's edge, about a kilometer downhill from the crash site. While rescuers climbed to the crash site, helicopter crews returned to the SF command post at *Point Salines*. From there, Major Lewis "Bucky" Burruss, their Forward Air Guide, sent AH-6s to the TF-160 crash site to provide fire support.

---

26 Col (Ret.) Carney, *No Room for Error*, 146.

At 0800, while air-land operations were ongoing, Lima 57 arrived at their holding point at 6,500 ft altitude. About the same time, Lima 58 had fired all their 40mm and 20mm ammunition and had a broken 105mm gun. After being advised ammunition was available at Roosevelt Roads, Puerto Rico, they set off for ammunition. Once Lima 58 departed, Major Burruss requested Lima 57 be sent to the TF-160 crash site to support the rescue effort. When cleared by ABCCC, a column of rising smoke led Lima 57 directly to the crash site. Upon arrival, sensor operators TSgt Bill Kerwin and SMSgt Don Boudreaux began a perimeter search around the downed helicopter. After making radio contact with CPT Beatty, it didn't take long to detect PRA forces approaching, report findings, and receive clearance to fire. Lima 57 then fired 20mm and 40mm HEI between the crash site and the PRA, causing aggressors to retreat. During the rescue effort, Lima 57 remained overhead until all survivors and the injured were recovered and transported to the *USS Guam*. Lima 57 was sent to *Calivigny Camp* to search for military activity, but they found the camp to be quiet.

By 0815, *Lima 56* returned from the tanker fully fueled and was placed in a holding orbit. By 0830, the airfield was secure and phase 1 and phase 2 elements were landing on *Point Salines*. As the morning progressed, three Ranger platoons advanced across the runway towards the north. A/1/75 Platoon Sergeant Michael Ramsey's element engaged a PRA soldier concealed in a dump truck on the open airfield. After the soldier surrendered, the prisoner was secured while the platoon took cover behind the dump truck, waiting for a transfer team. A few minutes later, they began receiving heavy machine gun fire from a concealed position about three hundred meters north. Trapped on the open runway behind the truck, Rangers exchanged fire with rifles and M72 Light Anti-tank Weapons (LAW), but the PRA gun site was difficult to hit since it was under an elevated house foundation on the side of a hill. As both sides exchanged fire, a near-constant hail of PRA bullets riddled the truck and snapped past the Ranger position. In the melee, Specialist 4 (SP4) Mark Yamane was killed and several Rangers were wounded. The Platoon's USAF TACP, TSgt Robert "Scotty" Scott, contacted *Lima 57* for immediate fire support.

> "We were waiting behind this vehicle to transfer this person to a collection team. We or I took too long for this transfer to complete and became a target in the open for the PKM fire and other direct fire weapons. We couldn't move. Thankfully, Scotty was there low crawling toward my position, in the open. Once in shouting range, he adjusted the AC-130 fire for me. We were all weaving and ducking assisting in adjustment. Thanks Scotty and of course the AC-130 and crew." **1SG (Ret.) Michael Ramsey.**

Sensor operators located both Ranger and the PRA positions and *Lima 57*'s navigator Capt Brad Broyles determined the target was inside "danger close" parameters for 105mm HE. To avoid fratricide potential, Lt Col Sims directed use of 40mm HEI and within a minute, *Lima 57* fired on the house. Unfortunately, 40mm projectiles exploded on the roof without penetrating the structure and the PRA gun site continued to fire. The crew realized their sole capability to defeat the gun position was a 32-pound 105mm HE projectile with its fuze set for delay function, but there was a chance Rangers could be hit by shell fragments. Realizing the criticality of the situation, Sgt Ramsey accepted danger close parameters, then directed TSgt Scott to clear *Lima 57* to fire 105mm. *Lima 57*'s response was immediate and Lima 57 fired their first 105mm round before TSgt Scott was able to finish his radio transmission. Their first round penetrated the house's roof, traveled about ten feet, then exploded above the floor. Hundreds of high-speed fragments penetrated the floor, eviscerating the PRA gunners underneath while blast overpressure blew pieces of the building outward. When a second round was fired, the entire structure collapsed on top of the PRA gun position.

Though Ramsey's immediate problem was negated, there was a high probability more PRA positions would be encountered as A/1/75 continued their advance. Aware that crossing the open expanse of terrain north of the runway exposed Rangers to more PRA gun positions, Ranger SSG Manous "Chip" Boles commandeered a bulldozer, raised the blade to block incoming fire and drove towards the ridgeline while other Rangers fell in behind.[27] While en route, they passed the house destroyed by *Lima 57*.[28]

---

27 Email from Historian GySgt Joe Muccia to Author, 2014.

28 Official 1983 After Action Report of TSgt Robert Scott, provided to Author, 2014.

> "Doc and I wrapped Sgt Yamane in his poncho and moved him out to the runway for evac. Sgt Ramsey yelled for us all to fall behind the bulldozer and move up the hill to the north. As we passed the first building, I saw what was left of the two soldiers and their weapons." **MSgt (Ret.) Robert "Scotty" Scott**

About 20 minutes later and 250 meters further east, another A/1/75 platoon was crossing the runway when they came under heavy machine gun fire. Tell-tale muzzle flashes were seen from the second story of a house about 130 meters to their front and the Rangers were caught in the open. With no cover and fully exposed on the open airfield, one Ranger had taken a direct hit and was bleeding badly. There was nothing but open runway behind them and their only cover was the eighteen-inch dirt berm in front of them.

> "Captain Abizaid needed to get eyes across the runway and I was the fire support piece of that team. That's where we were pinned down in the open with an 18-inch berm of dirt in front of us and the ditch running the length of the runway with us looking up the hillside and bare asphalt behind us from the runway." **1SG (Ret.) Sgt Richard Trundy**

In desperate need of fire support, A/1/75 Fire Support Team NCO, Sergeant Richard Trundy contacted Captain Eisenbarth at TOC-1 who authorized him to work directly with *Lima 57*. Without hesitation, Trundy talked *Lima 57* onto the target via walk-on 40mm fire. Once *Lima 57* was on target, they began firing for effect and hit a propane tank, resulting in a large secondary explosion and fire temporarily silencing PRA fire. During this time, Rangers quickly moved off the open airfield towards a rise in terrain called "Goat Hill."

Captain Abizaid led A/1/75 Rangers to the top of "Goat Hill" where they found a loaded, but abandoned M53 12.7mm AAA gun overlooking Calliste Camp about a kilometer to the northeast. While orders to surrender were broadcast towards the camp, Rangers gathered around the captured gun, trying to figure out how to fire it. Since the gun would not traverse, they accidentally fired the gun trying to unlock it, but eventually trained towards the camp and fired several bursts. In response, Cubans ran into a building as large-caliber tracers passed overhead. Attempts to engage the camp directly were not possible since the M53's barrels would not depress low enough for direct fire.[29] Shortly afterward, the Ranger position began receiving small arms fire from a large building, prompting Abizaid to contact TOC-1 for fire support.

> "I was in TOC-1 when the request for 105 fire on the main building came in, since the folks firing at Abizaid's troops had run into the building. I looked at Lieutenant Colonel Taylor, for his authorization, and he said, 'One round of 105 in

---

29 Email from Historian GySgt (Ret.) Joe Muccia to Author, 2014.

> the center of the building.' That's what *Spectre* did, and it produced a white flag and a lot of prisoners. I claimed the POWs as Air Force prisoners, but that only got a chuckle in the TOC."
> **Col (Ret.) James Roper**

After Lima 57 fired a single 105mm HE round into the building, hostile fire subsided and a white flag of surrender was seen. While A/1/75 continued to advance towards the camp to secure their prisoners of war, TOC-1 diverted Lima 57 to Calivigny Camp while fire support for A/1/75 was provided by USMC *Cobra* gunships.

By 0930, Lima 56 was called in to support A/1/75 as they advanced into the *Little Havana*' camp. Rangers attempted to convince the Cubans to surrender, but they refused. When Captain Abizaid cleared Lima 56 to fire on the camp, Maj Couvillon fired several rounds of 105mm HE into the jungle near the compound, but there was still no response from the Cubans. Switching to the 20mm guns, Maj Couvillon had his thumb on the trigger when a ceasefire was called. Unknown to both Captain Abizaid and Major Couvillon, a B/1/75 reconnaissance platoon was on a ridgeline, dangerously close to Lima 56's previous shots. From that point on, Lima 56 remained on station while the situation was resolved. In short order, Rangers entered the camp and Cubans surrendered with little resistance.

At about 0945, Major Burruss tasked Lima 56 fire on the police headquarters within *Fort Rupert* to suppress activity before a planned raid. The fort was located on high ground overlooking St. George's harbor and situated in a heavily populated area. The only round capable of damaging the structures was the 105mm, so extreme precision was needed to prevent collateral damage to civilian structures and personnel surrounding the fort. After firing about 25 rounds of 105mm into the courtyard and buildings, the police headquarters was out of commission without collateral damage outside the fort.[30] Later, the raid planned for Fort Rupert was scrubbed.

From there, Lima 56 was tasked to find Richmond Hill Prison, but had difficulty locating it with the maps they had, so they returned to Point Salines to await further tasking. About this time, Rangers secured the True Blue campus and advised them there were many more students across the island at St. George's University Grand Anse and Lance Aux Pines campuses. This was a complete surprise and an incredible intelligence failure that called for rapid development of a plan to rescue them.

Throughout the morning, SEALS trapped in the governor's mansion repeated transmissions on their low-power intra-team radios, hoping someone would hear them. Only after Captain Gormly hitched a helicopter ride from the *USS Guam* to Point Salines airport was he able to contact the embattled SEALs via intra-team radio. Switching to an airport phone in TOC-1, he called the Governor-General's mansion to talk to his SEALs. By then, it had been several hours since insertion, with most of that time being surrounded and

30 Couvillon, *Grenada Grinder*, 76.

Soviet built ZU-23 AAA located at Ft Rupert. (Credit: National Archives)

under fire from the PRA. Once the situation was known, Captain Gormly elevated his concerns to VADM Metcalf who directed two USMC Cobra gunships to the Governor-General's mansion, but they could not locate it or communicate with TOC-1, so they returned to the *USS Guam*. At the same time, Gormly contacted Lima 56 and Lima 57 directly via VHF radio to relay targeting information from the team under siege.[31]

When Lima 56 rolled in over the Governor-General's mansion, both sensor operators identified numerous hostile personnel surrounding the building. Lima 56's fire control officer, Lt Col Paul Wonderly directed the IR as primary sensor and navigator Capt Kirby Locklear confirmed the tar-

31 Col (Ret.) Carney, *No Room for Error*, 148.

gets. Maj Couvillon began firing 40mm HEI first, followed by 20mm HEI, which caused PRA soldiers to scatter. Within about five minutes, soldiers regrouped and resumed their advance towards the mansion. This Cat & Mouse situation continued throughout the morning until the PRA became hesitant to assault the mansion for fear of retaliation. From that point on, supporting the SEALs trapped in the mansion became the number one priority for all AC-130 aircraft.

By 1100, after about 30 minutes on station, Lima 56 departed for fuel at Roosevelt Roads and Lima 57 took their place over the mansion. Almost immediately after rolling into orbit, Lima 57 detected a BTR-60 Armored Personnel Carrier (APC) at the gate, firing a 14.5mm machine gun into the compound.

Lima 57's fire-control officer, Maj Richard Rudolph, was aware the only weapon capable of killing a BTR-60 was 105mm HE, but because of close proximity to the SEALs and ROEs to limit collateral damage, he selected the 40mm gun. Lima 57 opened fire, hitting the APC several times. The BTR-60 immediately ceased fire, turned around and disappeared into the jungle.

> "Upon arriving, I discovered a BTR-60 in the courtyard raking fire at the Governor- General's mansion. Due to the proximity of the mansion, it was decided to use the 40mm vs the 105mm to reduce collateral damage. Our original ROE was: 'No damage to the mansion,' although that changed dramatically in the next few hours. I

> got several direct hits on the BTR and it broke off the attack and turned and wobbled erratically in an attempt to escape. It disappeared in the jungle." **CMSgt (Ret.) Don Boudreaux,** Lima 57 LLLTV sensor operator[32]

Just past noon, Lima 57 departed for Grantley Adams Airport, Barbados for fuel. At that time, there was no AC-130 coverage over Grenada. At Roosevelt Roads, Puerto Rico, Lima 56 and Lima 58 crews discovered the 20mm and 40mm replenishment ammunition they were promised was unlinked 20mm Target Practice (TP) and low powered 40mm grenades, which were not usable by the AC-130. Both crews were then ordered to fly to Grantley Adams Airport, Barbados to be closer to Grenada.

Since Lt Col Sims was aware ammunition was not available at Roosevelt Roads, he hoped replenishment ammunition had arrived on Barbados, but after landing and refueling, it was not there. Undeterred, Lima 57 took off for the Governor-General's mansion at 1430 with only three thousand rounds of 20mm and forty rounds of 105mm.

At the same time, two more AC-130s and three crews were on their way to Grenada. Maj Don Kemper's crew deployed from Hurlburt on *Excalibur* while Maj Lawrence Strelau's crew was flown via C-141 to Barbados. Capt David Tarpley's crew was re-deployed from Howard AFB, Panama on *Ghostrider*.

32 Email from CMSgt (Ret.) Don Boudreaux, to Author, Oct 2014.

Reinforcement Operation *Urgent Fury* AC-130 Crews		
Call Sign	Aircraft	Aircraft Commander
Lima 59	69-6569 "Excalibur"	Maj Don Kemper
Lima 60*	69-6575 "Wicked Wanda"**	Maj Lawrence Strelau
Lima 61	69-6567 "Ghostrider"	Capt David Tarpley

By about 1500, Lima 57 remained in orbit over the Governor-General's mansion scanning for activity, when flight engineer CMSgt Gene Eller noticed a flurry of activity in the distance. Shortly afterward, they received a request for fire support from A/1/75 TACP SSgt Scott informing them that three BTR-60s had just charged a Ranger patrol. Two were stopped in their tracks by a Ranger fire team with 90mm recoilless rifles but a third BTR-60 turned around and disappeared behind terrain, so SSgt Scott tasked Lima 57 to locate and eliminate it.

When Lima 57 rolled in overhead the Ranger position, Eller visually acquired a BTR-60 moving at a fairly high rate of speed, then talked both sensor operators onto it. Lima 57 tracked the BTR-60 for about one-half mile before firing to ensure safe separation from the Ranger element. When clear, Lima 75 fired one round of 105mm HE just as the vehicle rounded a bend in the road. When the projectile detonated nearby, its driver lost control and the APC ran off the road then rolled over two or three times until it came to rest on its side.

* Maj Strelau's crew initial mission used Maj Couvillon's aircraft and call sign, Lima 56. Subsequent missions used call sign Lima 60.

** Maj Strelau's crew deployed via C-141 and flew their first mission on 6575 after Maj Couvillon's crew day was complete.

BTR-60 engaged by Lima 57. (Credit: Dr. Robert Jordan)

Satisfied the vehicle was no longer a threat, Lima 57 returned to the Governor-General's mansion just in time to find another PRA attack in progress. They began a wide perimeter search, ultimately locating and firing on two 12.7mm AAA positions. As Lima 57 continued to search for PRA positions, sensor operators detected muzzle flashes coming from the Prime Minister's residence about 100 meters from the Governor-General's mansion. PRA soldiers had taken up firing positions in the building, but because of proximity of friendly forces, Lt Col Sims selected the 20mm guns. Henceforth, he fired short bursts of 20mm HEI onto the Prime Minister's residence. After firing about 1,200 rounds, hostile fire had ceased and a small fire was burning. Though the situation was quiet, Lima 57 remained overhead until about 1630. Upon the realization Grantley Adams

Airport was overwhelmed with aircraft and supplies arriving, Lt Col Sims headed for Roosevelt Roads. Two hours later, after an excruciating 28-hour duty day, Lima 57's mission was complete.

Both AC-130s at Barbados were being prepared for follow-on missions. When Maj Lawrence Strelau's crew arrived at Barbados via C-141, they were quickly briefed by Maj Couvillon's crew while gunners and maintainers transferred 105mm ammunition from *Heavy Metal* to *Wicked Wanda*. By 2130, Maj Strealu's crew took off for Grenada using the call sign Lima 56 and were sent directly to the Governor-General's mansion.

About the same time Lima 56 reported on station, Maj Kepner's crew (Lima 59) reported on station. Col Fister first directed Lima 59 to the Governor-General's mansion to assist Lima 56, then redirected them the Radio Free Grenada remote transmitter to reattack the facility abandoned earlier by the Navy Special Operations element.

> "We proceeded to Grenada using the same route and flight profile as the preceding mission aircraft with two heavyweight air refuels. Upon arrival, we were directed to support the SEALs at Government House, followed by direction to attack the Radio Free Grenada (RFG) station and enemy forces at Beausejour." **Maj (Ret.) Don Kemper**

Lima 59 located the radio transmitter and targeted the transmission tower. After firing several dozen 105mm

HE rounds, two vehicles were destroyed but they achieved limited success in damaging the tower. After about thirty minutes, Lima 59 was sent to search for the missing SEAL platoon who were overrun at the transmitter station earlier that day. Lima 59 searched, but did not find the platoon. Late in the evening, the entire platoon was recovered by the *USS Caron;* two by helicopter and the rest after swimming several miles across the open ocean.

PRA resistance continued into the early morning hours of October 26. Captain Tarpley (Lima 61) arrived on station after midnight with an inoperable navigation system and non-functioning SATCOM radio. Though Capt Tom Gallagher navigated from Panama to Grenada solely by sextant and celestial navigation, a slight error placed them in orbit over Carriacou Island, about 23 miles from Grenada. As Lima 61 orbited Carriacou, Lima 56 was searching for targets near the Governor-General's mansion. Confusion and miscommunications relayed over non-secure radios resulted in Lima 61 being cleared to fire on any vehicle going towards the mansion. Believing they were in the right place, Tarpley's crew searched the road below and found a sole vehicle traveling on a straight road and began to track it. The situation beneath Lima 61's orbit, however, was quiet and dark. Something didn't look right to Lima 61's fire control officer, Lt Col Paul Singleton, who inhibited the fire-control system to prevent firing. When right scanner SSgt Jeff Drummond noted a high level of activity in the distance, Gallagher realized they were orbiting over the wrong island. Considering the inoperable navigation system and secure communications problems, Capt Tarpley decided it was best to land on Barbados for repairs.

While Lima 61 sorted out their navigation problem, Lima 56 continued to monitor the perimeter of the Governor-General's mansion. When sensor operators TSgt Dan McClintock and SSgt Roger Vanstee detected muzzle flashes originating from the Prime Minister's residence, it appeared the PRA was about to make another attempt to overrun the Governor-General's mansion. Attempting to break contact and suppress PRA fire, Lima 56 fired about one hundred rounds of 40mm HEI on and near the building. PRA soldiers fled the building, running through a hail of 40mm explosions. When Lima 56's attack was complete, a large fire engulfed the Prime Minister's residence. Continuing their perimeter search, Lima 56 located and attacked 15–20 PRA soldiers and a BTR-60 located about 250 meters southwest of the Governor–General's mansion, setting the APC on fire and causing PRA soldiers to flee. Once the situation appeared to be quiet, Lima 56 was released to begin clearing a path for a Marine rescue force scheduled to launch later that morning.

During their search, Maj Strelau's crew searched a road leading to Fort Rupert, engaging numerous PRA fighting positions along the road. Their last target was an AAA gun at Fort Frederick, presumably one of the sites that engaged the TF-160 formation during the aborted Richmond Hill prison raid. After Lima 56 destroyed the gun with 40mm HEI and 105mm HE, they rolled out and headed for Barbados, ultimately landing about 0630 on October 26.

About 0400 on October 26, a Marine amphibious force assembled off the northwest coast of the island near Grand Mal, destined to rescue those under siege at the Governor-General's mansion. Just past 0530, Maj Twiford's crew (Lima 58) took off and flew directly to the Governor-General's mansion while thirteen Marine Amphibious Tracked vehicles and five M60 tanks made their way from Grand Mal to the mansion.

Though Lima 58 found the situation at the Governor-General's mansion to be quiet, they remained overhead until 0700 when the SEALs, the Governor-General, his family members and staff were rescued and taken to the USS Guam.[33] With the rescue complete, Lima 58 tracked the Marine force as they pushed further inland. Sensor operators TSgt Jerry Andersen and TSgt Buddy Sexton watched PRA fighters flee from their positions as the armored column approached and, eventually, Fort Rupert was taken without opposition. The mission was not over, however. A few kilometers from Fort Rupert on the western coast near St. George's, 224 medical students were still locked down on Grand Anse Campus.

About mid-morning on October 26, Lima 58 landed on Grantley Adams International airport and could barely find a place to park since the small airport had become the primary support base for *Urgent Fury*. Supply pallets and support equipment were off-loaded anywhere a bare spot of concrete could be found. Communications antennas,

33 Russell and Mendez, *Grenada, 1983*, 5.

power units, and cables were set near the terminal building, resembling a county fair midway. Dozens of C-141's loaded with military supplies poured in alongside commercial jets loaded with tourists. The scene was semi-organized chaos, complete with wide-eyed tourists caught by surprise.

Though the sun was up on a new day, there were still American students trapped on Grenada. Though TF-120's number one priority was the rescue of students at Grand Anse, there was no easy solution to the problem. MG Schwarzkopf and VADM Metcalf realized rescuing a large number of people from the campus was a challenge and PRA soldiers had surrounded the campus. Overland rescue of the students was risky since the terrain between Grand Anse and Point Salines was optimum for PRA ambush. To decrease risk, MG Schwarzkopf recommended a helicopter-borne rescue by Rangers inserted by Marine helicopters. This "crossing of swords" proposal was not welcomed by the TF-124 command structure, but nevertheless, VADM Metcalf ordered USMC CH-46 crews from HMM-261 to support the rescue, which was set for the afternoon of October 26.

While TF-123 and TF-124 planned their combined mission, students at Grand Anse were contacted via phone and instructed on what to do when Rangers arrived. Meanwhile, Lima 56 and Lima 61 were preparing to launch to support the rescue.

The basic battle plan was to bomb, strafe and shell PRA enclaves near the campus for thirty minutes to suppress PRA threats to the incoming helicopter formation.

After thirty minutes, firing would cease but Lima 56 would remain overhead to provide on-call fire support. A formation of CH-46 helicopters would then approach from the sea to insert Rangers onto Grand Anse beach to set up a defensive perimeter. Rangers would then secure the students, rush them onto CH-53 helicopters and take them to Point Salines. After all students were rescued, CH-46 crews would return to pick up the Rangers.

At 1302, as Rangers boarded the CH-46s, and Maj Couvillon's crew (Lima 56) departed Barbados en route to Grenada. Once overhead their target area, they established a search orbit near the Grand Anse campus. A Navy Forward Air Controller (FAC) then cleared Lima 56 to fire on forty Carifta cottages and a police training building near the campus. Maj Couvillon selected the 20mm guns, and for the next twenty minutes, fired 50–70 round bursts at each cottage. Sensor operators didn't see anyone fleeing the area and all seemed quiet. When done firing on the cottages, IR sensor operator, SSgt Anderson, located the police training building and the crew shifted their fire to that structure. While firing on the building, Navy A-7s flew low through their orbit, strafing the cottages. Near the end of Lima 56's time window, an AAA gun site began firing at them. Maj Couvillon returned fire with a thirty-round salvo of 40mm HEI, silencing the gun.

> "Me, my student friend's pregnant dog, Brandy, and a lady Histology Demonstrator, Debbie Franklin (who wore leg braces and used a cane

> because of polio) then ran past Dorm 1 toward my Anatomy building about 50 yards away. Half way there, the first explosion occurred to my left, i.e., just North of our perimeter fence, toward the sea and nearly knocked us off our feet. Found out later it took out a PRA AA gun positioned in one of the rooms of an old roofless hotel. Upon reaching our building and diving under my office desk all hell really broke loose. The sounds were deafening. In what seemed like about 20 minutes, the AC-130 took out the two Carifta cottages across the street from me blowing out all the windows in my building."
> **Dr. Robert Jordan**

When Lima 56's time window ended, the police building was on fire and the situation appeared quiet. At 1615, *Sea Knights* landed in three ship formations under light PRA opposition, deployed Rangers onto the beach, then departed to a holding area. Rangers set up a defensive perimeter and the students were quickly escorted to the arriving CH-53s, then flown out as planned. Rescued American and British citizens were taken to Point Salines, then flown to Roosevelt Roads, Puerto Rico on C-141 *Starlifters*.

When CH-46s returned to retrieve the Rangers, Chalk 8 was constricted to a narrow landing zone between the surf and a group of palm trees. Unfortunately, rotor wash caused one of the palm trees to flex, then break and fall on the helicopters' rotor system, rendering it unflyable. Maj Dick

Gallagher and the crew of Chalk 8 had no choice other than to abandon their Sea Knight on the narrow strip of beach and fly out on another CH-46.

After the loss of a helicopter and departure of the rescue force, one Ranger squad manning a remote blocking position missed the call for extraction and was left behind. Waiting until dark, the squad removed life rafts from the abandoned helicopter and began paddling out to sea. Shortly after the Rangers left the beach, Lima 61, commanded by Capt David Tarpley, now flying *Heavy Metal*, was called in to fire on the helicopter to prevent exploitation of cryptographic equipment and weapons onboard.

As Lima 61 set up a firing orbit over the CH-46, fire-control officer Lt Col Paul Singleton selected the 105mm gun which still had a defective firing solenoid from the previous day. Realizing the limitation, gunners rigged a manual firing lanyard just like Lima 58 gunners did during the airfield seizure. Likewise, the pilot used verbal commands to direct gunners to fire the gun manually when firing parameters in the HUD were met. Unfortunately, that makeshift tactic was not ideal for accuracy. Henceforth, Lima 61 fired multiple 105mm HE rounds that exploded around the helicopter, in the surf and on the beach, but a direct hit was not achieved. Switching to the 20mm guns, Capt Tarpley fired successive bursts totaling about 750 rounds that raked across the CH-46. After firing for about 30 minutes, the helicopter was heavily damaged, but it did not catch fire as desired. Unwilling to continue the attack and conserve ammunition for emergency fire support requests, Lima 61 broke off their attack and remained over the Island on airborne alert until reaching minimum fuel conditions.

Abandoned CH-46 on Grand Anse beach engaged by Lima 61 on October 26, 1983. (Credit: National Archives)

On the evening of October 26, C-141s arrived at Barbados with war reserve supply kits, additional maintenance personnel and the much-anticipated ammunition resupply pallets. Forklifts were not yet available, so pallets were dumped directly on the parking ramp far away from the gunships. This made ammunition loading onto AC-130s difficult since several tons of large caliber ammunition needed to be hand carried to each aircraft by gunners and maintainers one can or round at a time.

AC-130 missions continued all day on October 27. Lima 59 flew a daylight armed escort mission in support of the

82nd Airborne near Frequente and found PRA troops firing at US troops from a tree line.

> "We attacked the enemy positions by firing 20mm and 40mm rounds (as directed) up and down the tree line for almost an hour until the hostile firing stopped. During the attack, we observed someone approaching from the east. Upon closer observation, he was wearing a long, white coat, and this is probably what saved his life. We think one of the students was attempting to get some pictures for whatever reason."
> **Maj (Ret.) Don Kemper,** pilot

Lima 59 continued to escort the 82nd Airborne as they maneuvered towards St. George's on True Blue-Grand Anse road. Near Ruth Howard, they encountered a large crowd of celebrating civilians, who welcomed US soldiers as liberators. Suddenly, PRA soldiers began firing on the group causing them to disperse. 82nd Airborne Soldiers returned fire and called in Lima 59 to suppress hostile fire. When complete, Lima 59 continued to escort the 82nd towards St. George's. As they fanned out over the island, many Cuban military officers fled to the Soviet Embassy to avoid capture.

Along their route, 82nd Airborne soldiers met with Air Naval Gunfire Liaison Company (ANGLICO) Marines at a crossroads. The ANGLICO element believed a hostile target was ahead and opted to call in Navy A-7 attack aircraft, while Lima 59 remained overhead. The A-7 pilot flew through the gunship's orbit and mistakenly bombed the

82nd Airborne 2nd Brigade headquarters command post, causing 17 casualties.[34] In the midst of the chaos on the ground, the remainder of Lima 59's armed escort mission was cancelled.

At about the same time, Rangers were preparing to attack Calivigny Barracks and other enemy positions south of St. George's. A flight of eight Blackhawk helicopters from B Company, 82nd Airborne Combat Aviation Battalion was assembled to carry 2/75 and C/1/75 Rangers to their objective. At 1555 hrs, Maj Twiford's crew was called in to fire on the barracks and surrounding woods. While firing, they scored a direct hit on a large fuel tank adjacent to the camp's power generator causing a large secondary explosion.[35]

The airborne raid began shortly afterward with Lima 58 overhead providing suppressive fire and monitoring the situation with their sensors. The UH-60s approached in groups of four from over the water in trail formation. Coming in fast, the first helicopter made a hard landing on the LZ. The second helicopter took small arms fire as they approached the LZ, wounding one of the pilots and several Rangers, but still landed successfully. The third helicopter came in way too fast for the small LZ. As the pilot attempted to land, the UH-60 hit the ground hard and spun into the second helicopter. The fourth UH-60 veered to avoid the crash and also set down hard, damaging its tail rotor. Apparently

34 Richard W. Stewart, *Operation Urgent Fury: The Invasion of Grenada, October 1983* (Dept. of the Army Center of Military History Publication, 2008) https://history.army.mil/html/books/grenada/index.html.

35 E-mail from Historian GySgt (Ret.) Joe Muccia, to Author, Oct 2014.

unaware of the damage, the helicopter crashed when its pilot tried to lift off. In just a few minutes, three UH-60s were destroyed, and more than a dozen Rangers were either killed or wounded.

After exploring the camp and finding no resistance, the barracks were declared secure at 1800 while Rangers remained on the camp overnight. AC-130 gunships remained overhead throughout the night on airborne alert in support of the Ranger force until they evacuated the camp. The next day, when 82nd Airborne Soldiers approached the camp, Lima 61 was called in to take out a sniper position, essentially eliminating the last remnant of PRA resistance at Calivigny.

With the last major military objectives secured on October 28, the 82nd Airborne and Marines began mop-up operations. Warehouses were discovered containing millions of rounds of small arms ammunition and thousands of weapons, most still in their shipping crates. All ammunition and weapons were of Communist Bloc origin and far exceeded the quantity Grenada would need for self-defense. As the 82nd Airborne searched the island and processed prisoners, a squadron of USAF A-10 Warthogs arrived in Barbados, making Grantley Adams airport operations more hectic. To lessen the burden of overcrowding, two AC-130s were sent to Roosevelt Roads. Unfortunately, the split operation placed large burdens on command and control, logistics and maintenance personnel. For the next few days, AC-130 gunships maintained a 24-hour airborne alert schedule until they were placed on 24-hour ground alert, sometimes parked near Cuban aircraft being used to repatriate Cuban POWs.

> "We periodically had to share the ramp when Cuban IL-76 aircraft would land to repatriate Cuban 'construction workers'. We were able to get TA to put *Spectre* decals on the transports' doors as they closed them for taxi." **Col (Ret.) Mike Byers,** AC-130 pilot

On the morning of October 29, Marines captured Coard, his wife, and Gen Austin, then took them to the USS Guam for incarceration. With PRA leadership officially defeated, Grenadian citizens assisted US forces in finding Cuban and PRA soldiers who were hiding.

On November 4, Operation *Urgent Fury* officially ended for AC-130 crews and maintainers, who returned to Hurlburt Field, FL.

MISSION DEBRIEF

Operation *Urgent Fury* and the reasons leading to US military involvement have gone down as one of the most critiqued and misconstrued set of circumstances in modern military history. Though politicians and arm-chair warriors may continue to ponder the "what ifs" forever, what cannot be discounted is the drive, fortitude, and commitment of the US military forces who conducted the operation.

The extremely short planning cycle and rush to combat operations contributed to a much-fractured Command,

Control, and Communications (C3) network. Ironically, the reliance on secure communications via SATCOM radios to maintain operational security actually hampered the mission by causing radio failures and either dropped or incorrect codes. Thankfully, communications from ALO, TACP, FSO, FiST and FO to AC-130 crews did not rely on SATCOM, but instead occurred over old-fashioned PRC-66 and PRC-77 radios on open frequencies.

The hastily-assembled plan began falling apart even before H-Hour and almost nothing occurred as planned. The operation was successful only because of the herculean effort and demonstrated adaptability of Soldiers, Sailors, Airmen, and Marines. AC-130 crews in particular flew long and tedious missions to support TF-123 and TF-121. Many fire missions were in close proximity to ground forces, which demanded careful and accurate fires. *Spectre* crews completed these missions without fratricide or high levels of collateral damage.

The combination of the AC-130's optical sensors, persistence, and lethality were exactly what ground forces needed on Grenada. All six AC-130 crews involved in the operation made significant contributions to mission success, but Maj Twiford's crew was singled out for their actions during the airfield seizure and was selected for the 1984 Tunner Award; the overall best aircrew in Military Airlift Command.

Lima 61's attack on the CH-46 abandoned on Grand Anse beach was largely unsuccessful, but many years after the operation additional facts were discovered. A short time after Rangers departed the beach on a life raft pulled from the helicopter, Dr. Robert Jordan, a faculty member at Grand Anse, accompanied by several others, walked out to the abandoned CH-46 to take a look when Lima 61 arrived overhead. Capt Tarpley's crew searched the area prior to opening fire and did not see any personnel. Unknown to them, Dr. Jordan, Debby Franklin, two Grenadians, and a pregnant dog named Brandy were on the helicopter when Lima 61 began firing. Fortunately for all involved, the degraded firing mode Lima 61 was operating under resulted in a sizable miss distance on their first shot, allowing the group to run for cover in the walk-in cooler of the Spice Island Inn. Had Lima 61's firing solenoid and fire control system been working properly, it was highly likely the gunship crew would have hit the helicopter on the first or second shot, injuring or killing those inside. This is one case where a degraded firing mode was a positive, albeit unintentional, aspect.

Overall, *Urgent Fury* combat operations cost the lives of 19 American servicemen and at least nine aircraft lost or damaged. The toll on Grenadian citizens and PRA soldiers was estimated to be 45 dead and at least 350 wounded, while 25 Cubans were reported killed and 59 captured. The AC-130s use of 20mm and 40mm guns during the opening hours of the mission resulted in a lower kill rate of both PRA and Cuban fighters, keeping within their orders to limit collateral damage and needless killing. The much more lethal 105mm HE round was only used when a lethal agenda or high level of material damage was desired.

Lieutenant Colonel (Ret.) Henry "Ike" Eisenbarth and Col (Ret.) James Roper summed up their opinion concerning AC-130 support in Grenada with the following:

> "There has always been a unique bond between Rangers and Gunship Crews...a strong bond of respect and trust, forged through hard realistic training, and honed on the field of battle. Every mission conducted by Rangers during Operation *Urgent Fury* was executed under the reliable weapons and sensor support umbrella of the *Spectre* Gunship, 'The Fabulous Four Engine Sniper.'" **Lieutenant Colonel (Ret.) Henry "Ike" Eisenbarth**

> "The AC-130 was particularly effective initially in silencing AAA, and from that point onward air power had high credibility. Ground commanders were proud and possessive of 'their own' capability to bring down heavy firepower from above. And the TACP was happy to oblige." After Action Report written by **Maj James Roper,** Nov 1983

After Operation *Urgent Fury*, the island of Grenada returned to its traditional peaceful lifestyle. Sir Paul Scoon was appointed interim head of government and appointed an advisory council, ultimately naming Nicholas Brathwaite as Prime Minister until elections could be held. The Grenadian people named Point Salines airport Maurice Bishop

International Airport and were so thankful for their liberation, they declared October 25th of every year a national holiday of thanksgiving.

> "I thank God you guys came in and that the US did what it did! Regionally and globally, it was the perfect chance and best timing to stop/crush the spread of Communism in our region of the world. And, to nip in the bud, the ascending aspirations and careers of some nearby petty Marxist leaning dictators. Great, great move on our part and I'll always be proud of us as Americans for doing it." **Dr. Robert Jordan**

> "The first Americans to be evacuated from Grenada since the United States invasion arrived here this evening. Some knelt and kissed the ground after they stepped from an Air Force C-141 transport plane and others whooped to express their pleasure to be home. 'I don't think there's any more beautiful sight than the United States,' said Jean Joel of Albany, N.Y. 'And the rangers who arrived to save us.' She was one of 69 Americans and two Britons, all of them students at St. George's University School of Medicine, who arrived on the first plane to bring people off the tiny Caribbean island since American Marines and soldiers invaded Tuesday." **Fay S. Joyce**, Special to *the New York Times*, published October 27, 1983

> "It was a morning to remember. I take my hat off to all those involved and lost in returning Grenada to freedom. It was a life changing day for all involved and made me even more proud to be an American." **Dr. Hank Collins**

In retrospect, Operation *Urgent Fury* was a critical turning point in post-Vietnam US military organization. Had operations in Grenada not occurred as disjointed and unorganized as they did, it is likely nothing in the US military command structure would have changed. Three years later, *Urgent Fury* was considered the catalyst of the Goldwater-Nichols Act and Nunn-Cohen Amendment of 1986 and the formation of the United States Special Operations Command (USSOCOM) in 1987.

The crew of Lima 58 was awarded the 1984 Tunner Award recognizing them as the best overall aircrew in Military Airlift Command.

AC	Maj Clement Twiford
AC	Maj Thomas Waylett
CP	1Lt Michael Phelan
Nav	Capt Bryan Lasyone
Nav	2Lt Rob Schmitt
FE	CMSgt Don Beardsley
FEM	MSgt Michael Hosenbackez
FCO	Lt Col Richard Dougherty
EWO	1Lt Sam Neal
SO	TSgt Jerry Andersen

SO	TSgt Albert Sexton III
AG	MSgt Ron Broyles
AG	TSgt Richard Smith
AG	SSgt Herbert Thompson
AG	SSgt James Habas
AG	Sgt George Celis
IO	MSgt Warren Allen Jr.
IO	SSgt William Jennings

SITUATION REPORT: 1987–1990

The 16 SOS maintained a constant deployed presence at Howard Air Force Base, Panama. Two aircraft and two crews alternated to fly nightly missions over El Salvador.

AC-130H crews home station training continued with Army Special Forces, Rangers and Navy SEALs during numerous exercises. Crews continued routine low-level training over Northwest Florida and Southeast Alabama at five hundred ft. Above Ground Level (AGL), spooking cattle and sheep in both states. Normally a live-fire training event would culminate at the end of the low-level route with the AC-130 climbing to normal firing altitude a short distance from the live-fire range. During the late 1980s, AC-130 crews began to attend Advanced Airlift Tactics Training Center (AATTC) training at Rosecrans Air National Guard Base, St. Joseph, Missouri. The nine day course included low-level flight training in tactics and evasion of fighter aircraft. To allow a gunship crew member a wide field of view overhead the aircraft, a large Plexiglas bubble was installed in the forward overhead escape hatch. The training was valuable to AC-130 crews for specific mission plans.

Maintaining the AC-130A/H 20mm guns became increasingly difficult in the 1980s. Nickel-Cadmium battery voltage would drop off, causing slow firing rates, jams and malfunctions. In the late 1980s, the Ni-Cad batteries were replaced by Lead-Acid batteries. The voltage drop-off problems went away, but the amperage dump was so powerful at the beginning of the burst that ammunition belts were being pulled apart and hard stoppage feed malfunctions were more likely to cause damage to ammunition and/or the gun compared to use of the Ni-Cads.

After it was suspected a Minuteman rocket was hit by sniper fire during launch, AC-130 gunships were tasked to provide surveillance of launch sites prior to satellite launches at Vandenberg AFB, CA and Cape Canaveral, FL. The 16 SOS covered Vandenberg launches while the 711 SOS took Cape Canaveral launches. Crews would normally deploy several days before a scheduled launch, search the area surrounding the launch site for several hours, then withdraw to a safe distance just prior to the launch. Typically, two additional crew members would deploy to operate radios and perform ground liaison duties with security personnel. Missions occurred on an infrequent basis until 1989.

By 1987, Air Staff was convinced AC-130 capabilities had to be retained and realized much had to be done to upgrade the overworked fleet. The first major effort to update the AC-130H began in 1987 as the Special Operations Force Improvement (SOFI) Program. This effort replaced the out-of-date ASCU Fire-control Computer (FCC) with two state-of-the-art computers to ensure redundancy and reliability. These components were designed to be modular line replaceable units (LRU) to facilitate easier installation and maintenance and reduce the need to hard wire equipment in the traditional manner. Engineers also focused on software development to permit substantial system upgrades without hardware changes. This allowed much more rapid improvements in the aircraft itself as well as its training systems.

Development of the AC-130U began in 1987. Many years had passed since the original development of the AC-130 and limited experience remained within the Systems Program Office (SPO) at Wright-Patterson Air Force Base, OH. North American Rockwell was awarded a contract to modify twelve existing C-130H aircraft into AC-130U gunships.[36] By Air Force standards, it was an unconventional acquisition since the Air Force provided the C-130H (a.k.a. Super-H) aircraft while the newly-formed United States Special Operations Command (USSOCOM) funded the conversion to AC-130Us.

North American Rockwell had no gunship experience so Air Force Systems Command recruited members of the 16 SOS and 1 SOW as development team members to assist Rockwell engineers. Many of these personnel were eventually assigned to Edwards Air Force Base during the flight

---

36 After AC-130H 6567 (Spirit 03) was shot down during Operation *Desert Storm,* the Air Force added an additional aircraft to the AC-130U production order as a combat loss replacement. This event added a "white tail" C-130 intended for commercial sale to the Rockwell modification line. This event resulted in tail number 92-0253 going down in history as the very first "new production" AC-130. This aircraft became affectionately known as "8-Ball" by crew chiefs.

test phase. As the program evolved, SPO representatives, Rockwell engineers and test crews put forth their best intentions to cure the operational woes of the legacy AC-130, especially fire-control, sensors and avionics. Modifications were completed in California at the North American Rockwell plant, Palmdale, CA and aircraft flight tested at Edwards Air Force Base. As a parallel effort, AC-130H aircraft 69-6568 (*Night Stalker*) was the first SOFI gunship delivered in 1990.

CHAPTER FOUR

OPERATIONS ELABORATE MAZE, NIMROD DANCER, BLUE SPOON, JUST CAUSE, AND PROMOTE LIBERTY, 1987–1990

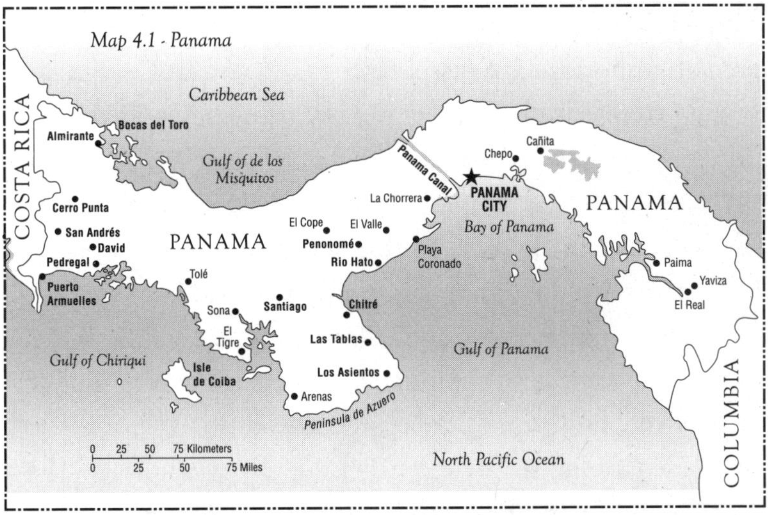

The Panama Canal Area of Operations (Credit: Carl Mauro II)

Starting in the mid-1970s, the situation in Panama slowly slid towards a dictatorship after President Jimmy Carter negotiated a treaty for a transfer of the Panama Canal to the Government of Panama. There were numerous US military bases on the isthmus and the Panama Canal Treaty stipulated the US had a right to protect its interests and intervene militarily to protect the Panama Canal. Starting in 1977, AC-130 gunship crews from the 16 SOS routinely deployed to Panama for training and were included in OPLAN 6000-86 (Defense of the Panama Canal).

By the mid-1980s, under the regime of a largely symbolic civilian government, General Manuel Noriega appointed himself as the commander in chief of the Panama Defense Forces (PDF) and was recognized by his appointed civilian cronies as the de facto leader of Panama. Noriega was well trained in military intelligence operations and was considered an important U.S. asset by the CIA and DoD, who were willing to overlook Noriega's many transgressions to maintain his intelligence value.[1] Noriega was clever, resourceful, and knew how to manipulate both US and Panamanian governments for personal gain. He maintained his position in Panama by threats and intimidation and was suspected of sanctioning several political murders. He militarized the PDF, purchased new equipment, and increased training levels. At the same time, government-sanctioned corruption, organized crime, and drug trafficking ran rampant. By 1987, Noriega was still on the CIA payroll when US government politicians felt Noriega had to go.

On June 26, The US Senate passed a resolution that called for the government of Panama to restore the constitutional rights Noriega had suspended, ensure free elections,

---

1 Lawrence Yates, *The US Military Intervention in Panama: Origins, Planning and Crisis Management, June 1987-December 1989* (Washington, DC: US Army Center of Military History, 2008), 20.

remove the PDF from non-military activities and organizations and investigate a murder Noriega was suspected of directing.[2] Noriega and his staff responded by directing the Panama Defense Force (PDF) to take out their frustrations on American citizens and military personnel stationed in Panama. Accordingly, Americans were regularly threatened and detained for minor traffic offenses and sometimes for completely fabricated charges. As tensions between the US and Panama increased, Panamanians upset with Noriega organized and participated in large public protests. The 1st Company of Public Order, located within the PDF's La Comandancia headquarters in downtown Panama City, used strong-arm tactics to break up protests. This PDF organization named "*The Dobermans*" was quick to respond with tear gas, rubber hoses, shotguns loaded with bird shot, and water cannons.

As anti-Noriega sentiment increased, a group of pro-Noriega Panamanian citizens formed an armed militia under the auspices of protecting the sovereignty of Panama. Calling themselves The Dignity Battalion, this group wore para-military/police uniforms and marched in formation through the streets brandishing weapons and attacking anti-Noriega Panamanians. The Dignity Battalion was essentially Noriega's goon squad who wreaked havoc on anti-Noriega citizens and Americans. Because of the threats posed by these hostile Panamanians, military installations were placed on Threat Condition (THREATCON) "Charlie" highly restricting off-installation travel.

---

2 Ibid, 19.

Shortly after the US Senate made their demands to Noriega, a group of pro-Noriega demonstrators gathered around the US Embassy, threw rocks and paint-filled balloons at the building, broke windows, and damaged cars in the area.

In 1987, US Army General Frederick Woerner Jr., Commander in Chief Southern Command (CINCSO) recognized the effect of political tensions between the US and Panama and raised the question of how Southern Command (SOUTHCOM) should deal with Noriega on a day-to-day basis. With few avenues of approach remaining, Woerner regularly met with Noriega in discreet and unofficial fashion at Noriega's headquarters on Ft Amador.

In spite of efforts to remedy the situation, relations between the US and Noriega continued to deteriorate. Intelligence analysts of the US Army's 470th Military Intelligence Brigade believed Noriega was intentionally provoking US forces to create a military confrontation that would expose the US as an aggressor and result in the US withdrawing from Panama. If a hasty withdrawal from Panama was required, leadership acknowledged the complexity and scale of such an operation would be monumental. At a minimum, a Non-Combatant Evacuation Operation (NEO) plan was needed, but with thousands of US citizens and military members living in Panama, the task of safely evacuating them would be difficult, time consuming and potentially dangerous. It was clear a single NEO plan was insufficient to protect US citizens and interests in Panama. The major dividing line between US and Panamanian forces was 4th of July Avenue, which defined the border of the former Canal Zone. Article IX of the Panama Canal Treaty prohibited PDF from crossing 4th of July Avenue.

In late 1987, a deliberate mission planning process began. What emerged was a CINCSO OPORD 2-88, a five phase operation for military intervention in Panama code named *Elaborate Maze*. AC-130 mission planners were tasked to begin developing classified compartmentalized plans ranging from support of a Non-combatant Evacuation Operation (NEO) through a full-scale military intervention. 16 SOS Commander Lt Col Howard Chambers assigned Captain Bradley Heithold as the lead planner for this effort.

By February of 1988, US grand juries had indicted Noriega for drug trafficking and relations between the US and Panama continued to decline. On March 16, Noriega survived a coup d'état attempt. Now fearless against the United States, Noriega increased PDF harassment of US citizens and the US military in Panama. The PDF also began hostile incursions into US-controlled facilities, which prompted SOUTHCOM concerns of PDF sabotage of US strategic assets.

Noriega's strategy of harassment continued to escalate in the spring of 1988. Particularly troublesome for SOUTHCOM were covert incursions into the Arraijan Tank Farm (ATF) located northwest of Howard Air Force Base. ATF maintained an inventory of thirty-seven large fuel tanks containing the entire US strategic fuel reserve for US forces in Panama. The tank farm was easily accessible from its northern perimeter via the Pan-American Highway.

> "The Arraijan Tank Farm resembled a "golf course" from the air. It was all hilly but some of it was clear, grassy area; short and tall. In between these "fairways" it was a dense jungle." **LCpl Mike Morrison,** Forward Observer, K 3/6, 2nd DIV, USMC

By March, the USMC Security Force Battalion based at Norfolk Virginia deployed a Fleet Antiterrorism Security Team (FAST) Platoon as part of *Elaborate Maze*. Upon arrival, their commander, Major Eddie Keith, decided to use the platoon to protect the tank farm. Soon after establishing a presence at ATF, patrols routinely spotted intruders at night in black uniforms, carrying weapons and wearing Night Vision Goggles (NVG). At times, intruders got close enough that Marines could observe them moving in tactical formations like professional soldiers, not like poachers or someone lost in the jungle. Daylight patrols discovered freshly-dug fighting positions, but reports of PDF activity within ATF were doubted by the SOUTHCOM staff who felt the holes were likely dug during earlier US training exercises. Generally, Marine reports of PDF activity within ATF were dismissed as ghost sightings. The Marine patrols, however, were confident of what they saw, but were unable to capture or produce convincing physical evidence to prove PDF activity within the ATF.[3]

---

3 Nicholas E. Reynolds, *Just Cause: Marine Operations In Panama, 1988-1990* (Washington, DC: History and Museums Division, Headquarters US Marine Corps, 1996), 4.

By early April, a Marine Air to Ground Task Force (MAGTF) began flowing into Panama, supported by other Marine elements which were all absorbed into the newly established Joint Task Force (JTF) Panama. Shortly thereafter, the 6th Marine Expeditionary Brigade (MEB), Company 1, 3rd Battalion, 4th Marines, commanded by Capt Joseph Valore, was assigned to replace the FAST platoon at ATF. After meeting with Maj Keith and surveilling ATF, Capt Valore established two patrol zones, a command post for each, and established Rules Of Engagement (ROE) for patrols.[4] As an added security measure, remote battlefield sensors were installed throughout ATF.

There were several sightings on the nights of April 9–10, but events on April 11 proved to be an escalation beyond the shadow of doubt. That night, a squad-size element of Marines patrolling the northeast sector detected armed intruders entering ATF via a shallow creek bed that ran through the tank farm. While attempting to encircle and capture the intruders, a Marine accidentally ignited a trip flare, and the popping sound was mistaken for hostile fire. Tragically, one Marine patrol opened fire directly at another, seriously wounding Corporal Ricardo Villahermosa, who died in Gorgas Hospital a few days later.[5] To prevent the potential for another fratricide incident, Marine foot patrols were discontinued after dark. Instead, Listening Posts (LP) and Observation Posts (OP) were situated inside the tank farm in dug in, protected positions for nighttime operations.

---

4 Ibid, 6.

5 Ibid, 6.

On April 12, intruders probed Marine positions and initiated a firefight. An AC-130H crew commanded by Capt Mark Wildermuth was preparing for an unarmed *Blinking Light* mission when they were alerted and diverted to ATF to surveille the situation. The Gunship crew arrived overhead as Marines were firing dozens of 81mm illumination mortars to expose the intruders. Gunship sensor operators easily located widely-dispersed personnel inside the tank farm but were unable to differentiate friend from foe. Illumination seemed to have no effect on the intruders as they continued to advance towards Marine positions. When Capt Valore was advised via radio of the urgent situation, he authorized return fire with 81mm HE mortars and small arms. During this time, Wildermuth's crew remained overhead, unable to affect the ongoing firefight, but systematically located and videotaped the locations of all personnel in ATF. By the time the firefight subsided, Marines had fired sixteen HE mortars, 222 40mm grenades, and hundreds of rounds of rifle ammunition.

By 2200 hours, MG Bernard Loeffke, Commander US Army South, accompanied by PDF officer Capt Moises Cortizo, arrived to inquire as to what happened. Capt Cortizo denied knowledge of any PDF troops in the area and Gen Loeffke directed Marines to stay in position until daybreak. During the night, Marines watched through their NVGs as intruders administered first aid and dragged their wounded (and perhaps dead) to the Pan-American Highway. Throughout the night, Security Force Marines manning a roadblock position near the Bridge of Americas witnessed blacked-out ambulances and PDF buses speeding towards

Panama City, presumably transporting troops and casualties from ATF.

At daybreak, a sweep of the area failed to produce bodies of intruders or spent rifle casings; however, there were signs that bodies had been dragged through the area. Marines also found fresh foreign-made field dressings, scraps of uniforms, and chemical light sticks. An investigation ensued, resulting in Marines being accused of being overzealous. However, individual Marine accounts of the firefight were consistent. One Marine testified he shot an intruder twice at close range and saw him fall to the ground. The AC-130 video indicated there were more personnel in the ATF than the number of Marines on duty and it did appear they were maneuvering against static Marine positions. JTF-Panama staff acknowledged the Marines were probably correct, but could not identify who the intruders were. Nevertheless, as the investigation concluded, Capt Valore's Marines were temporarily stood down while US Army soldiers from the 193rd Infantry Brigade took over surveillance of ATF.

JTF-Panama staff reaction to the events at ATF resulted in security measures being added, including AC-130 surveillance missions over strategic US facilities. Fortunately, two AC-130H gunships and three aircrews were already in place at Howard Air Force Base flying nightly *Blinking Light* missions into El Salvador. To meet JTF-Panama tasking, missions to El Salvador were scaled back in frequency to accommodate increased mission tasking in Panama. Soon, additional AC-130H and AC-130A gunships and crews were deployed from the 16 SOS, Hurlburt Field, FL and the 711th Special

Operations Squadron, Duke Field, FL. Once on station, AC-130 crews inherited a 24-hour alert commitment and nighttime armed surveillance missions over specific points of interest including the perimeters of Howard AFB, Ft. Kobbe, Ft. Clayton, Albrook Air Force Base and Rodman Naval Station. Though gunships were fully loaded at all times, the Rules of Engagement (ROE) were highly restrictive and direct USSOUTHCOM Commander approval was required to authorize crews to fire.

While gunship crews were capable of the task at hand, there were not enough Ground Liaison Officers (GLO) to coordinate gunship missions from each site of interest. To meet the demand, AC-130 crew members from the 1 SOW Opposing Forces team (OPFOR) volunteered to perform GLO duties with Army and Marine Corps personnel. The volunteers were primarily sensor operators and gunners who were trained in land navigation and radio communications by SOF personnel from the Joint Liaison Office on Hurlburt Field. In the coming months, gunship crews routinely responded to on call alert tasking and kept watch on the Panama Canal locks, Arraijan Tank Farm and the Army ammunition supply point at Fort Clayton.

The fact that incursions into US-controlled facilities continued and the inability to identify who they actually were was concerning to SOCSOUTH commander Col Chuck Fry. With the sole purpose of capturing and interrogating and intruder for intelligence information, he established Task Force Gray (TF-Gray), composed of several 3-man Army Special Forces reconnaissance/surveillance teams from Company C, 3rd Battalion, 7th Special Forces Group (Airborne) (C-3/7 SFG(A)), stationed at Ft. Davis. TF-Gray's tactic was to position Listening Post/Observation Posts (LP/OP) in the heavy jungle near Arraijan where man-made trails were discovered during daylight patrols. To avoid detection, LP/OP teams would be inserted covertly during daylight, establish their positions, then wait for nightfall to capture an intruder passing by. The overall objective of the effort was to capture an intruder then secure him for questioning. Since small teams can be vulnerable to being overrun by numerically superior forces, several large Quick Reaction Force (QRF) teams from the C-3/7 SFG(A) and 1st of the 508th Airborne Infantry Bn were in alert posture whenever LP/OP teams were out. Furthermore, the teams were supported by Army Blackhawk helicopters and one AC-130 gunship that was on alert at Howard AFB.

Mid-day on April 20, two three-member reconnaissance teams consisting of SFC Imbrasia, SFC Puerto, and SSG Hulsey (OP-1) and SFC Brown, SFC Torres, and SFC Lopez (OP-2) were inserted into the jungle northwest of the Howard AFB runway. As OP-1 neared their objective area, they detected an individual dressed in an unusual military uniform approaching, prompting them to take cover in the heavy jungle growth. The intruder was armed with a shotgun and appeared to be reconnoitering the trail. About twenty minutes after the intruder passed, OP-1 relocated into a more advantageous position, waiting for nightfall. At the same time, OP-2 set up their position on the opposite side of a ridgeline about 200 meters from OP-1. Once settled into position, they placed three command-detonated M18 Claymore mines in a triangular fashion around their position for site security. Their position overlooked a well used path cut through the jungle, headed towards the Arraijan Tank Farm. During late afternoon, OP-2 detected a sole individual, dressed in an unusual military uniform approaching. The intruder was armed with a rifle and appeared to be reconnoitering the trail.[6]

> "To our front, there was a path that we were observing for any foot traffic. At one point during the afternoon, we observed an individual wearing non-U.S. camo, carrying a long gun making his way through the path. We took several photos of the individual and once he left the area, we contacted HQ and relayed the event."
> **SFC Noe Lopez**

Just before sunset, SFC Brown prepared his NVG's for night ops. Shortly thereafter, he noticed movement coming from the path and alerted the team of the activity. Expecting a small squad element, the team was surprised when a platoon-sized element was headed directly towards OP-2. Now cloaked in complete darkness, the Special Forces team remained still to see if the intruders would pass by, but as they neared OP-2 it appeared the intruders were headed directly towards them.

---

6 Email from CW3 (Ret.) David Hulsey, in coordination with MSG (Ret.) Noe Lopez, and MSG (Ret.) Rick Criste to Author, 2020.

> "We remained still to see if they would continue along the path and would eventually pass. As we waited, it was clear the group was coming directly toward us and that we would have to engage them." **SFC Noe Lopez**

The OP-2 team remained motionless and concealed as the opposing force neared their position. As the intruders closed in, it was obvious they were using night vision equipment and OP-2's position was compromised. Now, vastly outnumbered and certain they would be engaged or captured, the team detonated the Claymore mine facing the opposing force to stop their advance. The resulting explosion and flash caused about half of the group to flee over a ridgeline, while the other half dropped to the ground, moaning and groaning in pain. The SF team opened fire with small arms, hitting one intruder in the head, shattering his Night Vision Goggles. The team then initiated another Claymore to clear their egress route, then withdrew to their rally point about 200 meters away. Once there, the team contacted the TOC, requesting AC-130 and QRF support.

> "Knowing that the OPFOR was going to look for us we requested mortar or AC-130 support. As we laid there, we began to hear movement in the area. Shortly thereafter we were told that an AC-130 was on station and heading to our area for support. As the bird flew overhead the movement of the OPFOR ceased momentarily. As we communicated with HQ the AC-130 crew was

> able to identify our team and also a large group close to our area. As we were running low on ammo we requested support fire from the gunship." **SFC Noe Lopez**

An AC-130A (call sign Runny 85) was diverted by the Joint Command Center to support OP-1 and 2, however, the aircraft was not equipped with SATCOM secure communications radios. When Runny 85 arrived overhead, sensor operators located all three members of the team. Forced to communicate with the team on an open frequency, Runny 85 searched the area in question and located two groups of unidentified personnel who appeared to be moving towards OP-2. The gunship crew searched with both IR and LLLTV with the GLINT while describing the locations of the two groups of intruders. With the gunship's LLLTV, illuminated by the GLINT trained on a group of intruders, Runny 85 requested clearance to fire. Almost immediately, both groups of intruders began to move away from the reconnaissance team. After carefully considering his options, the SOUTHCOM commander did not authorize Runny 85 to fire because of uncertainty of who the intruders actually were.[7] Whether the intruders were monitoring radios, or were intimidated by their positions being illuminated by the GLINT is unknown, but the end result was the same.

When Runny 85 landed on Howard AFB to refuel, an AC-130H crew commanded by Maj Don Kemper (call sign Psalm 23) was alerted. Psalm 23 was on station over the

---

7 Yates, *The US Military Intervention in Panama,* 80.

Special Forces team in less than 15 minutes but could not locate the intruders. Psalm 23 was then redirected to search for 20 intruders reported to be west of the runway, near a munitions storage area. Heavy foliage and bad weather hindered their ability to locate the intruders, but the crew located a truck and a small patrol boat south of the Howard runway that appeared to be in suspicious locations and may have been used to infiltrate the intruders. When Psalm 23 was cleared off target, OP-1 and 2 remained at their rally points until sunrise waiting for extrication by the QRF. The next morning, a thorough search of the area failed to reveal any bodies, but there were blood trails and drag marks found. Later, HUMINT sources reported an ambulance being escorted at high speed across the Bridge of Americas that night.[8]

Incursions into the Arraijan Tank Farm continued on a regular but unpredictable rate. Intruders seemed to probe Marine positions at times when no airborne alert aircraft were heard overhead. Ground alert crews responding from nearby Howard AFB took time to respond and the sound of engines starting could have been their signal to exfiltrate before a gunship could arrive overhead. Intruders were surprised, however, on the night of April 26 when *Grave Digger*, commanded by Maj Kemper, was flying a local training mission.

> "On 26 April, we were recalled from a dry fire to respond to an intrusion at the Arraijan tank

8 Ibid, 78.

> farm. We stopped at Howard and picked up one of the Command Post controllers, Maj Miles Batt (also a personal friend of mine). We did find the intruders, but were not armed at the time. Two Cobra helicopters were in the Howard traffic area, so I called them and asked if they were armed. When they replied positively, I told them we would lead them to the intruders and if shot at they could take out the intruders. They did not want to participate, so we went back overhead as an observer. The intruders were obviously on NVGs, because when our sensor operator lit them up (with the GLINT), they took off running and left the farm." **Maj (Ret.) Don Kemper**

The lessons learned during previous events in and around ATF highlighted the need for a better method of determining friend or foe. Gunship tacticians recommended the tried-and-true method first used by gunship crews in Thailand and well known to the SOF community: reflective tape commonly known as GLINT tape. A one-inch square of GLINT tape pinned on someone's hat or sleeve would be barely noticeable with the unaided eye, but would glow like a flare under the covert illumination of the GLINT. This method enabled easy passive identification of friendly forces without the need for strobes, beacons, flares or lighting their position with overt illumination. In the event the PDF would catch on to the GLINT tape tactic, gunship crews could request authentication via radio by having US forces remove or hide their one-inch square, thus exposing aggressors as those with visible GLINT tape. These tactics could have been considered low level Cat and Mouse, but they worked well, and crews didn't need to request "tape down" authentication.

As planning evolved, the original *Elaborate Maze* plan was broken into five separate plans that fell under the code name *Prayer Book*. The first three plans, named *Klondike Key*, covered nonpermissive evacuations of Panama. The fourth plan covered offensive military operations plans and was named *Blue Spoon* (OPORD 5-88). The final plan dealt with post-invasion tasks to stabilize Panama and was named *Promote Liberty*. AC-130 crews continued to fly armed surveillance missions over Panama. Incursions continued, but no substantive evidence was found to substantiate claims. Noriega took political advantage of the situation by creating and distributing propaganda to discredit US forces by claiming they were aggressive, untrained, and shooting at swaying palm trees.

After the April incidents of incursions, intruders routinely harassed OPs before firing a few rounds indiscriminately and retreating. On the night of October 31(Halloween), however, remote battlefield sensors situated through the tank farm detected approximately forty personnel approaching through the jungle. An AC-130 crew was alerted to investigate and videotaped intruders in ATF. Marines spotted intruders and verbally challenged them. The intruders opened fire and the Marines exchanged fire for about two and a half hours. Instead of retreating and departing like they normally did, the intruders regrouped and reengaged. Multiple individual firefights occurred that night.

After daybreak, substantial evidence of intruders was detected, but still no bodies or spent shell casings.[9] It was apparent the intruders understood American ROES well and knew how to manipulate the situation in an attempt to bring discredit to SOUTHCOM. Noriega exploited a Halloween propaganda scheme in the Panamanian media, but the JTF-Panama Staff had indisputable proof a PDF incursion had occurred and were prepared to defend their actions on the world stage. From that point on, Noriega's propaganda plan to condemn US forces as an untrained and undisciplined force was no longer viable outside of Panama.

The JTF Panama staff was confident Noriega had no intent to sabotage fuel supplies at the ATF and believed his incentive was harassment of US forces. Thus, operations were scaled back to a single platoon and fixed fighting positions were eliminated in favor of patrols and laying of ambush sites. Intruders and Marine tactics were now on relatively common ground, which increased the risk to intruders. The plan worked and, during the following months, large scale incursions ended. Thankfully, 16 SOS Ground Liaison volunteer efforts, coupled with AC-130 airborne alert assets, were successful. By 1989, even small level of effort intrusions were few and far between, but some did occur. In early 1989, AC-130 gunner SSgt Robert "Bobby" Daniel was at ATF performing routine liaison duties when he and the

9 Yates, *The US Military Intervention in Panama*, 117.

platoon he was supporting was "lit up" by intruders. SSgt Daniel said the attack seemed random and was over before the gunship arrived overhead. No casualties were experienced, and no intruders were identified.

In May of 1989, a Panamanian national election was held between Guillermo Endara and a Noriega puppet named Carlos Duque. Noriega first rigged ballot counts to make it appear Duque won. When Duque discovered he had actually lost by a landslide and refused to accept the office of president, Noriega voided the election. Noriega remained in power until he named another crony—Francisco Rodriguez—as president.

In reality, Rodriguez was a powerless figurehead and Noriega secretly remained the de facto ruler of Panama. In the days that followed, Noriega blamed American influence for the failed election. Nevertheless, the US recognized Endara as the duly elected president. Noriega directed increased threats and harassment towards the US personnel and facilities. The PDF made a special point to stop US military personnel and charge them with made-up crimes and fines. Some were incarcerated, threatened and humiliated before being released.

Unfortunately, the Panama Canal Treaty gave Noriega the upper hand while dealing with anyone in the country outside of the US-controlled areas. Harassment and intimidation was not solely directed at US personnel, however. Dobermans and members of the Dignity Battalion roamed the streets of Panama City, tear-gassing, beating, shooting, and hosing down anti-Noriega Panamanians.

Considering the continually escalating tensions, President George H. W. Bush enacted Operation *Nimrod Dancer* to reinforce US presence in Panama and protect US interests. More than fourteen thousand troops were sent to Panama as part of this effort. At the same time, AC-130 operations continued, but crews were moved from base housing units to a Harvest Bare area near the edge of the jungle. The Harvest Bare shelters were essentially collapsible composite shelters equipped with air conditioning units. The proximity to the unsecured jungle was a concern for security; but, over time, no incidents occurred.

A subset of *Nimrod Dancer* was *Task Force Bayonet*, established to train joint US forces in Panama for a potential invasion and to demonstrate a show of force to Noriega and his PDF soldiers. AC-130 crews participated in multiple TF Bayonet exercises, code named *Sand Flea* and *Purple Storm*, under the authorization of OPLAN 6000-86. As the weeks passed, tensions continued to rise between the US and Noriega who waged psychological warfare on each other during *Sand Flea* exercises. Both sides took every opportunity to manipulate the situation to their favor. The PDF continued to harass US citizens and interfere with US military exercises while SOUTHCOM pushed the limits of the Panama Canal Treaty.

Though the PDF had the upper hand on most civil law enforcement issues, the treaty stipulated SOUTHCOM was required to notify the PDF ahead of time for all planned exercises. Surely when an exercise began, the PDF would arrive to interfere and harass. Adopting a strategy to wear down the PDF, SOUTHCOM bombarded the PDF with exercise notifications causing the PDF to constantly alert their troops to both real and fabricated exercises. AC-130 gunships were sent to orbit above PDF facilities to establish a routine and collect intelligence of PDF actions. After weeks of constant alerts, the PDF became desensitized to most SOUTHCOM exercises. These exercises were valuable to demonstrate a show of force and demonstrate SOUTHCOM freedom of movement within Panama according to the treaty. The exercises were also valuable intelligence collection activities.

As *Nimrod Dancer* progressed, Capt Bradley Heithold and his team of AC-130 mission planners created contingency plans of varying intensity for OPORD 5-88. The overall *Blue Spoon* plan called for AC-130 support of Army and Navy special operations elements during a highly complex and lightning-quick invasion taking down multiple targets in one period of darkness. AC-130s were specifically chosen for their accuracy, precision, and the ability to limit collateral damage and danger to Panamanian citizens surrounding the objectives. SOF units trained and rehearsed their portion of the plan individually through October of 1989.

On October 1, 1989, PDF Major Moises Giroldi, who had helped suppress a coup d'état attempt against Noriega in 1988, proposed leading his own coup d'état. Using his wife as an emissary, he requested US support and protection for his family. SOUTHCOM Commander US Army General Maxwell Thurman did not trust Giroldi and described his plan as "ill conceived, ill-motivated, and ill led." [10] A major sticking point was the fact Maj Giroldi refused to harm Noriega and thought he could talk him into resigning his position. US government and military officials refused to commit US forces to support Giroldi and were convinced Noriega would not resign without a fight.

On October 3, Noriega was apprehended by Giroldi and his group, but they refused to turn Noriega over to US forces. Remarkably, Noriega was able to contact his command and control element who alerted loyal units at Rio Hato and Fort Cimarron. Noriega loyalists flew over US roadblocks into Panama City, landed at Paitilla Airport in Panama City and made their way to La Comandancia to fight Giroldi and his supporters. Two AC-130H crews orbited overhead watching the situation unfold, but were not authorized to fire. After several hours of tense drama, Noriega talked Giroldi and his supporters into surrendering. Afterward, Noriega ordered Giroldi and an undetermined number of conspirators to be incarcerated, tortured, interrogated, and murdered. At least seventy-four were incarcerated in the notorious Coiba prison colony eighteen miles off Panama's southwest coast.

> "We had a front row seat to the surrender and saw them file out of the building single file with their hands in the air to the back side of the

---

10 Ronald H. Cole, *Operation Just Cause, The Planning and Execution of Joint Operations in Panama, February 1988-January 1990* (Washington, DC: Joint History Office, Office of the Chairman of the Joint Chiefs of Staff, 1995), 14.

> building and get on their knees. We were told the coup troops surrendered...they were talked into it. No one really knew (as far as I know) what happened to the prisoners until after Just Cause."
> **MSgt (Ret.) Bill Jackson,** AC-130H sensor operator

The coup d'état attempt caught TF-Panama by surprise. While it created a distraction and presented an opportunity to rescue Kurt Muse, an American citizen and political prisoner of Noriega, no plan or forces were in place to do so. Muse was held in Carcel Modelo, an overcrowded and heavily guarded prison located in downtown Panama City, near La Comandancia. As a result, the *Blue Spoon* plan was amended to include OPLAN 90-2, Joint Special Operations Task Force (JSOTF) for the sole purpose of conducting special mission activity. From October to December 1989, JSOTF 90-2 special mission plans were developed.

OPERATION *BLUE SPOON* PLANNING FACTORS

The monumental task of taking down the entire PDF in one night was daunting. The plan called for precise timing and strict arrival times over assigned targets with aircraft arriving from many CONUS locations. The on time launch and arrival of a mass formation of AC-130s, MC-130s, C-130s, C-141s and KC-135s appeared to be overly optimistic, even on paper. But there were no other options.

The overall plan was incredibly complex and multilayered. Twenty-three different locations were to be assaulted simultaneously in the middle of the night. Included in the plan were 253 fixed wing airplanes and 80 helicopters; seven AC-130s were to be among them.[11] The overall plan required coordination of ground and naval forces, who would accomplish independent tasks simultaneously. The JSOTF was subdivided according to the assignment of responsibility.

> <u>Threat Assessment</u>: AC-130 crews based their tactical plans on the training level of the PDF and capabilities of known PDF weapon systems.
>
> <u>The PDF Skill set</u>: The average PDF soldier/sailor was trained and equipped to perform military duties. Members were patriotic to the sovereignty of Panama, but not all were loyal to Noriega. Some elements of the PDF were well trained and equipped to perform guerilla warfare and special operations. These units were fiercely loyal to Noriega. Elements of the PDF were trained by Cuban and Israeli advisors and the US Army at the School of Americas at Ft Benning Georgia.
>
> <u>Identification Friend or Foe</u>: Concerns of fratricide were high and extreme care needed to be exercised by all involved to prevent it. From an AC-130 perspective, basic AC-130 Identification of Friend or Foe (IFF) would be accomplished by

---

11 Tom Clancy, Carl Stiner, and Tony Koltz, *Shadow Warriors: inside the Special Forces* (New York, NY: Berkley Books, 2003), 318, 334–35.

covert lighting provided by the gunships Gated Laser Illuminator for Night Television (GLINT). Its rectangular beam of illumination would only be visible to those possessing night vision equipment, a rare capability in the PDF. Furthermore, all friendly forces were instructed to pin a one-inch square piece of reflective tape on their uniform and affix tape to all four corners of their vehicles. This method enabled gunship crews to quickly determine friend or foe with the GLINT. As a counterpart to the GLINT, JSOTF operators employed several variants of electronic beacons to identify their positions, but these beacons were not available to conventional forces.

Anti-Aircraft Artillery (AAA): The PDF was equipped with an unknown number of 14.5mm ZPU-4 four-barreled guns and some single-bareled ZPU-1 AAA. Both types were confirmed at Rio Hato, Fort Amador (a joint US and PDF base) and Torrijos-Tocumen airport. The guns were manually aimed and optically sighted and capable of reaching planned gunship altitudes but the probability of PDF soldiers hitting an AC-130 flying blacked out at five thousand–six thousand ft. altitude was low. The ZPU-4s posed a significant threat to low flying airlifters and helicopters however, and therefore were the number one AC-130 targeting priority.

Armored Vehicles: The PDF possessed a number of Cadillac Gage V-150 and V-300 armored cars. Some V-150s were capable of carrying mortars and some V-300s were armed with large cannons. Because of the threat they posed to dismounted infantry, crews were briefed to quickly eliminate these threats as soon as they were detected.

Man Portable Air Defense Systems (MANPADS): The PDF was suspected of possessing the SA-7 missile, but there were no confirmed sightings of the capability.

Vehicles, Small Arms, Mortars, RPGs: The PDF was equipped with diverse weapons originating from the US, Taiwan, and East Germany.

Nifty Package: A critical sub-task of the JSOTF and overall *Blue Spoon* plan focused on an effort to capture Noriega and eliminate the PDF command and control facility at *La Comandancia* while inflicting minimal collateral damage to Panamanian infrastructure and citizens. This effort was known as *Nifty Package*. Two AC-130s were specifically assigned *Nifty Package* responsibilities to neutralize *La Comandancia*, while all task forces shared collateral responsibilities to capture Noriega.

Acid Gambit: The most secretive element of *Blue Spoon* was a stand-alone JSOTF mission

> code named *Acid Gambit*. Their mission was to rescue Mr. Kurt Muse from Carcel Modelo. The *Acid Gambit* team was composed of US Army Special Forces, 160th Special Operations Aviation Group (SOAG) AH/MH-6 helicopters, two AC-130 gunships, and USAF Combat Controllers from the 24th CCTS. *Acid Gambit* planning and rehearsal operations occurred in compartmentalized secrecy. Mission parameters for *Acid Gambit* were challenging since Carcel Modelo was located in a densely populated urban area and close to La Comandancia. Further complicating any rescue plan was the fact that Noriega had issued orders for Muse to be executed at the first sign of trouble. This meant the rescue had to be precise, swift, and most importantly, the first action of *Blue Spoon*. Operation *Acid Gambit* rehearsals began at the old Spanish Fort Fuerte de San Lorenzo, Panama, then transitioned to Howard Air Force Base Elementary School, a mere three miles from the actual prison.

Early planning identified a limitation to provide the fire support required in the tight confines of the working area in downtown Panama City congested with closely-spaced military targets, civilian residences, and obstacles. These limiting factors prompted AC-130 FCO Maj Emmett "Otis" Redding to develop and refine a tactic he named *Top Hat* especially for the mission—two gunships in orbit over a single target at the same time separated by one thousand feet of altitude.

> "The key was the nominal selection. The nominal turn radii was slightly larger than the maximum diagonal distance between corners of La Comandancia. This ensured that both aircraft could fire completely around their orbits without endangering the other. Additionally, there was some fudge factor I built in so there was some limited ability to freely engage targets slightly outside the walls." **Maj (Ret.) Emmett "Otis" Redding,** 16 SOS Weapons & Tactics

Top Hat called for two gunships to orbit above *La Comandancia* at H-Hour and fire on pre-planned targets near the Carcel Modelo to create a diversion and suppress, weaken, and confuse PDF soldiers nearest the prison. As the diversion was in progress, 160th SOAG MH-6 Little Bird helicopters and Army SF Soldiers would land on the Modelo rooftop, breach the cupola with explosive charges and make their way downstairs to Muse's cell. Once they had Muse secured, they would bring him to the roof for extraction via MH-6.

The urban landscape of downtown Panama City was a three-dimensional maze of closely-spaced structures of different heights, electrical poles and wires. MH-6 pilots using night vision goggles were concerned landing obstacles on the prison roof may be difficult to detect and could present major problems. To mitigate the issue, an AC-130H crew was tasked to temporarily illuminate and mark the roof with their GLINT for the MH-6 pilots until they landed. After the assaulters were on the roof, the gunship would begin firing on pre-planned nearby targets to create a diversion. After Muse was rescued, both AC-130s would be on call for fire support while TF-Gator systematically surrounded Carcel Modelo and La Comandancia. After initial planning and training was complete, two AC-130H gunships and crews remained on station in Panama at all times while two more were on a short leash at Hurlburt, ready to swap positions as needed. The level of secrecy for *Acid Gambit* was high and nobody outside the small team, even those within the squadron, had any exposure or knowledge of the plan.

> Task Force-Green: TF-Green was composed of US Army Special Forces, 160th SOAG and USAF Combat Controllers from the 24th CCTS. TF-Green was committed to *Nifty Package* and the capture of PDF officials and was supported by one AC-130 gunship.

> Task Force-Black: TF-Black consisted of the US Army's 7th Special Forces Group, supported by one AC-130H gunship, two MH-60, one UH-60 and USAF Combat Controllers. They were assigned the task of disabling a television broadcast tower, capturing key PDF leaders, protecting Panamanian opposition leaders, and establishing a roadblock at Rio Pacora Bridge to

prevent Noriega's Battalion 2000 from reaching Panama City.

Task Force Red: TF-Red was a large strike package composed of the US Army's 1st, 2nd and 3rd Ranger Battalions, the 75th Ranger Regiment Headquarters element, followed by the Division Ready Brigade of the 82nd Airborne Division. Two AC-130H gunships, US Air Force Combat Controllers, Pararescuemen, Tactical Air Control Party, AH/MH-6 helicopters, C-130 and C-141 Special Operations Low Level II (SOLL II) troop carriers, C-130 Adverse Weather Aerial Delivery System (AWADS), MC-130 Combat Talons, and four F-117 fighters supported the Task Force.[12] Both AC-130H and AH-6 crews were tasked to provide CAS for ground forces at Rio Hato military airfield and the Torrijos military complex co-located adjacent to the Tocumen International Airport.

TF-Red was subdivided with TF-Red-Tango, which was responsible for the airfield seizure at Torrijos-Tocumen International Airport, and TF-Red-Romeo, which was responsible for the airfield seizure at Rio Hato. Because of the potential for civilian casualties, rules of engagement at

12 The original plan indicated four F-16s would drop bombs at Rio Hato. Two were to be primary and two were back-up aircraft.

Torrijos-Tocumen were restrictive, requiring the AC-130 crew to minimize collateral damage and prevent blockage of runways and taxiways. Rio Hato was far removed from Panama City, along the coastline about sixty-five miles southwest of Panama City. There were civilians located near the airfield in the village of Rio Hato and Farallon, but most were well clear of any risk of collateral damage from AC-130 fire.

Rio Hato was home base for the PDF 6th Mechanized Infantry, the PDF 7th *Macho De Monte* (Panamanian Special Forces) and the PDF's Military Academies. The *Macho De Monte* was considered the most disciplined PDF unit and the most loyal to Noriega. It was important to prevent a recurrence of PDF rapid response to the October coup d'état attempt when a loyal PDF unit flew from Rio Hato to Panama City to squelch the coup d'état. Task Force Red at Rio Hato was composed of Soldiers from the 2/75 and 3/75 Ranger Battalions and the 75th Ranger Regiment Headquarters Company, who would set Rio Hato as a staging base for follow-on missions once it was seized and secured. Additionally, Rangers were charged with *Nifty Package* commitment to capture Noriega at his Farallon Beach House near Rio Hato if intelligence indicated he was there at H-Hour.

Task Force Blue: (Navy Special Operations Unit) One AC-130 was assigned to support TF-Blue during *Nifty Package* tasking of the search and capture of Noriega to prevent him from escaping from airfields and shipyards in Panama. Since Noriega's whereabouts were difficult to ascertain, given that he slept in a different location every night, the TF-Blue needed the ability to quickly adapt to real-time intelligence reports once military operations began.

Task Force White: US Navy SEAL Team 4 was assigned the task of disabling Noriega's watercraft and aircraft at Punta Paitilla airfield to prevent his escape. One AC-130H gunship was assigned to support TF-White as they seized control of the airport on the edge of Panama City.

Task Force Bayonet: TF-Bayonet was a large multi-aspect force consisting of multiple units under command of SOUTHCOM, 193rd Infantry Brigade. It was responsible for operations to protect U.S. lives, property, and vital Panama Canal facilities.

Task Force Gator: This sub-set of Task Force Bayonet was designed to contain PDF in the La Comandancia compound. It included two Mechanized Infantry Companies (B, D) of the 4th Battalion, 6th Infantry, Ft Polk, LA, elements of the 193rd Infantry Brigade, two Military Police platoons, one platoon of four M551 Sheridan light tanks (3/73 Armor, Ft Bragg, NC), one platoon of four USMC Light Armored Vehicles (Company D, 2nd Light Armored Infantry Battalion, USMC), one combat engineer platoon, and a Psychological Operations Group loudspeaker team. TF-Gator was supported by one AC-130 gunship.

The number of troops and friendly vehicles surrounding the ten-foot tall wall of the La Comandancia compound in such a tight urban area was concerning. The potential for collateral damage and fratricide was high, and a high level of fire discipline was required from both ground and air weapon systems. To prevent inadvertent targeting of Task Force Gator M113 Armored Personnel Carriers (APC) and M551 Tanks were marked on all four corners with reflective tape. Soldiers and Marines pinned a small patch of reflective tape to their uniforms to enable an AC-130 crew to identify them via reflection of covert illumination of the AC-130s GLINT.

<u>Task Force Semper Fi</u>: This USMC task force was responsible for security at the ATF, Bridge of Americas, Canal Locks, La Chorrera area, the PDF 10th Military Zone Headquarters and the area west of the Howard AFB runway from

ATF south the coastline including the town of Vera Cruz.

In early December 1989, AC-130H *Acid Gambit* aircraft and crews on alert in Panama returned to Hurlburt to join five more AC-130H aircraft to participate in Joint Readiness Exercise (JRT) Mod 4, a full-scale dress rehearsal of *Blue Spoon*. The exercise was conducted on and near the Eglin Air Force Base Reservation and Camp Blanding, FL. *Acid Gambit* crews trained on a full-scale replica of the top two floors of Carcel Modelo, specifically built by the JSOTF on Eglin AFB Auxiliary Field 7. All Task Forces participated in the weeklong exercise that ended on December 15. When the exercise concluded, the JSOTF was at peak proficiency.

Meanwhile, AC-130A crews in Panama flew operational "preparation of the environment" missions. Crews were tasked to fly reconnaissance missions and record sensor footage of select areas. Their tapes were delivered to Intelligence officers at Albrook, analyzed, and sent to JTF-Panama planners to enhance situational awareness and facilitate mission planning. Some of these missions required penetration of established no-fly zones over Noriega's home and Panamanian Defense facilities. They also escorted Intelligence officers to a prison in Colon, providing a show of force with their 2KW spotlight while overhead the prison.

By December 15, a defiant Noriega was broadcast on television at a Podium, swinging a machete and declaring the United States had invoked a state of war against Panama. In reality, Noriega could not have picked a worse time to

Full scale replica of the top two floors of the Carcel Modelo Prison built on the Eglin AFB reservation. (Credit: Author)

ratchet up tensions and was apparently unaware that a plan to extricate him from power was planned, rehearsed, and ready to execute.

On December 16, PDF soldiers fired on a vehicle approaching a roadblock near La Comandancia. US Marine 1Lt Robert Paz was killed and a Navy officer and his wife, who witnessed the shooting, were beaten and interrogated before being released the next day. The death of 1Lt Paz and the violence demonstrated by the PDF was the trigger event that prompted President Bush to act immediately to protect American lives and remove Noriega from power.

> "I took this action only after reaching the conclusion that every other avenue was closed and the lives of American Citizens were in danger."
> **President George H. W. Bush,** Dec 17, 1989

At that point, the code name Operation *Blue Spoon* was changed to Operation *Just Cause* for historical reasons.[13] Mission objectives were to:

1. Protect American lives.
2. Capture Manuel Noriega and deliver him to competent authority.
3. Preserve American resources and canal vital elements.
4. Contain the Panama Defense Force (PDF).
5. Support the democratic government of Panama as recognized by the United States.
6. Rebuild the Panama Defense Force (PDF) along the lines specified by that government.

On December 18, 1 SOW Wing Commander, Col George Gray III received a warning order and initiated a recall directing all crews to report to the squadron for a mass briefing. Mission Planner Captains Brian Dougherty, Gary Holland, and Scott Kory briefed the overall *Just Cause* plan to all crews. Afterward, two AC-130H *Acid Gambit* crews went home, packed their bags, and returned to the squadron for immediate deployment to Panama. Col Gray and 16 SOS Squadron Commander Lt Col Billy Napier deployed to Panama with crews commanded by Capt Charles "Greg" McMillan, Capt James Hughes, and a small maintenance and support team. For security reasons, the *Acid Gambit*

13 The name "BLUE SPOON" was not held in high esteem by Generals Kelly and Lindsay who asked Kelly if he wanted to tell his grandchildren he participated in Operation *BLUE SPOON*. Cole, *The Planning and Execution of Joint Operations in Panama*, 32.

deployment occurred under the guise of a normal rotation to relieve the AC-130A crews already on station in Panama. As the two crews were on their way to Panama, five additional AC-130 crews completed final mission planning that afternoon. After being briefed on operational security requirements and show time, they were sent home for crew rest.

Once *Acid Gambit* crews arrived at Howard AFB, AC-130A crews were briefed they would not be returning to CONUS as planned, but would stay at Howard and participate in *Just Cause.* Coincidentally, AC-130A crews were neither briefed on *Acid Gambit* nor added to the JSOTF. Instead, both crews remained under the control of SOUTHCOM's Air Operations Center (AOC) as on call alert assets.

On December 19, crews were ready and morale was high. Activity on the Hurlburt flight line was high, but a casual observer would likely assume the activity was nothing more than a continuance of the recent MOD 4 exercise. Five AC-130s were scheduled to depart at 1700 from Hurlburt Field, led by 16 SOS Operations Officer Lt Col Mike Guidry. These crews were tasked to fly directly from Hurlburt to their targets in Panama, complete their missions, then return to Hurlburt. To protect aircraft transiting the Yucatan Channel near Cuba, an AWACS aircraft and a Combat Air Patrol (CAP) consisting F-15 and F-16 fighters made sure Cuban fighters didn't try to interfere.

Gunship missions were expected to take between 18–20 hours, so crews were augmented with additional pilots and flight engineers who would take turns at the controls (while one flew, the other rested). High Explosive ammunition was delivered directly to the normal aircraft parking area near the Eason Hangar instead of loading in the usual Hot Cargo area. Munitions Line Delivery (Line-D) technicians and gunners loaded each aircraft to a maximum rack/can capacity of 100 rounds of 105mm HE and WP, 256 rounds 40mm HE and HEI, and 3,000 rounds of 20mm HEI. Additional cans of 40mm and 20mm were loaded and strapped down in the aisle way of each aircraft. Since fire-control computers suffered a high failure rate, several crews loaded spare computers onboard.

An emergency wartime maximum weight waiver was approved and some aircraft were loaded to 175,000 lbs., ten tons over peacetime maximum allowable weight. As pre-flight activities were ongoing, Captain Joseph Adams and Captain Hall—US Army Ranger fire support Liaison Officers (LNO)—arrived from Fort Benning. Adams boarded Capt Transue's aircraft and Hall boarded Lt Col Guidry's aircraft. The LNOs would play a crucial role in support of Rangers during the airfield seizures of Rio Hato airfield and Tocumen/Torrijos airport.

All gunships were heavy. Many of the crew members were veterans of *Urgent Fury* six years prior and vividly remembered the risk involved taking off at such a heavy weight. If all went well, they would lift off after a long takeoff roll, rotate, then slowly climb to altitude. If an engine was lost during takeoff roll at any time after the reject point, the gunship would either run off the end of the runway or crash between the end of the runway and the shoreline of the Gulf of Mexico. With no other options available, crews accepted the risk.

When the time came to start engines, there were no major issues as five AC-130s roared to life. After completion of before taxi checks, pilots taxied to the north end of the runway, in line for takeoff. To maintain absolute com-out security procedures, Capt Bob Hockman and Maj Tim Schafer coordinated communications with Eglin Air Traffic Control to ensure silent take off procedures. At precisely 1700, Lt Col Guidry received radio silent, green light takeoff clearance from the Hurlburt Field Tower, pushed *Hell Raiser's* throttles forward and slowly accelerated down Runway 18. The take-off roll was dramatically long, and controls were sluggish as the grossly overweight aircraft lifted off the runway and disappeared into a cloud deck 500 ft. over the Gulf of Mexico. Four more gunships took off in five-minute intervals without experiencing any major problems.

	Operation *Just Cause* AC-130 Crews			
Call Sign*	Aircraft	Aircraft Commander	Task Force	Mission Assignment
AP-01	69-6576	Lt Col Michael Guidry	Red	Torrjios/ Tocumen Airport
AP-02	69-6573	Lt Col Bernard Frakes	White	Paitilla Airport
AP-03	69-6577	Capt Francis Gabreski	Black	Rio Pacora Bridge

* At a point after D-Day, all AC-130s were assigned AMASS call signs however, to alleviate confusion in this chapter, day one call signs are used for the first day and identified by aircraft commander for the remainder of the deployment.

AP-04	69-6569	Capt Mark Transue	Red	Rio Hato Airfield
AP-05	69-6567	Capt Philippe LeBrun	Blue/ Green	Colon/Farallon/ La Escondida
AP-06	69-6570	Capt Greg McMillan	Green/ Black	Acid Gambit/ Airborne Alert
AP-07	69-6575	Capt James Hughes	Green/ Gator	Acid Gambit/ Panama City
AMASS 11	55-0046	Maj Clay McCutchan	N/A	Alert
AMASS 12	56-0509	Capt Michael Wilson	N/A	Alert

"Departing HRT comm out was surreal and something I have only done once in my entire aviation career. We taxied past the squadron building and those not going were all lined up out front watching us go by. Some were waving, some were flipping us off. We watched Air Papa 01 and 02 go, then it was our turn. The green light was observed from the tower, maximum power was applied, and we headed down the runway. After a lengthy take-off roll, we skimmed over the shoreline and headed out to sensor align and join up in the formation. Something the FEs discussed at length were what preparations to take in the event of an engine failure on take-off with various techniques compared. A 175,000lb gunship will not fly on three engines, therefore fuel dumping was priority number one and we were ready should the need arise." **CMSgt (Ret.) Mike Longe,** flight engineer, AP-03

It took an unusual amount of time for each aircraft to climb to altitude over the Gulf of Mexico to enable harmonizing (known as tweaking) of their fire-control systems. Once at altitude, crews jettisoned targets including salt water activated red phosphorus MK-25 markers and SDU-5/E strobe lights taped to Styrofoam blocks for aiming references on the water surface. While tweaking, AP-04 gunners discovered a problem with their 40mm gun mount, so they manually cranked the gun into position and locked it down for fixed-gun firing operations. Four gunships successfully tweaked their fire-control/guns, but AP-02 experienced a fire-control computer failure, dumped fuel to reduce weight, then returned to Hurlburt for repairs.

While the formation headed south, AP-02 remained on the ground with engines running while Fire-control Specialists worked hard trying to repair the problem. The problem was elusive, and after a long delay, specialists determined the fire-control computer could not be repaired. While specialists brought a new fire-control computer to the aircraft, aircraft Commander Lt Col Bernard "Bernie" Frakes requested and received engines running hot ground refueling, a first for an AC-130 crew. Once the computer was onboard, there was no time to perform installation and check-out, so Lt Col Frakes decided to take the aircraft as is and switch out the computers in flight. After almost an hour after they had returned to Hurlburt, AP-02 took off and headed south at maximum continuous power trying to catch up with the rest of the formation.

> "After an impromptu hot refueling we were at 180,000 a first for me. Mentioned it to Frakes as I handed him the TOLD card with speeds on it that were literally off the charts and he didn't bat an eye. It was a long takeoff roll and this was before they cut the trees that were in the flight path south of 98. We didn't miss them by much, 573 was struggling. Since it was cold the engines were making good power we actually had a 3 engine climb capability." **MSgt (Ret.) Alan Garrett,** Flight Engineer, AP-02

The communications-out, lights out refueling was scheduled to take place at six thousand ft. under clear weather conditions, but the weather didn't cooperate. At six thousand ft. MSL, the four gunship formation entered a solid cloud deck resulting in zero-visibility conditions. The situation added another dimension of risk since no procedures or training had been accomplished for IFR formation, and crews had only trained in visual flight conditions during Mod-4.[14] Now under zero-visibility conditions, in the dark, and in a cloud bank, they had to not only find the tankers, but keep from running into each other. At the refueling track, KC-135s were positioned at nine thousand ft., also in zero-visibility conditions. If unable to refuel, five AC-130 CAS missions planned for H-Hour would fail.

Considering the weather situation and potential for mission failure, Lt Col Guidry had no choice other than to break

14 Email from Col (Ret.) Mike Guidry to Author, Jan 2014.

radio silence to contact the lead KC-135. Communicating over secure SATCOM, the gunship formation and tanker formation began a series of maneuvers to break into the clear.

> "The weather conditions for the 1st air refueling were so dire, the command in Panama didn't think we'd make it and wanted to re-plan close air support using only the 4 AC-130s at Howard. Col Gray convinced the Commander that AP-01 lead would get the formation to Panama on time on target and the planned AC-130 CAS plan didn't need to be changed." **Col (Ret.) Mike Guidry,** Aircraft Commander, AP-01

Lt Col Guidry requested the KC-135 formation descend to 7,500 ft. and look for clearing visibility. The tanker crews found weather was socked in at 7,500 and 7,000 ft. Now with only 1,000 ft. between the tanker and gunship formations, Lt Col Guidry asked if the KC-135s could drop down to 6,500 ft., only 500 ft. above the AC-130 formation. At 6,500 ft., the tanker lead reported a broken cloud deck and felt a rendezvous might be possible. Lt Col Guidry directed all gunships to climb to 6,500 ft. AC-130 crews were unable to see the tankers as they ascended, but TACAN indicated the tankers as slightly ahead. Fortunately, as the gunships broke into a narrow clear area between cloud decks, the tankers were spotted one-mile dead ahead. The weather was barely workable as three KC-135s and four AC-130s broke in and out of the clouds. The potential of a catastrophic in flight collision was high, but crews pressed on and began refueling.

> "As the lead Navigator on the lead aircraft (AP-01), linking the formation together in IMC conditions was what I could only describe as 'controlled chaos.' The task was very demanding and risk was high, but we still hit the Aerial Refueling TOA exactly on time and course. This was a perfect example of professional and skilled crews adapting to real time conditions where finite elements of timing, communication and flawless execution were absolutely mandatory." **Col (Ret.) Gary Holland**, Mission Planner/Navigator AP-01

> "It was very hairy, all 7 aircraft in tight formation going in and out of the clouds…one gunship tried to join on another gunship thinking it was the tanker." **Col (Ret.) Mike Guidry**, Aircraft Commander, AP-01

The white-knuckle refueling took longer than anticipated. The mission plan mandated descent to 500 ft. at a specific point north of the Yucatan Channel to avoid detection by Cuban radar. Since the refueling was supposed to be complete before reaching that point, the plan was for the KC-135s to break away from the gunship formation prior to reaching the pre-planned descent point. That plan, however, had to change since AP-04 was still receiving fuel. Instead of disconnecting and breaking away from the gunship, the pilots of tanker #2 remained connected, passing fuel as they descended along with the AC-130 formation. Fortunately, KC-135s and AC-130s had developed "tobogganing" refueling tactics in the past to overcome airspeed issues, but it was rare to toboggan at such a high gross weight. After both aircraft descended to 500 feet and some tense minutes on the refueling boom, AP-04 broke away from the tanker, fully fueled.

Once past the Cuban radar, the formation climbed back to six thousand ft. and continued on, in clear weather. AP-02 caught up with the formation just before the second air refueling track and took his place as number 2, deputy lead. All aircraft took on maximum fuel, and then headed to their staging point just off the north coast Panamanian city of Colon, where AP-02 performed a quick tweak in international waters. About the same time, AP-01's fire-control system failed, prompting the crew to replace it with a spare they had taken with them.

As the five-ship formation closed in on Panama, *Acid Gambit* crews prepared to take off. Unfortunately, Noriega had been tipped off of the impending invasion. Intercepted PDF transmissions indicated a convoy of PDF's Battalion 2000 was starting to depart Fort Cimarron towards Panama City. It was crucial to stop Battalion 2000 since the rescue of Muse might result in disaster if the PDF security force at *La Comandancia* was reinforced. General Stiner requested H-Hour be moved up one hour, but it was impossible to fly the formation any faster to meet the requested time. Concerned for Kurt Muse's safety, he directed the *Acid*

Gambit operation to commence 15 minutes before H-Hour. Thankfully, both AC-130 crews supporting *Acid Gambit* were already in place and able to adjust accordingly.

THE START OF OPERATION *JUST CAUSE* AND *ACID GAMBIT*

Two hours before H-Hour, the SOUTHCOM AOC alerted AC-130A, call sign AMASS-11. Their mission was to support Kilo 3/6 Marines of TF-Semper Fi (Operation *Spartan Gap*) as they moved into position on a ridgeline west of Howard AFB. The ridgeline was tactically significant since the high ground exposed the entire base to potential PDF threats.

> "Operation *Spartan Gap* was to protect the ridgeline west of Howard AFB: from the ATF at the north end, down to the town of Vera Cruz at the southern end. This operation kept the ridgeline overlooking Howard AFB clear of PDF forces looking to set up mortar or sniper positions. On the night of 20 Dec 1989, two hours before H-Hour, we relocated from the ATF Command Post to the ridgeline and maintained our position for the next 10 days." **LCpl Mike Morrison, Forward Observer,** K 3/6, 2nd DIV, USMC

Immediately after AMASS-11 took off, crews commanded by Captains McMillan (AP-06) and Hughes (AP-07) took off. After tweaking their guns offshore, they proceeded to their holding point. While AMASS-11 orbited over the field conducting scans of the base perimeter, an unknown individual on an open radio frequency contacted them for fire support. Maj McCutchan's crew was requested to engage a set of coordinates that plotted to the Mission Control hangar on Howard AFB. Immediately detecting a PDF ruse, McCutchan and his FCO, Maj James Strength played along with the requester in an attempt to locate him for capture by ground forces. The requester must have realized they were onto him and broke off further communications.[15]

> "We attempted several times to contact the unknown party that had requested fire on the 'Mission Control' hanger at Howard AFB…and made several attempts to use FM homing however, the signal was too weak, indicating a significant distance or weak power." **Lt Col (Ret.) James Strength,** fire-control officer, AMASS-11

Meanwhile, the five ship AC-130 formation holding near Colon dissolved as each gunship departed on a specific timeline to meet H-Hour Time On Target (TOT) requirement. While scores of aircraft approached Panama from CONUS, AP-06 and 07 departed from their holding point early to meet their newly adjusted TOT. Arriving overhead their working area blacked out, AP-06 IR sensor operator TSgt Glenn LeMay located and searched the roof of a nearby 16-story high-rise building close to Carcel Modelo to ensure it was clear of snipers. Once the roof was determined clear, McMillan rolled into orbit above Panama City as his sensor

15 Email from Lt Col (Ret.) James Strength, to Author, Jan 2015.

operators located and tracked target A-8, Carcel Modelo. LLLTV sensor operator MSgt Jerry Andersen illuminated the roof of the prison for 30 seconds with the GLINT to give inbound MH-6 pilots a visual reference of the exact location of their landing point. At the same time, AP-07 ensured their GLINT was turned off to ensure there were no inference problems with AP-06's GLINT.

While AP-06 kept a close watch on the area surrounding the prison, four MH-6s, formed in two-ship formations spaced 30 seconds apart, closed in on Carcel Modelo from the west. When the helicopters overflew a TF-Green sniper and machine gun position located within an observation house on Quarry Heights, the fire team immediately killed three Dignity Battalion members manning an RPG position on 4th of July Avenue. As the first flight of MH-6s headed for the densely-packed urban terrain, they were able to quickly locate Carcel Modelo's roof via AP-06s GLINT. The helicopters were met with small arms fire from *La Comandancia* and the 16-story apartment building southwest of the Carcel Modelo. It only took three seconds for the first two helicopters to insert twelve TF-Green Soldiers onto the roof of the prison.

While the first two helicopters flew to their designated holding points, the second two MH-6s inserted eleven more TF-Green operators onto the roof, including a command and control element and security team. One member of the security team (call sign Hotel-55) placed a TEMIG beacon on the roof to mark their position and was in radio contact with AP-06. TF-Green Soldiers quickly enacted their well-rehearsed plan. Immediately after landing, TF-Green breacher SSG Dale Comstock emplaced an explosive charge on the rooftop cupola of the prison. As soon as the last MH-6 landed, McMillan and Hughes's crews shifted focus to their pre-planned targets designed to distract attention away from Carcel Modelo.

> "Knowing you guys were orbiting above and keeping vigilance for me and my fellow soldiers on the ground was like having a guardian angel sitting on my shoulder...with a cannon"
> **MSG (Ret.) Dale Comstock,** TF-Green

Precisely on time, AP-06's Navigator, Capt Bill Lane, radioed "clear," directing the beginning of the attack on La Comandancia complex. Seconds later, two AH-6 gunships armed with M134 miniguns and 2.75 inch HE rockets swept in from the west at low altitude. Their target was the main La Comandancia building, designated B-1 on planning maps and only about 100 meters from Carcel Modelo. On their first pass, lead pilots CPT George Kunkle and CW3 Fred Horsley were firing a long burst of 7.62mm when their helicopter was hit by PDF fire, resulting in loss of flight controls. Seconds later, they crash landed inside the La Comandancia compound, and remarkably, both pilots survived the crash without major injuries.

Meanwhile, the other AH-6 crew fired a long burst of 7.62mm and 2.75 inch High Explosive rockets into the front door of La Comandancia. Simultaneously, AP-07 began to fire on targets B-5 and B-6 (transportation barracks and personnel management office), while AP-06 began firing on B-11 and B-12 (PDF 1st Company of Public Order; the Dobermans).

Approximately one minute into the mission, TF-Green Soldiers, led by Major Gary Harrell blew the door of the rooftop copula and made their way down a staircase to Muse's cell. After SFC James Sudderth killed the guard assigned the responsibility of executing Muse and captured another, SSG Kelly Venden and SSG Pat Savidge breached Muse's cell door and began to fit him with a flak jacket and helmet.

> "The initial explosion rocked me awake. I quickly dressed and laid flat on the floor below the barred window, tucked into the 'bathroom's' opening. I would sneak peeks around the corner through the darkness, watching nervously for the silhouette of the executioner coming to kill me. The explosions continued to rock the prison, briefly illuminating my cell with its bright white flash. I saw only more debris on the floor and still no one at my door. After a few minutes of continued bombardment, one particular impact lit up my little corner of hell, only this time allowing me a brief look at two heavily armed lethal looking figures in the hallway. They were American Soldiers who had come to take me home." **Mr. Kurt Muse**

On the rooftop and third floor, the TF-Green security element confronted several armed guards and quickly cut them down with small arms fire.

About four minutes into the attack, neither AC-130 crew was advised an AH-6 was down in the compound, so they continued firing on their pre-planned targets unaware CPT Kunkle and CW3 Horsley were inside the very compound they were attacking. The downed pilots made repeated attempts with their PRC-90 survival radio but were unable to reach anyone. Kunkle and Horsley were in a bad position. Though they knew which buildings were being targeted, it was difficult to recognize the buildings from a ground perspective. While AP-06 and AP-07 continued firing on their assigned targets, a PDF ZPU-4 AAA gun located on a baseball field southeast of La Comandancia opened fire. AP-06's Illuminator Operator, MSgt Larry Bower, determined the AAA was not accurate, so Capt McMillan remained in firing orbit.

About one minute before the planned extract of TF-Green and Mr. Muse from the Carcel Modelo rooftop, PDF fire from La Comandancia and the 16-story apartment building increased dramatically. There was heavy small arms and RPG fire coming from the top floor of La Comandancia which had potential to wreak havoc on MH-6s during extraction. Hoping to silence incoming fire, Hotel-55 attempted to contact AP-07 for fire support, but the noise of gunfire and explosions masked his request and AP-07 was not able to decipher who was attempting to contact them. Fortunately, AP-06 was able to determine it was Hotel-55 calling for a fire mission on La Comandancia.

With only about one minute remaining before extraction, AP-06 accepted Hotel-55's request and quickly fired about 35 rounds of 40mm Misch Metal, and 3 105mm HE delay fuzed rounds directly into La Comandancia. The attack was violent and overwhelming as showers of 40mm Misch Metal sparks spewed from the windows of the top floor and 105mm High Explosive detonations blew out big chunks of concrete. A particularly unlucky PDF soldier was hit directly with a 105mm HE round less than two seconds after firing an RPG from an upper floor.

> "I asked him (AP-06) to start at one end (of La Comandancia) and work to the other. Night became day when they opened up. That was the best fireworks display ever! Next thing I remember is the call from the AC saying they were complete, and after that it was time to leave the roof. I remember thinking afterwards, that was the first time since I was in the unit I had AC-130 fire impact that close to our position. I believe it was at or under 100 meters; sweet." (Hotel 55, Name withheld)

Both AC-130 crews ceased firing on their pre-planned time while TF-Green Soldiers brought Muse to the roof for extraction. It had been a long five minutes of continuous fire from both AC-130 crews and the rescue had taken only six minutes. There was a short lull in activity, but the mission was far from complete. Two MH-6s landed on the Carcel Modelo roof, then TF-Green Soldiers and Muse boarded the first helicopter, commanded by CW3 James Dietderich.

All seemed to be going according to plan, but as the pilot lifted off, he saw utility wires near the edge of the rooftop, directly in his flight path. To avoid hitting the wires, Dietderich pulled up to clear the wires but lost main rotor RPM and lift; a condition known as rotor droop. Unable to climb, the MH-6 descended until it hard-landed on the street between two apartment buildings about 50 yards north of Carcel Modelo. The rescue element jumped off their pods to establish a security perimeter while CW3 Dietderich manipulated engine controls to recover power to lift off. H-Hour was approaching fast and everyone knew the situation would become even more violent the closer Task Force Gator got to their blocking positions.

> "MH with Muse crashed due to poor intel. We asked if there were wires above the street on the departure route and were assured by S-2 that there were none. The pilot did a super job avoiding a crash but drooped the rotor and landed in the street." **Col (Ret.) Richard Bowman**, MH-6 Pilot, Chalk 3 during *Acid Gambit*

Now three minutes before H-Hour, the MH-6 sat on the street with rotors turning, north of Carcel Modelo while Task Force Gator rapidly departed Quarry Heights to move into eleven predesignated blocking positions. In less than a minute, they began crossing 4th of July Avenue at high speed and began taking small arms fire from the 16 story hi-rise apartment complex west of La Comandancia. TF Gator elements immediately returned fire with their .50 caliber and 7.62mm machine guns. TF-Gator M113s plowed through obstacles, vehicles, PDF small arms and RPG fire, while Track Commanders and gunners fired to suppress and defeat PDF resistance.[16]

PDF and Dignity Battalion fire from the 16-story apartment building increased in intensity as TF-Gator formations drove down the narrow streets surrounding La Comandancia. The first to encounter a roadblock was TF-Gator's 2nd Platoon, D Company 4/6 Infantry, commanded by 2LT Douglas Rubin. Several vehicles were parked across Balboa Avenue, about 200 meters west of 4th of July Avenue. As the M113 charged towards the position at 30 miles per hour, PDF small arms fire was ineffective against the 13-ton APC. The first M113 hit the vehicles at full force, crushing one PDF soldier while TF-Gator gunners shot three more. TF-Gator's tactic relied on speed and overwhelming firepower, both of which they had as they rolled across 4th of July Avenue.

---

16 The only element of TF-Gator read-in to the Acid Gambit plan was Team King, the back-up ground rescue element. TF-Gator elements assigned blocking positions were not aware of Acid Gambit operations and had no idea a friendly helicopter would be encountered.

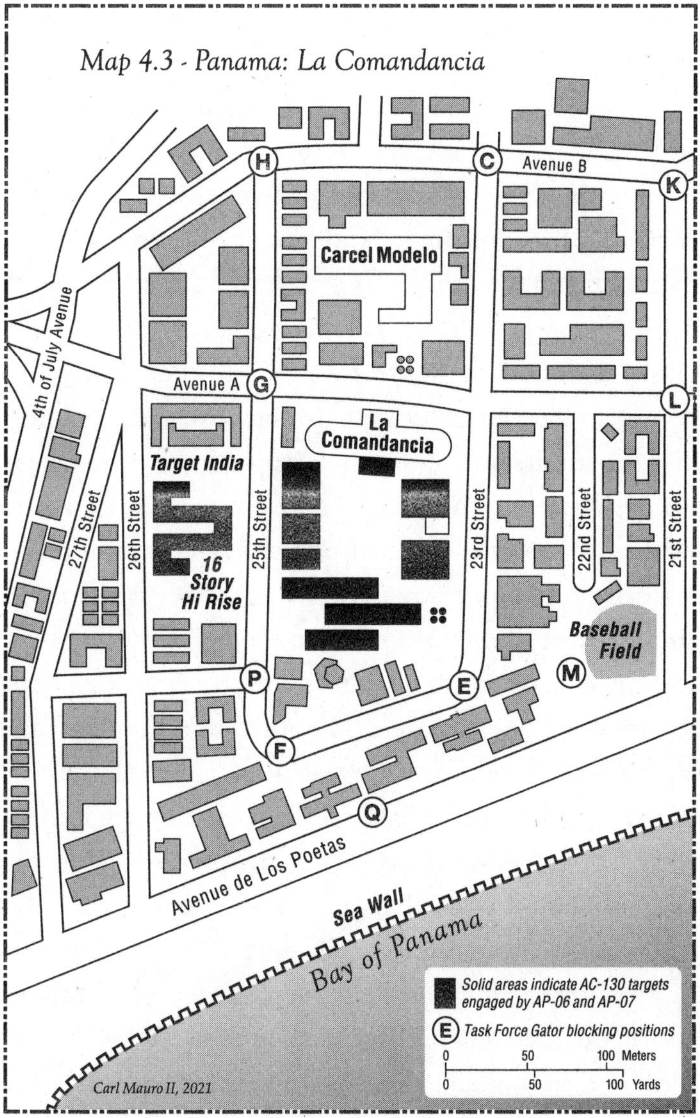

Basic sketch of the La Comandancia compound. The shaded boxes indicate AC-130 targets engaged by AP-06 and AP-07. The lettered circles are locations of TF-Gator blocking positions. The compound was surrounded by densely packed civilian housing areas. (Credit: Carl Mauro II)

Meanwhile, about 300 meters north of *La Comandancia*, CW3 Dietderich was ready to attempt another take off. All five operators and Muse re-boarded the helicopter but SSG's Venden and Savidge forgot to secure themselves to the aircraft. When Dietderich attempted to take off, the heavily-loaded helicopter could achieve only a few feet of altitude. Unable to climb from a hover, he needed forward airspeed to gain altitude. Having no other choice, the pilot literally drove down the street in ground effect in a desperate attempt to gain lift.[17] Obstacles and a short street negated any gain in altitude. Now at a major intersection near *La Comandancia*, he turned left and away from the entrance to the prison. With sufficient power available and facing an open street, he drove down the street to the north, gradually gaining airspeed and altitude. As the helicopter cleared the rooftops, it took machine gun fire on the left side, the main rotor struck a power pole, and both Venden and Savidge fell about 15-20 ft. onto the street below.[18] The MH-6 crashed onto the middle of 24th Street almost immediately afterward. Of the eight aboard the helicopter, everyone except Muse and co-pilot CW2 Don Fox were either wounded by hostile fire or injured during the crash.

With the main rotor still turning, the crew attempted to turn off their engine but were unable. When SFC Tom Caldwell dismounted to lead Muse to safety, he was struck on

---

17 Ground effect is a condition of improved performance encountered when operating near (within 1/2 rotor diameter) of the ground.

18 A persistent theory exists that it was actually a TF-Gator who shot down the aircraft, but this theory cannot be proven.

the head by the rotor blades and was knocked unconscious for a short while. SFC Sudderth's foot was trapped under the helicopter and in a great deal of pain. SFC Sam Joseph and CW3 Dietderich fanned out to establish a security perimeter near an apartment building while dragging Venden, who was knocked out, away from the crash site. When Caldwell regained consciousness, he led Muse away from the helicopter, waiting for ground extraction. Meanwhile, a special formation of three M113s led by 1LT David King known as *Team King* was on its way but was hindered by roadblocks, obstacles, and PDF/Dignity Battalion fire.

About three hundred meters south of *Team King*, 2LT Rubin's twenty-six man platoon continued a high speed route to their pre-planned blocking positions, either defeating or squeezing by road blocks including dump trucks and cement blocks. As they neared a known PDF 75mm recoilless rifle position on Avenue De Los Poetas, the formation stopped briefly to dismount Private Louis Miller and Sergeant Matthew Pickett to eliminate the position. When Miller and Pickett found the recoilless rifle abandoned, they remained in place to destroy the site while the formation continued towards their objective positions. After arriving at position "E" (Echo) on 23rd Street just outside of the southeast corner of the La Comandancia compound, 2LT Rubin's soldiers dismounted in the darkness to place forty pound breaching charges on the exterior of the concrete barrier wall.

During this time, Track Commanders fired continuous .50 caliber bursts of suppressive fire at muzzle flashes seen on multiple floors of the 16-story high-rise buildings a short distance to the northwest. As they fired, a number of tracer rounds missed the building, continuing northwest towards the AH-6s flight pattern. During this time, AP-07 was searching for CW3 Dietderich's downed MH-6 helicopter when Aircraft Commander Capt Jim Hughes saw a burst of large caliber tracers pass below the gunship from the 9 O'clock position. Suspecting it was a PDF AAA fire, Capt Hughes used his Head Up Display (HUD) to talk the LLLTV sensor, SMSgt John "Jack" Hollyfield, onto the exact point the tracers originated. Heavy smoke emitting from the Chorrillo District hindered the ability of the LLLTV sensor to resolve the gun site. Since the IR sensor was not affected by smoke, AP-07 FCO Maj Emmett Redding, directed IR sensor operator TSgt Ron Marshall to search for the gun site. Within a short time, TSgt Marshall located three vehicles near the walls of the La Comandancia complex, but his sensor lacked the clarity needed to determine exactly what type of vehicle they were. In an effort to identify the vehicles, SMSgt Hollyfield slaved his sensor to the IR sensor and scanned for GLINT markings, but the vehicles appeared unmarked. Unfortunately, the gunship crew forgot to power on the GLINT after the *Acid Gambit* mission and without an active GLINT, markings that would normally light up like a beacon were faint and nearly unrecognizable. Tragically, this single-point failure of IFF quickly evolved into the worst possible situation for 2LT Rubin's soldiers at position Echo.

What followed was a classic error chain dilemma. Reacting to what appeared to be hostile fire from a PDF position and lack of detectable GLINT markings, the crew of AP-07 were convinced the vehicles were PDF.[19] Furthermore, in the smoke and urban terrain, the crew misidentified the tracked M113s as 6-wheeled V-300s. Because of the lack of GLINT signature, AP-07's Nav, FCO, LLLTV sensor operator and IR sensor operator determined they had valid targets firing at friendly helicopters. Hoping to eliminate a perceived AAA threat to the helicopter traffic, 1Lt Steve Sartore, AP-07s navigator, contacted TF-Green FSO Major Henry "Ike" Eisenbarth (call sign Zulu-58) explained the situation, and requested clearance to fire. From the command and control UH-60 flying over Ancon Hill, Eisenbarth noticed large-caliber tracers passing near his helicopter. Convinced there was PDF AAA within La Comandancia compound, he cleared AP-07 to fire under the condition they use 40mm HEI only because position Echo was close to a residential area. For the next four minutes, AP-07 attacked all three vehicles with 40mm HEI-P Misch Metal.

> "As I positioned my vehicle on the side of a building, two sparkly bursts exploded in front of my vehicle. I adjusted my position a little further back alongside the building and off-loaded the troops from the rear. Next, I prepared for the explosion from the 40 lb. charge that was going

19 In the haste to squelch what was believed to be a PDF AAA position, the crew mis-identified the three M113 tracked APCs as Six wheeled V-300 armored cars. After-action review of the video clearly resolved M-113s, not V-300s. This was a significant IFF error which was avoidable had the crew not been intently focused solely on GLINT tape for IFF.

> to be used blow the wall. As I lowered my seat into the vehicle, I noticed my shadow in front of me, which was strange because we had no lights on. I turned to find the back of my APC on fire and my TC (track commander) evacuating the turret. Following his lead, I exited the vehicle. Initially I was going to jump off of the front of the track but quickly remembered the explosions in front of me, so I ran past the flames coming out of the rear hatch where the troops had been. I jumped off and onto the ground. Still not knowing exactly what was going on, I searched for soldiers in order to re-group because something most certainly had gone wrong." **SSG (Ret.) Darin Marcinkevicius**

AP-07 fired about 20 rounds believing they were engaging a PDF position, but instead of PDF, they were US Army Soldiers assigned to TF-Gator. When they ceased firing, sixteen TF-Gator soldiers were wounded, one M113 was burning, another was damaged, and a third was undamaged. Confident the perceived PDF AAA threat was suppressed, AP-07 ceased fire on position Echo to await further tasking.

On position Echo, the situation was dire to say the least. Soldiers lay wounded, ammunition was cooking off inside the burning APC, and the once dark area was illuminated by fire. 2LT Rubin advised his Fire Support Officer, call sign Charlie-58 his platoon had been attacked by PDF mortars. Concerned with the potential for another attack,

Charlie-58 contacted the TF Gator commander who put his Battalion Fire Support Officer, CPT John Guidry in contact with AP-07. Guidry then sent Hughes's crew to search for a mortar position suspected to be on a nearby baseball field. While AP-07 was searching the ball field, TF-Gator Soldiers loaded the most seriously wounded into the undamaged M113 to be driven to a medical aid station.

Believing position E had been attacked by PDF mortars, 1LT Robert Nabb (call sign Charlie-58) came to position Echo to assist the remainder of 2LT Rubin's platoon. Once the seriously wounded were evacuated, the remaining Soldiers withdrew about 100 meters to the south near the sea wall. Meanwhile, unknown to 2Lt Rubin, TF Gator Commander Lieutenant Colonel James Reed directed one Sheridan and an LAV to reinforce position Echo.

At 7,500 ft. above the commotion they had inadvertently created, the crew of AP-07 was unaware they were chasing their own fire, not mortars as reported. Clearly, AP-07 searched for the non-existent mortar position on the baseball field without success, but did find an abandoned ZPU-4 gun site which they engaged with 22 rounds of 40mm. After engaging the AAA gun, Zulu-58 sent AP-07 to target India, the same 16-story high-rise building TF-Gator Track Commanders were firing on that was mistaken for AAA fire.

More than 25 minutes after H-Hour, Kurt Muse and his rescuers awaited extraction by *Team King*. Unfortunately, the convoy was hindered by multiple roadblocks and PDF positions. When turning onto Avenue B near La Comandancia, *Team King* encountered heavy small arms fire coming from the 16-story high-rise building. One of *Team King*'s USAF Combat Controllers, MSgt Steve Jones, requested AP-07 fire support. Cleared by the TF-Gator FSO, AP-07 opened fire on the apartment building and La Comandancia headquarters causing a temporary lull in hostile fire.[20]

Unfortunately, *Team King* moved only a short distance before encountering two large dump trucks blocking Avenue B. The vehicles were too heavy to move with the M113s and the formation began to take heavy fire from a nearby building. Reversing course, they plowed through an ineffective roadblock on Avenue A, turned north on 26th Street, then right on Avenue B and to position Romeo, near the crash site.

> "We heard over the radio that an MH-6 had crashed. So when I got to the crash site and saw Muse standing there, I realized that the entire reason for our mission was standing directly in front of me." **MSgt (Ret.) David Schnoor,** Combat Controller, 24th Combat Control Squadron

About 40 minutes after H-Hour, with Muse and his rescuers onboard, *Team King* backtracked their entrance route, crossed 4th of July Avenue and arrived at the landing zone near Balboa High School. Muse and the wounded were transferred to medical helicopters and *Team King* received a TF-Green follow-on mission at the US Embassy. AP-06 was tasked to escort *Team King*, through streets of Panama

---

20 Email from SMSgt (Ret.) Steve Jones, to Author, Jan 2014.

City, scanning for threats and roadblocks and AP-07 was tasked to remain overhead La Comandancia for TF-Gator fire support.

While AP-07 searched the La Comandancia compound for PDF activity, CPT Kunkle and CW3 Horsley used the break in activity to maneuver towards one of the TF-Gator positions, encountering PDF fire and accepting surrender of one less than enthusiastic PDF soldier along the way.[21]

Near position Echo, the lull in activity prompted PVT Louis Miller and SGT Matthew Pickett to retrieve the damaged M113 to enable use of its 50-caliber gun and its high-powered communications radios. While Miller and Pickett approached the M113, the remainder of Rubin's platoon and FSO Nabb followed some distance behind to set off the cratering charges on the perimeter wall. Meanwhile, AP-07 detected activity at position Echo, which they believed were PDF reinforcements. Again, since the GLINT was off, SMSgt Hollyfield did not detect markings and misidentified the vehicles as PDF V-300s. 1Lt Sartore reported the activity to the fires network, and AP-07 was cleared to fire.

SGT Pickett was standing near the rear of the APC as PVT Miller started the M113. When a volley of 40mm rounds began exploding in front of his M113, Pickett hit the ground, wounded, along with four more from his platoon. Undeterred by flash and explosions, PVT Miller put the APC in gear and backed out of position so fast across Avenue De Los Poetas that he nearly collided with the sea wall.

21 They eventually made contact with a TF-Gator position, were rescued and their prisoner secured.

> "Almost as soon as the track began to move the same sparkly explosions went off in front of the vehicle. Pvt Miller, the driver, backed the vehicle up and almost drove through the seawall barrier and into the water evading the explosions."
> **SSG (Ret.) Darin Marcinkevicius**

Once in the open, sensor imagery on both IR and LLLTV revealed the vehicle was obviously an M113 and not a V-300. Tragically, the lack of detectable GLINT markings had apparently "stove-piped" AP-07's situation awareness to the point they believed the vehicle was PDF, so they continued to fire.

While Private Miller frantically sped to the west on Avenue De Los Poetas, AP-07's 40mm explosions trailed the vehicle aft, then walked forward, causing Miller to slam on his brakes and reverse direction. AP-07's pursuit ended when SMSgt Hollyfield detected three M113s led by Lieutenant Colonel Reed approaching PVT Miller's track from the opposite direction. All three inbound M113s were spotted as they passed directly under a street light which brightly illuminated GLINT tape on all four corners, validating them as friendly vehicles. At about the same time, TF-Gator Battalion Fire Support Officer, CPT Guidry, suspected something was wrong and directed AP-07 to cease fire.[22]

At that point, AP-07 believed they had fired on a PDF armored vehicle and troops, and 2LT Rubin's men thought

---

22 The three M113s carried Medics and staff sent to tend to 2LT Rubin and his wounded men.

they were being attacked by PDF mortars, but both were wrong. While 1LT Nabb, 2LT Rubin and the rest of his platoon were tended to by medics at nearby position Quebec, AP-07 was re-tasked to Ft Amador.

At Ft Amador, AP-07 worked with the Task Force Bayonet FSO to find a lone V-300 with its turret gun pointed directly at the entrance of Ft Amador. The FSO cleared them to fire; but, since the vehicle was close to occupied base housing units, Maj Redding directed firing of the 40mm gun to limit collateral damage potential. Just before they opened fire, AP-07's IO SSgt Tom Parker, spotted AMASS-11 directly beneath him, heading directly through AP-07's firing orbit. SSgt Parker called a cease fire and AMASS-11 passed right through SMSgt Hollyfield's narrow TV monitor.

Target B-1, La Comandancia Headquarters building (foreground) after being heavily damaged by AC-130 fire. (Credit: US Air Force photo)

> "It was during the CAS work over Ft Amador that AP-07 darn near shot down AMASS-11. They were flying well below us and we were just about to go hot with the 40mm when the AC-130A passed through the LLLTV's dot quad!" **Maj (Ret.) Emmett "Otis" Redding,** Fire-control Officer, AP-07

When AP-07 engaged the V-300 with eight rounds of Misch Metal, PDF soldiers dismounted and fled the area. Capt Hughes and Maj Redding elected to cease fire since the threat was negated and additional firing would only increase risk to US personnel nearby. When they advised the Task Force Bayonet FSO their mission was complete, he disagreed and insisted AP-07 continue to fire with 105mm HE to kill the target. At that point, AP-07 refused to fire and a short argument ensued. Determining there was no tactically sound reason to accept additional risk to innocent bystanders, they declined the fire mission. Now low on fuel, AP-07 refueled via KC-135 and reported to their designated hold point. With no further mission tasking, they landed at Howard Air Force Base.

The battle near La Comandancia continued throughout the night. The Chorrillo District surrounding La Comandancia may have been spared from direct AC-130 fire, but the exchange of gunfire between PDF soldiers, Dignity Battalion militants, and US Military units wreaked havoc on the civilian area. Tracer bullets from both sides impacted the closely-spaced wooden buildings, some of them dating back to the origin of Canal construction. Witnesses reported PDF

Dignity Battalion henchmen were intentionally setting fires also. Within a short period of time, a large fire was burning that ultimately consumed the entire area. Smoke rose thousands of feet in the air and obscured a large portion of the district.

AC-130A ALERT OPERATIONS

After conducting an initial scan of Howard AFB's perimeter, AMASS-11 landed and resumed a ground alert posture. Shortly after H-Hour, the developing ground situation resulted in Maj McCutchan's crew being launched again to search for, and engage a mortar position on the golf course at Fort Amador. The target was located underneath some transmission lines and near the tomb of General Omar Torrijos, but AMASS-11 successfully engaged the target without causing collateral damage. After several hours of airborne alert, AMASS-11 was called back to Ft Amador to investigate a report of three armored cars. Within a few minutes of arrival, both sensor operators acquired the vehicles and found as many as 100 personnel nearby. A Fire Support Officer assigned to Task Force Bayonet directed AMASS-11 to fire on the vehicles, but both sensor operators and the FCO agreed that something didn't look right.[23] GLINT tape reflections could be seen on the personnel throughout the entire orbit, indicating friendly forces. AMASS-11 FCO, Lt Col James Strength, discussed the situation with McCutchan,

---

23 This was the same FSO who later directed AP-07 to fire on a V-300 in close proximity to occupied base housing.

and they agreed the personnel were not PDF. Though the FSO insisted the target was valid, Maj McCuthan knew they were tracking friendlies, so he refused to fire. What followed was a verbal battle between the TF Bayonet FSO and AMASS-11 with the FSO demanding AMASS-11 engage the personnel and gun site. McCutchan refused the FSO's order to fire three times before rolling out of orbit and returning to Howard Air Force Base for fuel.[24]

Capt Wilson's crew (AMASS-12) remained on ground alert during the early hours of the operation. The crew was ready for a rapid launch, suited up in survival vest, life preserver units (LPUs) and parachute harnesses, and the copilot was pre-positioned in his seat, listening to radio transmissions. A decision was made to send Capt Wilson's crew who quickly spun up the aircraft and started to taxi only to find themselves holding on to the taxiway while a flight of twelve blacked-out C-130s were recovering in close interval. Once all twelve aircraft had turned off the active and taxied past, Wilson's AC-130A was cleared to take off.

Immediately after takeoff, they were tasked to Punta Paitilla Airport to replace AP-02 in support of SEAL Team 4. When they arrived, they were requested to reconnoiter several positions around the airfield, including the hangar where Noriega's personal jet was stored.

During the afternoon of December 20, USSOUTHCOM received a report that a group of hostile Panamanians were holding about twenty-nine hostages inside the Marriott

---

24 They later learned friendly forces had indeed overrun the site and their decision to not fire had saved the lives of many US Army soldiers.

hotel in downtown Panama City. Resolution of hostage situations was typically handled by JSOTF Special Mission Units, but they were heavily engaged in ongoing missions. In their place, a specially trained element of the 82nd Airborne Division was chosen for the mission. Henceforth, the 2nd Battalion, 504th Infantry hastily planned a mission supported by an AC-130A Gunship to take place before midnight. AMASS-11, commanded by Maj Clay McCutchan was chosen to perform route reconnaissance ahead of the rescue force and provide fire support if required during the movement to the Marriott.

AMASS-11 took off shortly after 2130 and arrived on station overhead the rescue force's initial point and at 2215, as elements moved out on foot towards the Marriott. Carefully negotiating down the narrow streets and urban terrain, the first element was engaged by PDF small arms fire from hidden positions several times, but no casualties occurred and they pressed on towards their objective. Now close to the hotel, a truck loaded with hostile Panamanians charged straight at them, firing AK-47s from the side of the vehicle. After a few intense moments and exchange of gunfire, three men of the rescue force were wounded while the attacker's truck was destroyed and they suffered four dead and two wounded. About the time the rescue force resumed their advance, AMASS-11 detected two snipers on the roof of a building about a block away from the Marriot. The ground force was unable to engage the snipers, so AMASS-11 was tasked to fire 40mm at the snipers to eliminate the threat they posed. When sensor operators MSgt Walter Watley and TSgt James Dombrosky measured the distance from friendly forces to the snipers, they determined rescuers were eight feet inside Danger Close firing parameters. Navigator Capt Bruce Fernald radioed the ground force commander to move back at least eight feet while sensor operators tracked the center of the roof. Maj McCutchan carefully flew tight sensor guidance and fired a burst of three rounds of 40mm HEI. Seconds later, two rounds impacted the street surrounding the building and the third round detonated on the center of the roof, causing the snipers to scatter. With no further sign of hostile forces, AMASS-11 remained overhead, on call until low on fuel while the rescue team entered the Marriott, rescued the hostages and began a room to room search.

THE AIRFIELD SEIZURE OF RIO HATO

The PDF 6th and 7th companies located southwest of the Rio Hato runway. This was the primary working area for AP-04 on the night of December 20. (Credit: DoD photo)

Planners considered Rio Hato the hottest Landing Zone (LZ) of all PDF enclaves. More than five hundred PDF troops were estimated to be stationed there. Of these were the 6th Mechanized Infantry Company and the 7th Infantry Company *Macho De Monte* (PDF Special Forces). Soldiers of the 6th were considered loyal to the defense of Panama, but were not necessarily loyal to Noriega. On the other hand, *Macho De Monte* soldiers were fiercely loyal to Noriega as demonstrated during the October 1980 coup attempt. JSOTF leadership recognized the need to neutralize the *Macho De Monte* before they were able to respond to the H-Hour attack on La Comandancia and Noriega's headquarters on Ft. Amador.

Commander of the 75th Ranger Regiment, Col William "Buck" Kernan was responsible for all TF-Red activities, including the seizure of Torrijos-Tocumen airport in Panama City. Since Torrijos-Tocumen was surrounded by urban sprawl, it was not favored as a base of operations for follow-on activities. Instead, he chose the isolated base at Rio Hato as the best location to establish a command center and support base for follow-on missions. From the beginning, Kernan planned to conduct a mass airfield seizure operation of Rio Hato whereas six-hundred fifty Rangers would conduct a swift, overwhelming airborne operation. Rangers would be augmented by USAF TACP, CCT and Pararescuemen, who would parachute onto the airfield with Rangers to support the operation, establish an Air Traffic Control network, and establish Kernan's headquarters element. The Ranger fire support plan called for one AC-130 gunship, four AH-6 *Little Birds*, two F-117 fighters and two AH-64 *Apache* helicopters.

AC-130 roles and responsibilities for this mission were well defined during the MOD-4 exercise, right down to detailed timeline, radio frequencies, call signs, and altitudes. Included in the mission package were aerial photographs dated October 1989. Three AAA guns and clear images of all facilities and structures near the airfield were identified and marked with alpha-numeric code. Capt Mark Transue's AC-130 crew were assigned as the primary fire support mission for 2/75 while AH-6 *Little Birds* provided primary fire support for 3/75. Because of the number of individual mission objectives, anticipated speed of action and tight confines of the PDF compounds, Ranger Fire Support Officers (FSO) devised a simple, decentralized, and robust fire support plan including addition of a Ranger FSO with extensive knowledge of the overall mission plan onto the AC-130 gunship.

The mission plan began at H-Hour with two F-117 fighters approaching from the south, each dropping a two thousand lb. laser guided bomb near the PDF 6th and 7th Infantry barracks. Bomb fuzes were set to penetrate the surface to contain fragmentation and act as large "stun grenades." The plan called for the F-117s to depart for home station immediately after the bombs detonated, with no follow-on activities in Panama. Simultaneous with the bomb drops, two AH-64 Apache helicopters hovering over water about one thousand meters south of the PDF compounds were to engage two ZPU-4 sites located on a cliff overlooking the ocean. After firing on the ZPU-4s, the Apaches were to withdraw from the area. The bomb explosions were the visual cue for AP-04 to engage a ZPU-4 AAA gun position located in the open alongside the runway. At H+3 minutes, the airdrop formation consisting of thirteen C-130s would approach from the south and begin dropping Rangers onto the airfield. At that point, the only fire support aircraft remaining would be one AC-130 and four AH-6 helicopters. The entire 2/75 Ranger Battalion and two companies of the 3/75 Ranger Battalion would parachute onto the airfield, assemble at predetermined rally points then move toward their objectives to overwhelm the PDF and secure the airfield. Drop altitude was set at ~500 ft., which would reduce jumpers "hang time" and exposure to hostile fire but would leave no margin for error in the event of a parachute malfunction.

Once on the airfield, a Ranger clearing team would remove obstacles from the runway and USAF Combat Controllers would assess the runway's status to facilitate air-land operations. The 75th Ranger Regiment Headquarters element would establish a Tactical Operations Center (TOC-1) and coordinate radio communications with fire support aircraft before Rangers began to advance towards their assigned objectives. The overall plan included B/2/75 moving south and west into the PDF compounds (objectives Cat and Lion), and A/2/75 securing the PDF Academies (objective Silver) west of the runway. C/2/75 would be held in reserve with an ancillary mission to either augment the other two companies if they suffered heavy losses or to seize Noriega's beach house at Farallon if required.

A/3/75 and B/3/75 would establish blocking positions on the perimeter of the east and west sections of Pan-American Highway 1 (which bisected the Rio Hato runway), establish a 180-degree security perimeter north of the highway and end of runway and seize a PDF armory northwest of the airfield (objective Iron).

MISSION EXECUTION

Capt Transue's crew was assigned aircraft 69-6569 *Excalibur* (call sign AP-04). During preflight inspections on the afternoon of December 19, Ranger FSO CPT Joseph Adams arrived on Hurlburt Field to act as AC-130 as onboard liaison. An hour later, AP-04 took off, headed for their first refueling track. Once airborne, CPT Adams detailed his fire support plan to the crew of AP-04 and discovered his coded maps were not in complete agreement with the maps issued to AP-04, however, problems were worked out while en route to Panama.

After a nearly six-hour flight, including two heavyweight aerial refuelings, AP-04 arrived at the hold point northeast of Rio Hato, completely blacked out to prevent visual acquisition by PDF ZPU-4 gunners. About two minutes before H-Hour, Capt Transue directed all guns to be armed. Henceforth, gunners TSgt Wayne White and SSgt Bernie Gilbert loaded and armed 105mm and 40mm guns while Sgt Barry Clark armed the 20mm guns. Shortly afterward, at an altitude of 5,500 ft, AP-04 headed for the assigned initial point over Rio Hato. The mission plan called for two 2,000 lb. bombs to be dropped from the south from high altitude onto Rio Hato exactly at H-Hour. Since risk of being shot down by a wayward bomb was not an appealing concept, navigator Capt Ed Appler timed arrival overhead to ensure AP-04 was on the northern arc of their orbit when the bombs were released.

Now closing in fast on the airfield and less than one minute before H-Hour, IR sensor operator MSgt Fred Kramer searched forward into the area where intelligence reported the ZPU-4 gun was, but it wasn't there. After a wide area search, it was found about one thousand feet to the south. Capt Transue took IR guidance and established a firing orbit on the ZPU-4. By then, H-Hour was less than ten seconds away. Appler counted down the seconds over the main interphone system and precisely at H-Hour, two bright flashes lit the PDF compounds near the beach while the *Apaches* fired a salvo of 30mm ammunition at two ZPU-4 sites near the shoreline, then departed.

At the same time, AP-04 opened fire on the ZPU-4 near the runway with 105 HE. As the first round exploded near the gun, LLLTV sensor operator SSgt Bill Jackson spotted what appeared to be either a V-300 or Military P-3 fire truck with an active rotary beacon on top, speeding to the north. Jackson tracked the vehicle, but before a shot could be taken, it had crossed the Pan-American Highway into a no-fire zone.

Now, at about H-Hour plus two minutes, one of the two ZPU-4 positions which were expected to be silenced by the *Apaches* was now firing at AP-04. Illuminator Operators

SSgt Mike McCarthy and SSgt Frank Demchenko watched the AAA site closely, but tracer fire was inaccurate. At that point, AP-04 set out to suppress the active AAA sites, but with less than a minute before the airdrop began, there wasn't sufficient time to locate and engage them. While AP-04 headed towards a gun site southwest of the runway, the first C-130 (Chalk 1) of the drop formation crossed the coastline at 475 to 500 feet altitude and Rangers began to parachute onto the airfield.

The C-130 drop formation met fierce resistance from the PDF. All thirteen C-130 troop carriers and three heavy equipment airlifters flew directly through a gamut of AAA and small arms fire. Some aircraft were hit more than a dozen times and Chalk 9 lost an engine to gunfire, but none broke out of formation. Several Rangers were hit while still inside the aircraft and more were injured on the drop. Meanwhile, LLLTV sensor operator SSgt Bill Jackson spotted a V-150 moving northeast towards the drop zone firing a machine gun at Rangers on the open airfield. Obviously, immediate action was required but unknown to AP-04, PFC Donald "Joe" Miller and several other Rangers had ducked into a patch of nearby elephant grass after taking fire from the V-150.

> "I distinctly remember one of AAA guns firing again before I crossed the runway; I remember because it sounded terrifying & thinking I better cross & go deal with them. Before I moved out, you guys dealt with it, I crossed the runway

anyway to head to my objective & that's when I ran into the vehicle." **SGT Donald "Joe" Miller,** 90mm gunner for A/2/75 on Rio Hato

Without hesitation, SSgt Jackson tracked the moving vehicle, then fired a single 105mm HE round. Seconds later, Captain Adams called a cease fire when parachutes could be seen on the wide-view TV monitor. Fortunately, the V-150 was hit directly on the front right corner near the driver's compartment resulting in a flash bright enough to momentarily black out the LLLTV sensor. When sensor imagery stabilized, the V-150 was seen rolling to a stop, apparently completely out of action. Shortly afterward, PFC Miller and his fellow Rangers emerged unscathed from the grass and headed towards their rally point.

As the thirteenth C-130 passed over the drop zone, more than 600 Rangers had parachuted onto Rio Hato creating a semi-organized scene of violence and, some may say, chaos. Rangers were scattered from one end of the runway to the other and it would take some time to find their rally points to organize and begin moving towards their objectives. Identification of who's who was difficult at times, especially since some PDF were intermingled with Rangers. To prevent fratricide, a pre-arranged running password (Bulldog) was used extensively and extreme fire discipline was required to ensure Rangers did not accidentally fire upon each other.

Meanwhile, AP-04 searched objectives Cat and Lion for PDF activity. MSgt Kramer spotted a V-150 moving west and tracked it directly to a gun site located on a bluff, west of the 6th Infantry compound. The vehicle was parked underneath a tree and within 50 ft. of an apparently unmanned ZPU-4. AP-04 opened fire with 105mm HE and WP, hitting two nearby buildings, but not the vehicle. In response, the V-150 quickly backed out of position onto the roadway and headed west at a high rate of speed. MSgt Kramer tracked and engaged the vehicle, but did not compensate with enough lead, so the HE projectile he fired exploded on the road about 50 feet in trail. Recalculating his lead with "Kentucky windage," a second round was fired. About the same time the round was fired, it appeared the V-150's driver abandoned the vehicle while still in motion. For the next few seconds, the driverless vehicle swerved, ran into a shallow ditch and stopped just as a 105mm WP projectile impacted the roadway next to it, covering it in burning white phosphorus and smoke.

Several minutes after engaging the westbound V-150, AP-04 returned to the gun site on the bluff and found another V-150 parked in an open area next to the gun. The vehicle's troop door was open, a light was on inside the vehicle and a PDF gunner was seated on the gun. It was now a contest between the ZPU-4 gunner and AP-04 as to who would get rounds on target first. In less than a minute, AP-04 engaged the ZPU-4 with 105mm HE scoring a direct hit on the gun, blowing off a wheel and tire. The gun tipped on its side and was clearly out of action, so AP-04 continued to search for additional threats in objectives Cat and Lion.

Now, about 45 minutes past H-Hour, AP-04 maintained active surveillance of PDF activity in the southern compounds. A commercial-type vehicle was seen leaving the *Macho De Monte* compound, heading west. AP-04 tracked the vehicle to the western perimeter of the Rio Hato reservation until it parked underneath a carport of a residential building. About 40 meters to the east, the IR sensor revealed at least two, maybe three hot spots believed to be PDF soldiers who had set up an ambush site. Confirming the target with CPT Adams, Capt Transue fired a volley of about sixteen rounds of 40mm HEI at the vehicle under the carport, but the rounds missed, ultimately exploding between the building and roadway about 100 ft. north.

While AP-04 switched to their 105mm gun, both sensor operators observed a PDF solider emerge from behind the building as if investigating the aforementioned 40mm explosions. Seemingly undeterred by the gunfire, he walked to the front of the building and stopped by the vehicle in the carport. Within seconds, SSgt Jackson fired a 105mm HE round at the vehicle, but the round fell short by about 30 ft. Compensating his aimpoint using "two shot" tactics, a second round impacted and exploded on the front corner of the house, producing a bright flash and hail of sparks on the building's concrete walls. A small fire ignited under the carport and it appeared the nearby ambush site had been abandoned. AP-04 then returned to objectives Cat and Lion to search for other targets and PDF ambush sites. As the mission progressed, AP-04 remained on call for fire support, orbiting and searching the southwest end of the airfield for PDF activity. MC-130E's landed to establish Forward Area Arming and Refuel Points (FAARP) east of the runway.

Shortly thereafter, C-130 troop carriers began to land with reinforcements and support personnel.

While Rangers assembled and began maneuvering to the south to clear and secure the PDF compounds, AP-04 remained overhead while AH-6 pilots engaged PDF positions near the 6th infantry barracks with 7.62mm and 2.75-inch rockets. During this time, AP-04 engaged a parked M35 truck with 105mm WP and a cartridge case became stuck in the gun's chamber and it took about ten minutes for the gunners and IO to extract the casing. Meanwhile, the two-story 6th Infantry barracks was completely engulfed in flames, lighting the entire area.

There was a lull in activity as elements of 2/75 systematically maneuvered across the open airfield to the south and southwest. AP-04 monitored Ranger formations moving towards objectives Cat and Lion to ensure PDF ambush sites were identified and suppressed before they became a problem. To bolster Identification Friend or Foe (IFF) individual Rangers were marked with a small square of GLINT tape pinned to their uniform. SSgt Jackson and CPT Adams kept a close eye on the LLLTV sensor display to identify any personnel not marked with GLINT tape.

While Rangers maneuvered towards their objectives, reactions of PDF soldiers varied. The PDF Academies (objective Silver) were supposed to be empty, but more than one hundred frightened and unarmed teenage Cadets were found inside. Many assigned to the 6th Infantry dropped their rifles and fled into the civilian village west of the Rio Hato reservation. Some stripped off their uniforms and were later discovered hiding in their underwear. This was not the case with the 7th Infantry *Macho De Monte*, however. Many chose to stay and fight using small unit, guerilla tactics, resulting in several close quarters engagements with Rangers. As the night wore on, it was no surprise the *Macho De Monte* was a formidable threat that had to be dealt with one by one.[25]

While B/2/75 Rangers systematically cleared buildings in the 6th Infantry compound and A/2/75 advanced toward the eastern chain link fence of the Macho de Monte compound, AP-04 remained overhead for on-call fire support. While Rangers used M72 LAW rockets to breach doors and fragmentation grenades as "housewarming gifts," they found the 6th Infantry buildings vacant. As the tedious process of clearing the buildings continued, Capt Transue spotted headlights of a vehicle traveling north in an open pasture about four kilometers west of the airfield. He had been watching it for some time as it crossed over a shallow spot in the river and headed north across an open cattle pasture. Since it was about 0445, and obvious to anyone nearby a full-scale shooting war was afoot, the vehicle was suspected to be loaded with PDF troops attempting to make an end-run attack on 3/75 positions to the northwest. Transue's request to investigate was approved and AP-04 rolled out of orbit heading for the truck. Illumination of the truck's headlights made it easy to track, so Transue flew directly to it and established a firing orbit. Sensor operators Kramer

25 Incidents of Macho De Monte ambushes and "hit and run" tactics continued for several days on Rio Hato.

and Jackson discovered it was an M35 "Deuce & a Half" truck packed with personnel armed with rifles. The position of the truck and the fact they were armed and mobile indicated hostile intent. Lack of GLINT markings confirmed they were not friendly forces. Once CPT Adams confirmed the target as hostile, he cleared AP-04 to fire.

Capt Transue began firing on the truck with the 40mm HE in the manual mode using LLLTV guidance. Initial shots impacted and exploded aft of the truck, causing some of the PDF soldiers to dismount and run across the pasture. The second volley of shots walked from behind the truck, into the bed with one round hitting a PDF soldier directly. As the attack continued, shell fragments knocked out a headlight and the truck rolled to a stop. It appeared the truck's engine had stalled since the remaining headlight was flickering as if the driver was attempting to re-start his engine.

After another volley of 40mm fire, more PDF soldiers dismounted. Some appeared to be assuming a defensive position and some ran across the pasture, clearly retaining their weapons. Transue continued to fire at the truck with 20mm HEI, eventually walking a long burst of 20mm HEI over the top. After this burst, PDF scattered in all directions away from the vehicle. Those who held weapons were engaged by AP-04 one-by-one as they ran. While this chase was on, B/2/75 ran into an issue as they entered the *Macho De Monte* compound and requested an urgent call for fire. AP-04 immediately broke off their attack, rolled out of orbit and headed towards objective Cat.

Returning to the *Macho De Monte* compound, B/2/75 3rd Platoon Leader 1LT Dave Haight advised AP-04 his squad was taking fire from inside the compound. Rangers returned fire, but the PDF were using their barracks building for concealment, firing through windows and using the concrete walls as defilade. Both sensor operators detected a group of PDF soldiers and a ZPU-4 south of the building near a bluff. SSgt Jackson spotted three *Macho De Monte* soldiers behind the barracks southern wall. The distance between the Rangers and PDF was less than 100 meters, but with the concrete building between the PDF and Ranger positions, 1LT Haight and his Forward Observer (FO), SPC Case, were confident the risk of fratricide was low, so he accepted danger close firing parameters. Capt Appler confirmed the target and fire-control officer Capt Phil Bradley directed the LLLTV sensor operator to engage with 105mm HE. Gunners loaded and armed the gun and SSgt Bill Jackson carefully fired into a small clearing behind the barracks.

On impact, the first round detonated causing a shower of sparks on the barracks wall and several fragments struck the ZPU-4. Almost immediately, a *Macho De Monte* soldier jumped out of position near the gun, ran about 20 ft. towards the barracks and fell onto the ground on the same spot Jackson was engaging. The next round fired hit him directly. When the dust cleared a few seconds later, his body was no longer visible and motion behind the barracks was no longer detected. AP-04 remained overhead while Rangers finished clearing the compound and no further difficulties were encountered.

By 0500, PDF resistance was fading fast while AP-04 remained overhead scanning for threats. Rangers continued systematically clearing buildings in both compounds, one by one. By 0530, AP-04 was low on fuel after almost five hours of persistent CAS. When AP-04 pulled off station for aerial refueling, AP-01 took their place at Rio Hato, but there were no additional calls for fire that morning. After refueling, AP-04 was sent to La Comandancia before landing at Howard AFB after being airborne for 15.7 hours.

Macho De Monte hold outs near this ZPU-4 gun in the 7th Infantry compound were engaged by AP-04. (Credit: MSgt (Ret.) Gordon Tully)

After sunrise, USAF Combat Controller Maj Mike Longoria sent a group of combat controllers into the 6th and 7th infantry compounds to assess damage of the two thousand lb. bomb drops. At the same time, Rangers searched residential areas near the airfield, capturing several hundred PDF prisoners. Ranger Medic SGT Frank Morales accompanied by Physician Assistant CPT Scott Buralli, a Chaplain, and a small team of Rangers set out to tend to the wounded and pick up remains of those killed in action. For the rest of the day, Rangers rounded up several hundred PDF prisoners, primarily members of the 6th Infantry and support personnel, in the civilian areas near the base. Few suspected *Macho De Monte* surrendered and those hold-outs mortared the airfield regularly over the next several days until fading away. With the field under control, Rangers then began the tedious task of inventorying PDF vehicles, weapons and munitions preparing them for transport to Howard AFB, then out of Panama.

THE AIRFIELD SEIZURE OF TORRIJOS-TOCUMEN AIRPORT

A few minutes before H-Hour, Lt Col Michael Guidry's crew (AP-01) arrived at their holding point near Torrijos-Tocumen Airport, identified in the fire support plan as Objective Condor. At the same time, soldiers from the 1/75 and 3/75 Ranger Battalions and the Division Ready Brigade of the 82nd Airborne Division were inbound to parachute onto the objective to seize the airfield. This was a difficult working area since the airport not only served the PDF, but was the civilian airline terminal for Panama City. Normally scheduled commercial flights were being serviced and many civilians were in the air terminal at H-Hour. Avoiding collateral damage was a high priority.

Complicating matters, AP-01 had only three minutes before the airdrop began to locate and destroy ZPU-4 AAA guns, FAP HQ buildings, and the Rifle Company Barracks.

Once Rangers landed, AP-01 would provide direct fire support if they came under fire from anyone on or near the airfield. Fifteen seconds prior to H-hour, AP-01 rolled into a firing orbit over the airport and immediately detected individuals and vehicles milling around the PDF aircraft hangers and their primary targets: the 2nd Infantry barracks and HQ buildings. Knowing their original tweak was not valid after changing the fire-control computer in flight, AP-01's LLLTV sensor operator, TSgt Fred Taylor, decided to use the two shot method to get shots onto the targets quickly.

Exactly on H-hour, AP-01 opened fire on the building complex with 105mm HE. As expected, their first round missed a target building by about forty feet, but scored a direct hit on a palm tree causing it to topple as if it were cut down with a chainsaw. Immediately, TSgt Taylor offset his aim point accordingly, and the crew fired seven rounds into the barracks before Lt Col Guidry called for a momentary cease fire to assess battle damage. Unbeknownst to anyone at the time, the first volley of fire from AP-01 alerted Noriega, who was less than one thousand meters away in the Tocumen recreation center.

As the smoke cleared, Lt Col Guidry called for both 20mm guns to be armed. The fire-control computer swap affected the 20mm guns also, so Guidry had to offset his aim point. After a short burst to determine where shots were impacting and correction applied, Lt Col Guidry fired 1,500-rounds of 20mm HEI, walking over the U-shaped barracks, creating a massive fire. The crew ceased firing at exactly 01:02:30 hours in preparation for the airdrop. Thirty seconds later, Noriega escaped in his limousine while eleven SOLL-II C-141s began to fly overhead and Rangers parachuted onto the airfield.

While Rangers maneuvered to their designated assembly areas, AP-01 observed Rangers aggressively engaged with PDF vehicles and personnel. Unfortunately, radio contact had not yet been established, so all AP-01 could do was observe and intercept PDF reinforcements approaching the area. Fortunately, Rangers quickly defeated their targets with small arms. Once radio contact was established, AP-01 remained overhead for several hours supporting the Ranger's airfield seizure operation and the follow-on arrival of the 82nd Airborne.

While the crew observed Rangers systematically clearing the buildings below, an Army Ranger Fire Support Officer called for assistance. A squad had spotted what appeared to be PDF reinforcements speeding towards the airport. AP-01 located and tracked a civilian sedan and bus. Unsure of vehicle's occupants, AP-01 fired a warning round at the road about 100 meters in front of the sedan. The sedan slowed and ran over a parachute on the road causing it to become tangled in its front fender. When the driver of the sedan stopped to clear the parachute, six armed personnel bailed out of the bus and took up defensive positions. Accordingly, AP-01 was cleared to engage. TSgt Taylor quickly fired two 105mm HE rounds at the sedan, scoring a direct hit on one PDF soldier and killing another with shell fragments. Unknown to AP-01 at the time, the convoy was dangerously close to a Ranger blocking position and USAF TACP SSgt Marty Klukas. After AP-01 and Rangers opened fire, the bus quickly reversed direction and ducked into a civilian housing area before the gunship crew could engage it. By that time, AP-01 was low on fuel and departed for their third heavy-weight aerial refueling of the night. When complete, AP-01 was directed to replace AP-04 at Rio Hato.

As the sun began to rise, the crew rolled into orbit over Rio Hato airfield for three hours for on-call CAS. The situation at Rio Hato was relatively quiet as Rangers searched for PDF hold-outs and captured prisoners. Upon reaching minimum fuel limits, AP-01 departed Rio Hato and landed at Howard AB completing a 16 hour mission.

> "I was about 75 meters from the Duster and the Ranger blocking force was even closer. I remember two 105mm shots in quick succession and it killed both guys that were trying to free the parachute from their left front tire. We looked at the Duster and two dead guys in the morning and the craters from the 105 were only a few yards apart. When the P-01 (Air Papa 01) rounds came down, the Rangers thought they had been rocketed and opened fire on the vehicle. Myself and four other Rangers were on the far side of the vehicle in the drainage ditch watching the blocking force fire go whizzing past us." **CMSgt (Ret.) Martin Klukas,** USAF TACP at Torrijos-Tocumen

Combined effects of two 105mm rounds fired by AP-01 and Ranger small arms fire on a sedan approaching a Ranger position near Torrijos Tocumen Airport. Rangers covered the remains of the two PDF soldiers near the vehicle. (Credit: Martin Klukas)

THE RIO PACORA BRIDGE

The PDF Battalion 2000 was located at Fort Cimarron, about 30 kilometers from Panama City. The battalion was a PDF stronghold that could present significant resistance to US forces during the initial phase of *Just Cause*. Early in the planning stage, the Pacora River (Rio Pacora) was recognized as a geographical obstacle that isolated Ft Cimarron from Panama City. There was only one major bridge that crossed Rio Pacora; therefore, JSOTF control of the bridge would prevent PDF Battalion 2000 soldiers from crossing the span to reinforce PDF forces in Panama City. AP-03, commanded by Capt Francis (Robert) Gabreski, was tasked to support Task Force Black to prevent Battalion 2000 from crossing the bridge and interfering with the airfield seizure at Torrijos-Tocumen and destruction of La Comandancia.

Since the PDF was tipped off of an impending invasion, Battalion 2000 was nearing the bridge as AP-03 arrived overhead. Headlights from PDF vehicles were seen approaching while 23 soldiers from the 7th Special Forces Group led by A/3/7 Commander Major Kevin Higgins and supported by USAF Combat Controller MSgt John Eklof were inserted by two MH-60 and one UH-60 helicopter. As AP-03 approached the bridge, sensor operator MSgt Russ Spitzmacher detected a nine vehicle convoy of M35 trucks. AP-03 could not establish radio contact with TF-Black for clearance to fire, so they were unable to take any action.[26] As the first truck began to cross the bridge, TF-Black engaged the lead vehicle with Anti-Tank weapons and small arms, halting the column. By the time radio contact was established, Battalion 2000 troops were within danger close firing parameters of TF-Black and AP-03 was immediately cleared to fire by Major Higgins.

Capt Gabreski opened fire with 20mm HEI. Gunfire raked over the convoy, causing PDF soldiers to abandon their vehicles and retreat. Some fired their weapons wildly at US forces as they withdrew. A group of PDF took up positions along the tree line on both sides of the road and continued to probe US positions unsuccessfully for the remainder of the night. Every time they advanced, they were met with

---

26 Email from Lt Col (Ret.) Robert Gabreski to Author indicates there were actually nine trucks in the convoy approaching the bridge as opposed to reports of six.

fire from TF-Black and AP-03. When Gabreski's crew ran low on fuel, Capt LeBrun's crew (AP-05) took their place. Since the bridge spanned a major Highway, civilian vehicles continued to travel towards the bridge all night, most likely unaware of the military operation in progress. Accordingly, it was difficult to determine if vehicle occupants were hostile or just everyday Panamanian citizens in the wrong place at the wrong time. To limit the possibility of targeting innocent civilians, AP-05 resorted to firing 40mm rounds in front of vehicles to encourage them to stop or turn around. In one case, just after two rounds of 40mm HEI detonated in front of a Jeep, the driver slammed on the brakes, dismounted, ran into the tree line and disappeared. Later, AP-05 detected a Range Rover attempting to navigate around the bridge, but did not fire since the vehicle was unable to cross the river at any point anyway. LeBrun was subsequently ordered to terminate his mission and land at Howard AFB.

Through the night, the PDF retrieved their dead and wounded but were unable to cross the bridge. After sunrise, TF-Black soldiers swept the area and the damaged/destroyed trucks and captured 20 prisoners. Underneath the bridge, they discovered two dead PDF and one survivor with compound leg fracture.

> "Even though two gunships fired up the bridge and surrounding area, the morning body count was only three and they were all in the river below the bridge. Two dead and one survivor with a nasty compound fracture of his right

femur he suffered when he jumped off the bridge to escape gunship fires. Morphine really helped him out as we interrogated him before he went to Gorgas Hospital. Battalion 2000 was pulling out their dead and wounded all through the night as reported by Major Higgins. The estimates of total casualties vary by source." **Maj (Ret.) Mike Poddubny,** USSOUTHCOM Liaison Officer

Though Battalion 2000 was persistent in their attempt to cross the Rio Pacora bridge, their effort proved futile. TF-Black, AP-03 and AP-05 undoubtedly dealt a severe blow to the offensive capabilities of Norigea's PDF.

THE SEIZURE OF PUNTA PAITILLA AIRFIELD

AC-130H gunship AP-02 was tasked to provide fire support for Task Force White during US Navy SEAL Team 4 operations at Punta Paitilla Airfield, located on the coastline a few miles from La Comandancia. Three SEAL platoons and a USAF Combat Controller infiltrated the airfield via rubber raiding craft (Zodiacs). Their mission was to seize the airfield, disable Noriega's aircraft and secure the airfield for follow-on JSOTF operations. Early in the mission, AP-02's harrowing effort to repair 6573's fire-control system and an extremely heavy take-off from Hurlburt was stressful and tense, but they successfully arrived on time. Since they did not have much time to tweak their guns, they performed a quick combat tweak offshore before arrival at Paitilla.

While AP-02 orbited above Paitilla and observed SEALS coming ashore, they were unable to establish voice communications with SSgt David Sulak, an Air Force Combat Controller attached to the SEALS. They did, however, detect a signal from their TEMIG beacon and observed SEALs maneuver across open pavement towards a large hanger suspected of containing Noriega's aircraft. About the same time communications were established with SSgt Sulak, AP-02's fire-control system failed again, leaving Lt Col Frakes with no aiming reference except a standby reticle. Lt Col Frakes considered firing the 40mm gun in the blind but realized it could only be done at high risk to the SEALS and civilian houses nearby.

While AP-02 attempted to repair their fire-control system, ST-4 Golf platoon had problems of their own. As they approached a hangar, PDF soldiers verbally challenged them, took cover, then opened fire. Four SEALs were killed and eight more were wounded. Unable to provide fire support, AP-02 departed for Howard AFB for fire-control system repairs while remaining SEALs continued their mission to disable Noriega's aircraft. Much later, AMASS-12 was sent to Paitilla but, since the AC-130A was not equipped with SATCOM, could not contact the Combat Controller unless on an open frequency. By that time, all was quiet on Paitilla and fire support was not requested.

THE HUNT FOR NORIEGA

Capt LeBrun's crew (AP-05) was on aerial alert to support Task Forces Blue, Black, and Green, depending on intelligence reports of the whereabouts of Noriega at H-Hour. As the night progressed, both Farallon and La Escondida were confirmed negative at H-Hour, but a suspected Noriega sighting was made at Colon and AP-05 was tasked to chase down a suspect vehicle. After a lengthy chase, TF Green members stopped and searched the vehicle, but Noriega was not in it. TF-Blue and Green would face several more leads to run down, but Noriega was not found. Following 18.3 hours of flight and four in-flight refuelings, AP-05 was the last AC-130 to land at Howard AFB.

As the sun rose on Panama on the morning of December 20, most mission aircraft had landed on Howard Air Force Base. Lt Col Frake's aircraft required a level of maintenance and troubleshooting not available at Howard, so AP-02 was directed to return to Hurlburt. The small staff of maintainers who expected to see only a few AC-130s land on Howard AFB was surprised when all nine AC-130s recovered there. Since the parking ramp of Howard was overcrowded, five gunships were parked nose to tail on an abandoned asphalt parking apron west of the runway.

> "When we landed at Howard and the tower was looking for a place to park, we were told that our original parking spots were inadvertently taken by two C5s. As such, they had no other place to put us other than on the abandoned/

> condemned runway. When we taxied to our 'space,' I noticed the big yellow X at the entry to the runway, I pointed it out to Lt Col Guidry and he had me confirm with the tower that we were directed to park on a condemned runway (big yellow X). Tower's response was that they had no choice because of the C5 situation." **Col (Ret.) Gary Holland,** Mission Planner/Navigator, AP-01

Gunship maintainers and munitions support personnel scrambled to re-arm aircraft and prepare them for the next mission but were overwhelmed by the sheer number of tasks that needed to be performed. There wasn't much rest or sleep for any of the maintainers for the next two days.

> "At dawn, as combat aircraft began to land, delivery crews were dispatched to resupply AC-130 and MH53 aircraft. Personnel responded to various calls for downloading or resupplying as necessary. As expended munitions residue returned to the area, all delivery trailers were replenished and again dispersed. Personnel not actively supporting flight line operations spent the day unpacking and inspecting munitions, providing security, refueling vehicles and performing the various tasks required for continued mission support." **SMSgt (Ret.) Thomas "Ed" Fowler, 1** SOW Munitions Maintenance

Crews entering mandatory crew rest for follow-on missions were billeted in vacant family housing units spread out throughout Howard AFB. While making arrangements, a billeting NCO who had been directed to clear Shoppette coolers for use as temporary morgues, used exceptional creativity by trading cases of beer for spent cartridge cases from the night's missions. It seemed just about everyone on Howard AFB wanted a cartridge case as a souvenir, so the situation worked well for everyone.

During the afternoon of December 20, Capt McMillan's crew was alerted to search for sniper positions in the hills near Howard. AP-06's equipment was already on *Bad Company*, but it was fourth in line, parked behind *Death Angel*, *Grave Digger*, and *Hell Raiser*. Furthermore, *Death Angel* was down for a major hydraulic leak. The confines of the parking ramp were tight, and it would take a lot of time to tow the other aircraft out of the way. After a short discussion with Lt Col Napier, McMillan believed he could successfully taxi past the other aircraft. Once AP-06 began to taxi, Capt McMillan moved as far to the right as he could to clear the broken gunship, but brushed wingtips with *Death Angel*. Unfortunately, he pulled back power just as the aircraft's nose gear and right main landing gear rolled off the edge of the paved taxiway. McMillan re-applied power in a desperate attempt to free the aircraft, but it was mired in soft mud and would not budge. As the right gear sank into the mud, the aircraft listed to the right until the #4 propeller was just a few feet from contacting the surface, prompting an emergency shut-down.

> "I sat on the end of the cargo ramp (of *Death Angel*) and watched all the flight line activity going on. It wasn't long that we got word McMillan's crew was launching. I could see *Bad Company* start engines and the whole time I'm thinking, 'there is no way those guys are getting around these other birds.' Mac pulls out with a hard right turn to get around us and they quickly see they don't have the wingtip clearance to remain on the pavement. The plane goes further right and the right main gear and nose go off the pavement and the right wing drops hard. The ground was extremely soft and you could see the wheels starting to plow through the tall grass and mud. Immediately upon departing the pavement, the right main gear is sinking fast as is the nose." **CMSgt (Ret.) Mike Longe,** Flight Engineer, AP-03

With *Bad Company* haplessly mired in the mud, the crew quickly removed their equipment while maintainers towed *Death Angel* out of the way. Shortly after boarding *Grave Digger*, they took off. Later, as crew chiefs were in the process of towing *Hell Raiser* to a more stable parking apron, it broke through the ramp and became stuck also. The posture of both gunships was unusual since one wingtip of each was nearly touching the ground while the other was 30-plus feet in the air. From a distance, it appeared both aircraft were damaged by a mortar attack, but in reality, they were simply stuck in the mud.

While the rest of the gunships were towed to a more stable area, MSgt John Varner, Production Superintendent led his team of maintainers in the recovery of both gunships. Maintainers inspected the aircraft and found *Bad Company* (6570) was relatively unscathed, but *Hell Raiser* (6576) suffered some damage. They had 6570 repaired and ready to fly in 24 hours, but 6576 had a damaged main gear door and had to have a new one flown in from Hurlburt along with other spare parts. Two days after the incident, maintainers succeeded in repairing 6576.[27]

Bad Company being recovered after running off the taxiway on the afternoon of December 20, 1989. (Credit: Renae' L Ward, SMSgt (Ret.) USAF)

AC-130A crews were heavily tasked on the second night of the operation. Maj Clay McCutchan's crew responded to a crisis situation at the Marriott Hotel in downtown Panama

27 Email from CMSgt (Ret.) John Varner, to Author, May 16, 2012.

City to support Rangers. It was reported that elements of the Dignity Battalion were searching the hotel for Americans to take hostage. Rangers were infiltrated by helicopter then moved by foot several blocks to the hotel. During the movement, shots were fired from a rooftop location, injuring the element leader. McCutchan's sensors found several armed personnel on a nearby rooftop within 20 meters of the ground party. The crew was cleared to fire danger-close and placed 3 rounds of 40mm HEI on the target, with the 3rd round striking directly. When the dust cleared, there was no sign of any enemy personnel, and the ground team proceeded to the Marriot under armed escort. The ground party requested McCutchan's crew make an assessment of the rooftops after arriving at the hotel. Sensor Operators did not believe the roof would be suitable or stressed for a helicopter landing, forcing the evacuation by ground. When the aircraft was low on fuel, they turned for Howard to refuel. After refueling, they took off again to search for mortars reported at Ft Clayton, then the town of David on the other side of the Isthmus. Finding nothing at either location, they were en route to Howard and found two mortar carrier vehicles which they engaged with 40mm HEI fire.

Capt Wilson's crew was tasked to support elements of the 82nd Airborne Division, along with OA-37s from Howard AFB, in the assault of Fort Cimarron, home of Battalion 2000. The crew hand launched several LUU-2 flares to provide illumination for OA-37s to attack buildings on the fort. After launching a string of flares, Wilson flew into a nearby cloud formation to avoid being spotted by PDF gunners. [28] The Dragonflies then began their attack. After unsuccessful strafing attempts by the OA-37s, the ground party continued to receive effective enemy fire from the compound, so the AC-130A rolled in and Wilson began engaging the main buildings with 40mm HEI/AP mix.

> "The HEI seemed to glance off the roof, but the AP projectiles broke the clay tile. Once we had punched a hole in the tile, the HEI got into the ceiling and set the building on fire." **Maj (Ret.) Ken Moerscher,** gunner

As the hole grew, HEI rounds began to enter the ceiling structure and set fire to the building. Wilson's crew then engaged military vehicles in the compound and an additional structure with alternating 20mm and 40mm fire. With smoke pouring from buildings, the 82nd Airborne moved in on Fort Cimarron to accept surrender of Battalion 2000.

That same night, AP-04 and AP-05 were launched as airborne alert assets. Shortly after takeoff, AP-04 was directed to Rio Hato to fire on a sniper position near a suspected PDF weapons cache. A Ranger patrol about 250 meters from the house observed what appeared to be PDF activity in a residential concrete building surrounded by other houses. Concerned there was collateral damage potential for surrounding buildings and Panamanian civilians, the gunship crew selected the 40mm gun. After firing about thirty rounds

28 Email from Maj Ken Moerscher to Author, April 21, 2014.

on and around the building and witnessing no activity, they ceased firing and were cleared off station. About an hour later, Rangers again observed suspected PDF activity and requested AC-130 support. This time, AP-05, commanded by Capt Philippe LeBrun responded. A Ranger FSO talked AP-05 onto the target, and sensor operators TSgt Mike Dorris and MSgt Paul Buege measured the distance from the closest Ranger position to the target at less than 250 meters. Because of concern for collateral damage and unnecessary risk to the Ranger element, FCO Capt Mike Brennan suggested Capt LeBrun use the 40mm gun for the engagement, which he did. After firing upwards of eighty rounds, it was evident 40mm was not penetrating the roof or walls of the concrete structure. A short conversation between the FSO and AP-05 convinced everyone they had to fire 105mm HE to breach the structure. Though the nearest Ranger position was technically inside "danger close" firing parameters, the crew and Ranger FSO were confident AP-05 could lessen risk by setting fuzes to delay to allow surface breaching to regulate fragment dispersion. Lead gunner TSgt Bob Kane and gunner SSgt Bobby Daniel set four HE rounds on delay and loaded the gun as Sensor operators carefully tracked the target to ensure precision and lessen risk to the Ranger force. When all prerequisites to fire were complete, AP-05 began their attack. The first and second rounds exploded near the building while the third round penetrated the structure and exploded within. Just as the crew fired their fourth round, the Ranger FSO called a check fire. Within a minute, fire engulfed the building and secondary explosions were seen. Satisfied the weapons cache was no longer a problem, AP-05 remained overhead on call until low on fuel.

By night three, AC-130s remained on airborne alert, ready to respond to any location as required. Considerable effort was directed to operations at Rio Hato since more than six hundred Rangers and support personnel were on site. Though about three hundred PDF prisoners had either surrendered or had already been captured in nearby villages, small squads of *Macho De Monte* continued to wage hit-and-run mortar and small arms attacks from just outside the security perimeter. *Macho De Monte* troops specialized in guerilla warfare and encounters were expected at night. Rangers manning fighting positions on the perimeter were sometimes overwhelmed by the many natural sounds of animals moving through the jungle, masked by elephant grass or tree cover. Several times, AC-130 crews were tasked to search for *Macho De Monte* troops suspected to be advancing on Ranger positions, but the source of noisy movement turned out to be cattle. Nevertheless, AC-130 crews remained overhead as a deterrent since the sound of their props alone had a suppressive effect on *Macho De Monte* guerillas.

The overwhelming force subjected to the PDF during the first three days successfully subdued the majority of the PDF and Noriega was on the run. TF-Green and Blue were systematically rounding up Noriega's commanders, supported by AC-130 crews. Many reports of Noriega sightings were investigated but turned out to be false sightings. Soon, the hunt for Noriega was dubbed "the hunt for Elvis."

On December 23, Transue's crew flew a daylight mission in support of TF-Green during a raid of Playa De Coronado, capturing a high-ranking PDF officer, but Noriega was not there. After the mission was complete, a TF-Gator FSO requested a call for fire on a V-150 located in the middle of an open courtyard near 4th of July Avenue. His request was not urgent, and he explained the V-150 wasn't manned, but he wanted it to be taken out of commission to prevent anyone from using it. Capt Transue allowed his second pilot, Capt John Viglione, to take command of the aircraft for the fire mission.

Sensor operators found the target and the FSO cleared AP-04 to fire. Viglione called for 105mm HE to be used on the target as gunners loaded and armed the gun. The first shot impacted near the front of the V-150 and the primary sensor operator compensated for the miss via the "two shot" method. The second shot also resulted in a near miss. As gunners loaded a third round, the FSO came over the radio in a loud and commanding voice "*CHECK FIRE, CHECK FIRE, CHECK FIRE!*"[29]

Afterwards, the FSO explained Panamanian civilians who lived in the apartment complexes surrounding the target had asked him to put on a show for them by having the V-150 shot. Apparently, the whole neighborhood was glued to their windows to watch the fireworks. When the first round detonated near the target, fragments and blast broke out a majority of the neighborhood windows as they ran back into their apartments in panic.

29 Check fire is an artillery term used to advise gunners to stop firing.

Barely two days into the operation, TF-Red controlled Rio Hato Airfield and had processed several hundred PDF prisoners. TF-Red commander Col William "Buck" Kernan met with commanders of the PDF 5th Military Zone and gave them an ultimatum: surrender or be destroyed. PDF Commanders were then sent to outlying garrisons to advise their troops. At Rio Hato, Col Kernan directed the formation of an assault element to begin rounding up PDF soldiers from outlying areas.

On the night of December 22–23, an assault force consisting of a 12-man Special Forces Operational Detachment Alpha (ODA a.k.a A-Team) from C/3/7 SFG (A), Rangers from A/3/75, MH-47s, and MH-60s from 160th SAOG, and Capt McMillan's AC-130 prepared for a mission to Penonome. An unknown number of PDF were expected to surrender from the town garrison and nearby prison. About an hour before the mission launched, Col Kernan used the Panamanian public telephone system to call the garrison commander to tell him an assault force was on its way and warn him of consequences if they did not surrender. Some on the strike force thought the concept of warning the enemy was tactically unsound, but others felt it was a stroke of genius. Thus, it was the beginning of an effort named Operation *Ma Bell*.

The assault force departed in total darkness from Rio Hato on a short flight to Penonome. About the same time, Capt McMillan's AC-130H crew took off from Howard Air Force base to support the operation. Once overhead Penonome, McMillan's crew established an orbit and began searching the area, noting it appeared fairly quiet. A short time later, the assault force landed without a shot being fired from either side. Panamanian civilians flocked to the area to witness the operation while Rangers quickly established a 360-degree security perimeter about 100 meters from the PDF compound. PDF soldiers positioned themselves on a soccer field near the garrison, ready to surrender. Several soldiers from the ODA approached the group and commanded them to comply with their orders. The ODA organized PDF soldiers into elephant trail columns of 10–12, patted them down, and then marched them to Ranger element for a detailed search.

After Rangers processed their prisoners, they were secured in a holding area inside Penonome prison. Since there were nearly 200 PDF soldiers in the garrison, it took some time for the small team to process all the prisoners. The resulting bottleneck of surrendering PDF and the perception that they outnumbered the A-Team may have led PDF soldiers to think they could overpower US forces and escape without surrender. When the large group of PDF began to threaten the A-Team, they quickly became concerned.[30] The A-Team was stuck between the Ranger security perimeter and an enemy possibly willing to fight, so they called McMillan's crew orbiting overhead, advising them to be ready to fire on the group quickly if needed. Sensor Operators TSgt Glen Lemay and MSgt Jerry Andersen were already tracking the group and the crew was ready to fire.

30 Email from Richard Lamb, to Author, July 9, 2015.

The proximity of the group to the assault force and status of civilian rubberneckers in the area concerned Fire-control Officer Capt Mike Radford and Navigator Capt Bill Lane, who recommended not firing. Andersen suggested an idea worthy of merit: illuminate the group with the 2KW spotlight as a show of force.

> "The AC-130 illuminated the area with their searchlight and the PDF saw the larger force of Rangers deployed in the darkness; and they quickly understood that the aircraft above was in fact, a gunship! They immediately became compliant and all we had to do to keep order the remainder of the night was point our fingers skyward. Because of the significance of the target, we were glad to have the gunship…it was like having a security blanket, or night light! We didn't know what to expect and found a level of comfort hearing the drone of the engines orbiting above us." **CSM (Ret.) Richard Lamb,** 7th Special Forces Group

After illuminating the area, PDF prisoners fell quiet and sat down while civilian onlookers left the area in haste. McMillan's crew stayed overhead for the remainder of the evening until they ran low on fuel. The combination of the *Ma Bell* phone call and the threat of AC-130 fire squelched PDF opposition at Penonome, which was the largest surrender operation outside of Panama City and Colon. A 12-man ODA, Ranger security element, and one AC-130 gunship crew succeeded in negating the entire PDF Military Zone's command, control and communications infrastructure, while capturing 188 prisoners.[31]

The same night, another AC-130H crew flew a US Embassy protection mission while another flew a reconnaissance mission. Two more AC-130s searched for snipers over Panama City with one supporting a raid at Las Tablas, but Noriega remained elusive. Late that evening, AP-05 was launched from alert on *Hell Raiser* to assist a small contingent of TF-Black soldiers that had secured a radio transmission station tower to the north of Panama City on the side of a mountain. Reports were that troops were massing.

The crew of AP-05 searched and located several groups of people and two large trucks at the end of the prepared roadway that led to the radio station. Due to the thickness of the jungle, they could not track personnel into the jungle. Earlier, TF-Black had placed movement sensors throughout the jungle trails that lead to their position. Upon reports from the sensors, AP-05 obtained clearance to fire. The crew fired somewhere between 10 to 20 rounds of 105mm. As a sensor would sound, AP-05 would fire, then wait for another report from TF-Black. When all was silent for a period of time, they left their orbit as a feint of permanently departing. Establishing an orbit out of audible range, they waited until movement was reported again, and then returned fire by direction of the TF-Black FSO. When they were refueling on an offshore track, they were called back for an urgent fire support request.

31 Ibid.

As soon as they rolled in to orbit the radio station, all sensor movement stopped. At that point, TF-Black soldiers provided the precise position of their sensors and asked them to fire several rounds directly at the sensors. AP-05 stayed on station until near sunrise, landing on Howard after an 11.4-hour mission. This was the last firing mission of an AC-130 during Operation *Just Cause.* The true source of exactly who or what was activating the movement sensors wasn't discovered.

The day before Christmas, Noriega was still on the run, but it was inevitable that he would be eventually captured. The PDF and the Dignity Battalion were no longer functional. Panamanian citizens were reporting PDF hideouts and celebrating Noriega's fall from power. US forces were accepting mass surrender of PDF soldiers in Panama City. The log entry in Col Gray's December 25 report read:

> "Twas the night before Christmas, not a firefight in sight, PDFs big boss Noriega, was in a perilous flight
>
> When out of the SATCOM there arose such a clatter, that the radio operator screamed, 'what the Hell is the matter'
>
> From the Vatican Embassy, Came a voice all aghast, 'Noriega's right here,' and he says 'kiss my ass'
>
> The ground troops were dispatched, by rotor and fixed wing, overhead *Spectre* orbited, 'let us shoot the damn thing!'

> The clearance was given, to ground and above, to launch all the helos, show him push comes to shove
>
> The fighting would have been fierce; our spirits were high, but when the dust finally settled, we had to wonder why
>
> Unsure of his fate; either the death of a sissy, or a trip to the states, hopefully on Christmas morning
>
> Accompanied by a Doc, he will be sent to the US…Merry Christmas U.S.S.O.C."[32]

By December 24, only a few remote PDF enclaves remained intact. On Christmas day, Lt Col Del Cid, Commander of the PDF Western Region, sent a message to US forces stating he intended to surrender along with his entire unit at his headquarters in the city of David in western Panama. Del Cid was known to be untrustworthy, so some believed he may be attempting a ruse. To ensure they were not caught off guard, the JSOTF commander sent Soldiers from TF-Black escorted by elements of TF-Red to accept surrender of the PDF. After A/3/7 SFG (A) heloed into an Elementary School about ten kilometers away from David, Capt McMillan's crew orbited overhead the David headquarters and nearby Enrique Malek International airfield, ready to fire.

32 The author of this poem is purposely unknown.

From the elementary school, A/3/7 Commander, Major Higgins, used the elementary school phone in the principal's office to contact Lt Col Del Cid and warned him that if he did not surrender his forces they would be destroyed. Lt Col Del Cid agreed to surrender. Higgins, accompanied by Colonel Jacoby, SOCSOUTH TF-Black Commander and three Special Forces teams landed at the softball field outside of Lt Col Del Cid's headquarters to accept his surrender.

Three other Special Forces teams, directed by Captain Stu Bradin, flew to nearby Enrique Malek airfield (5 km outside David) to secure the area. Bradin directed PDF soldiers to abandon their ZPU-4 AAA guns on the airfield and stand in formation at the terminal. To ensure the PDF compliance, Colonel Kernan cleared the gunship crew to pick out an isolated spot of earth near the runway and "put on a show of force." McMillan's crew fired about 200 rounds of 20mm HEI near the runway and thirty minutes later, 2/75 Rangers arrived via MH-53. Del Cid surrendered his entire force without incident. With Del Cid out of the picture, US forces received another "gift" later in the day. Noriega surfaced near Paitilla Airport and quickly took refuge in the nearby *Nunciatura* (Vatican Embassy).

That night, 1 SOW personnel celebrated Christmas day in unconventional ways in their crew houses and barracks. After being allowed time to relax, they were able to break out the beer they traded for fired brass cartridge cases earlier in the mission.[33] Dirty gym socks taped to the wall, stuffed

33 Crews discovered fired brass was a more of a commodity, than a disposal issue.

with MRE fare was a common theme. One crew fabricated a Christmas tree from a palm plant and decorated it with Chem-lights.

Morale was high, but the *Nifty Package* mission was not complete. For the time being, Noriega was untouchable under international law while holed up in the Nunciatura. Word spread quickly as US forces and Panamanian citizens surrounded the embassy, demanding Noriega's surrender. Noriega proved stubborn, however, and Monsignor Laboda could not convince him to surrender. Shortly after Noriega entered the Vatican Embassy, AC-130 crews were directed to maintain at least one low altitude aircraft in orbit over the Nunciatura, 24 hours a day. Crews referred to these missions as operation constant noise.

Crowds surrounded the embassy demanding Noriega's surrender. SOUTHCOM commander General Maxwell Thurman met Monsignor Laboda at the front gate of the Nunciatura to negotiate terms of surrender but was not allowed inside. During these outdoor conversations, Thurman was concerned his politically sensitive discussions would be overheard by members of the media, complicating negotiations. To mask future conversations, he directed an Army psychological operations unit to set up high powered loudspeakers to play music outside the Nunciatura to defeat the media's eavesdropping microphones. A playlist of topical tunes was selected and loudspeakers began blasting loud rock and roll music towards the Embassy, twenty-four hours a day. On December 29, GEN Colin Powell felt the music was undue harassment and ordered the music stopped.

In the following days, Secretary of Defense Dick Cheney arrived for a static display of an AC-130H gunship and on December 30, an AC-130 supported Rangers during the seizure of the last major PDF unit located on Isla Coiba, a notorious Panamanian penal colony. When the Rangers arrived, they found many prisoners wandering freely. Most of the guards and seventy-four of the October coup d'état participants had already fled from the island in boats. The PDF guards who remained on site surrendered without a fight. Rangers cleared cells, finding prisoners being held in extremely deplorable conditions.

Ranger SPC Chuck Holton struck up a conversation in Spanish with one of the PDF guards. When the guard asked what his Night Vision Goggles (NVG) were, SPC Holton let the guard look through them. The AC-130 crew overhead was scanning the prison with their GLINT at the same time. When the PDF guard witnessed the rectangular beam of light sweeping across the prison, he was taken back. When he asked what it was, Holton replied, "that is the eye of God, and it can see everything you do, and kill you if you run," then pulled his NVGs back. After that, Rangers had no trouble keeping track of the guards.

On January 3, 1990, the PDF was in shambles and a large crowd of Panamanian citizens stood outside the Vatican Embassy chanting anti-Noriega statements. Monsignor Laboda threatened to lift Vatican Embassy diplomatic immunity if Noriega did not surrender.[34] Noriega

34 Kenneth J. Jones, *The Enemy Within: Casting Out Panama's Demon* (El Dorado, Panama: Focus Publications, 1990), 84.

feared the embassy would be overrun by protesters, who would lynch him. At 2050 hrs., an AC-130H crew orbiting overhead witnessed personnel boarding a helicopter near the Embassy, then departing towards Howard AFB. News quickly circulated that Noriega had surrendered. Shortly afterward, Noriega was examined by 16 SOS Flight Surgeon Major Darr LaFon, then flown on an AFSOC MC-130 to Homestead AFB, Florida to face trial for drug trafficking.

Following Noriega's surrender, AC-130A crews returned to the US, but AC-130H crews retained a presence for Operation *Promote Liberty* until the summer of 1990.

MISSION DEBRIEF

The objectives of *Just Cause* had been to capture Noriega, bring him to the U.S., protect American lives in Panama, restore order, minimize deaths all around, and promote a return to democratic government. These goals were achieved. Success did not come without a storm in the world of anti-American media, however. Many exaggerated claims of civilian deaths ensued, challenging the official SOUTHCOM estimate of 314. Polls were run that supposedly showed that the vast majority of Panamanians thought the invasion was a good thing—prompting media assertions that the polls were fatally flawed.

The 1st Special Operations Wing suffered no casualties and aircraft damage was minimal. Operations security was commendable considering the size of the operation, but the PDF had advanced warning they were about to be attacked.

AC-130 crews had a rare ability to assess BDA on the targets they had shot on D-Day. Lt Col Billy Napier and the crew of AP-06 walked through La Comandancia and the author was sent to Rio Hato via MH-53 to assess BDA and retrieve a trophy gun barrel from one of the ZPU-4 guns silenced on December 20.

INTRUSIONS INTO US-CONTROLLED FACILITIES

The question concerning size, scope and intent of incursions into the ATF and other US-controlled facilities was questioned by many. Captured PDF documents mentioned firefights at ATF on April 12 and October 31, 1988, but lacked detail as to what units were involved. Speculation however, centered on the 7th Rifle Company *Macho De Monte*, who were known to be loyal to Noriega. Though US Forces fired on and witnessed intruders being hit by gunfire during night operations and there was substantial evidence of blood trails and drag marks found after sunrise, no bodies were found. Since the Macho De Monte was known to employ Cuban advisors, it is possible Cuban casualties may have resulted during the incursions. If so, the details of potential Cuban casualties could not be published in this unclassified document.

Intelligence analysts believed PDF incursions were designed by Noriega as a morale builder and test of competence of his military elite and an opportunity to embarrass and belittle the US publicly.[35] Noriega's covert actions

35 Cole, *Operation Just Cause*, 10.

fueled his propaganda campaign, perhaps to create a high-level international incident that would force the US out of Panama. It was clear that Noriega was undeterred by US security activities, and soon after his anti-Marine propaganda began at ATF, he commented: "Never before has there been a more effective laboratory for armed men. Nor has the opportunity (ever) been so propitious for training in low intensity conflict, as that which exists today in Panama."[36]

The level of interaction between Noriega and high-ranking officers of JTF-Panama is unknown since General Woerner was under orders from Washington to protect American interests and to not exacerbate the situation. Noriega, on the other hand, seemed to want to escalate the situation, perhaps even to the point of wanting a high-profile Panamanian death to martyr to his cause.

THE CRITICAL TIMELINE

The in and out of weather affected aerial refueling capabilities and the AC-130's ability to reach Panama. This was the critical make-or-break point of the AC-130 mission. The fact that all gunships and tankers emerged from the cloud "sandwich" fueled, on time, and unscathed bears testament to their crew training, skill, and adaptability. The credit gunship and tanker pilots and the lead navigators deserve cannot be overstated. They succeeded in getting both formations to the exact rendezvous initial point on time under hazardous conditions. An exemplary crew effort occurred

36 Ibid, 10.

behind the throttles as gunship flight engineers kept engine turbine inlet temperatures at dangerous levels, on the brink of failure, to produce maximum power to remain connected to the tanker. The KC-135 pilots were outstanding in their ability to maintain level flight in zero visibility, mitigating the potential for a catastrophic in-flight collision.

> "The KC-135 pilots displayed exemplary aviation skills maintaining the visual flight conditions, in extreme weather conditions, that allowed all five AC-130 crews to receive full fuel on loads. Had this not been accomplished, the gunships didn't have the fuel to return to Hurlburt Field or proceed on to Panama. All five AC-130s would have had to make emergency landings somewhere in Mexico." **Col (Ret.) Mike Guidry,** 16 SOS Operations Officer

<u>Command Control and Communications (C2, C3):</u> SOUTHCOM was assigned C2 of the AC-130A gunships, but the JSOTF maintained C2 of all AC-130H gunships. There was confusion in the AOC as to who had ultimate tasking authority of each aircraft. This disconnect contributed to AMASS-11 flying directly through AP-07's firing orbit at Ft Amador. Since AC-130A gunships were not equipped with SATCOM, effective communications were negatively affected. There was an overt turf war between the JSOTF and AOC that negatively affected

C3 and coordination between both elements. The situation contributed to great consternation on the part of the Air Force commander, Maj Gen Peter Kempf, who took the issue to Lt Gen Charles Boyd, HQ USAF Assistant DCS Plans. The end result ensured future war plans would reflect single ownership of all gunships by the Air Force commander in theater.[37]

Weapons Effects at Rio Hato: Mission plans called for only three minutes of preparation fire before the airdrop, which was not sufficient to eliminate PDF AAA threats. This factor resulted in high risk for the airdrop formation. Also dubious was the performance of AH-64s at Rio Hato that fired on two gun sites with 30mm, then departed, suspecting they had accomplished their mission. Unfortunately, at least one gun remained active afterward, firing at the drop formation as they arrived over the field. Additionally, mission planners appeared to have placed too much confidence in the suppressive effect of F-117 dropping two thousand lb. bombs. If there was any effect, it ended shortly after the fighters departed. The AH-6s were effective however, one AH-6 accidentally fired on a Ranger position killing two and injuring four. The AC-130 capability was stand-alone in its ability to remain on sta-

37 E-mail from Lt Col (Ret.) Randy Durham.

tion for upwards of five hours with night vision sensors and a sufficient range of firepower to meet mission needs. By sunrise on December 20, TF-Red Romeo owned Rio Hato. During the operation, four Rangers were lost during combat action and more than forty were wounded or injured. PDF casualties included thirty-four killed in action and an unknown number of wounded. More than three-hundred-sixty were captured and several hundred escaped into the Panamanian countryside. In all likelihood, the number of Ranger casualties would have been higher without AC-130 fire support.

NIGHT CAPABILITY AND PSYCHOLOGICAL EFFECT OF THE AC-130

The use of the GLINT for IFF was critical at Rio Hato since friendly forces were interspersed with hostile forces. Fortunately, US forces were well-equipped with Night Vision Equipment and, with exception of the *Macho De Monte* and other specialized units, the PDF was not. Lacking this equipment, the vast majority of PDF soldiers fired on by AC-130 crews had no idea where fire was coming from. It appeared most believed they were under mortar attack and reacted as if they were. PDF who recognized the threat from blacked out AC-130s feared it and described the aircraft as the Devil in Disguise, since they could hear it but not see it. Once the gunship opened fire, there was little an adversary could do to escape and merely the sound of an AC-130 overhead was enough to prompt PDF surrender. Likewise, the sound of the AC-130's propellers overhead friendly positions resulted in a sense of security for ground forces that kept the PDF at bay.

"I would like to add my comments on the superb support that was provided to every Special Forces A-Team, Company, or BN and every Special Operations unit that I have been in and why they are such huge fans of the AC-130 *Spectre* Gunships. From Early Warning to devastating and complete destruction of the enemy forces the AC-130 'gets it done.' I well remember the covering fire on the Modelo Prison, and the Comandancia during operations in Panama. As we departed the facility with our precious cargo safely on one of our choppers, we all felt a sigh of relief as we watched the steady rain of fire on the enemy facilities. Those white rounds coming from the AC-130 silenced the enemy gunners trying to stop our departure. There are not enough words to adequately express the gratitude of all of us on the ground. Imagine a small split detachment moving in deep enemy territory and the comforting communications with our AF Brother on the other end of the radio as they orbited overhead clearing the way and providing covering fire as needed. Knowing what we had overhead, always gave us a sense of security that cannot be expressed unless you have walked in those shoes. Talk to any Special Ops or Special Forces troop and you will see a smile of delight when you ask about the capabilities of the mighty AC-130 and the accuracy of the covering fire only they could provide." Major General Gary L. Harrell, US Army (Ret.)

Overall Munitions Effectiveness: A BDA assessment of AC-130 targets engaged revealed the anti-personnel and anti-material capabilities of AC-130 ordnance were acceptable, but a need for a better capability against concrete structures was needed. The PDF Headquarters was badly battered and burned, but mostly on the upper floors because the AC-130's standard 105 High Explosive round could not reliably penetrate concrete.

BLUE ON BLUE/TF GATOR.[38]

The near-fratricide incident between AP-07 and the TF-Gator element at position Echo was thoroughly investigated. Research revealed difficulties in operating in complex urban terrain and a series of errors by multiple parties. It is also important to note TF-Gator soldiers were not informed of the *Acid Gambit* mission and, with exception of *Team King*, had no idea friendly forces were near their blocking positions as they surrounded the La Comandancia complex. The situation began when M113 Track Commanders on position Echo fired towards upper floors of the high-rise buildings and La Comandancia which was mistaken for PDF AAA fire. Though firing in the air was strictly prohibited by the Rules of Engagement (ROE) because of helicopter traffic at low altitude, TF-Gator gunners were suppressing PDF fire and likely not aware they were endangering helicopters, including the blacked-out Command and Control helicopter flying above Ancon Hill.

Regardless of this consideration, the primary contributing factor to the blue on blue event was a single point failure of IFF brought on by the crew of AP-07 who forgot to turn on the GLINT after the *Acid Gambit* mission. Contrary to AP-07 crew observations during the mission, the investigation revealed all three of 2Lt Rubin's M113s and personnel were properly marked with GLINT tape, but the markings were faint since position Echo was dark and the GLINT

38 The color blue is code for friendly forces, therefore, a blue force firing on another blue force is known as "blue on blue" fire AKA "friendly fire."

was off. Review of AP-07's BDA video recording revealed GLINT tape markings were visible during certain aspects of the gunships orbit via reflection from distant street lights, but were not bright as they would have been if illuminated by the GLINT, and went unnoticed. Furthering errors in IFF, smoke, and obstacles in urban terrain resulted in the fire-control officer and sensor operators' misidentifying the M113s as V-300s.

From a ground perspective, it is likely the attack could have been stopped after the first attack had AP-07's fire not been mistaken by 2Lt Rubin as PDF mortar fire; but, since he had not worked with an AC-130 before, it's understandable how that mistake could happen. LT Nabb was familiar with AC-130 fire and suspected Rubin's platoon was being attacked by AP-07, especially when PVT Miller was being chased down Avenue De Los Poetas. When LT Nabb radioed concerns to his Battalion Fire Support Officer, CPT Guidry, AP-07 had ceased firing because of approaching friendly vehicles. Nevertheless, suspecting something wasn't right, CPT Guidry directed a cease fire and AP-07 was re-tasked to Ft Amador.

A few days later, 16 SOS commander Lt Col Billy Napier met with the Lieutenant Colonel James Reed, TF Gator commander. After reviewing AP-07's Bomb Damage Assessment (BDA) video tapes, it was painfully clear Capt Hughes crew had in fact fired on 2LT Rubin's platoon during two separate engagements. Lessons learned via this tragic event included the need for more positive Identification Friend or Foe (IFF) including marking beacons and covert strobes on friendly vehicles. Clearly an overreliance on GLINT for IFF was a single-point failure that was an unforeseen factor. The 40mm HEI Misch Metal restriction directed by Major Eisenbarth prevented collateral damage, but since it was the least lethal round on the AC-130, it was the primary reason nobody was killed.

In the end, 21 TF-Gator soldiers were wounded (one seriously) by AP-07's fire. Though everyone involved shared some level of responsibility for the near lethal outcome, the crew of AP-07 shouldered the brunt of responsibility for single-point IFF failure.

SEAL support at Punta Paitilla Airport: AP-02 made every effort possible to support SEAL team 4's mission, but their aircraft proved to be irreparable, even after changing fire-control computers. Lt Col Frakes was a highly skilled pilot with extensive combat experience in Vietnam. He realized the risk of firing "in the blind," which could have been done, but only with increased risk to the SEALs. When Golf platoon closed within danger-close parameters of the PDF and began taking fire, Lt Col Frakes faced a tough decision. Without an operational fire-control system, nobody could be certain where AP-02's shots would go and the risk of fratricide to the SEALs already wounded and those maneuvering to assist them were unacceptable. Had AP-02 fired in the blind and ironically injured or killed the SEALS they were trying to protect, the situation would have been much worse than it already was. After AP-02 was replaced by AMASS-12, there were no requests for fire support from the SEALs and the ground situation was under control.

ACCOLADES AND MAJOR LEVEL AWARDS

The 1st Special Operations Wing won the Schilling Award for 1990 from the Air Force Association for its actions.[39] The 16th SOS crew led by Capt Charles "Greg" McMillan received its MacKay Trophy at the Pentagon on July 15, 1990. Capt Transue's crew was awarded the William H. Tunner Award for their actions at Rio Hato. Capt Gabreski earned the USAF Academy's 1989 Jabara Award for his actions at the Pacora River Bridge.[40] The crew of AMASS-11 was recognized as the Air Force crew of the year for 1990 and LT Col James Strength was recognized as Air Force Reserve Navigator/FCO of the year. An added note: AMASS-11's refusal of the order to fire is posted in the entrance lobby to the Air National Guard commissioning school in Nashville, TN, as an appropriate example of when it is legal to refuse to follow a legal order and is taught as such in the school itself.

1990 MacKay Trophy Recipients/AP-06 Crew

AC	Capt Charles McMillan
CP	Capt John Hicks
NAV	Capt William Lane
FCO	Capt Michael Radford
EWO	Capt Phillip Ladd
FE	SMSgt Michael Hosenbackez

39 "History of the 1st Special Operations Wing, 1 January 1990-31 December 1990," vol I, 29, 34. (all extracts are unclassified).

40 Capt Gabreski is the son of WWII and Korean Fighter Ace, Francis S. Gabreski.

TV	MSgt Jerry Andersen
IR	TSgt Glenn Lemay
AG	TSgt Derral Skinner
AG	SSgt Mark Johnson
AG	TSgt Bruce Greishop
AG	SSgt Stephen Jones
AG	TSgt Tony May
IO	SSgt Larry Bower
MC	Lt Col Billy Napier

1990 Tunner Award Recipients/AP-04 Crew

AC	Capt Mark Transue
CP	Capt Scott Taylor
PIL	Capt John Viglione
NAV	Capt Edward Appler
FCO	Capt Phillip Bradley
NAV	1Lt Dennis Beatty
EWO	1Lt Stephen O'Connor
FE	SSgt William Jennings
FE	TSgt Guy Davis
IR	MSgt Fred Kramer
TV	SSgt Bill Jackson
AG	MSgt Steven Hicks
AG	TSgt William Walter
AG	TSgt Wayne White
AG	SSgt Bernard Gilbert
AG	Sgt Barry Clark
IO	SSgt Frank Demchencko
IO	SSgt Michael McCarthy

1990 Air Force Reserve Crew of the Year/ AMASS-11 crew

AC	Maj Clay McCutchan
CP	Maj Michael Milton
NAV	Capt Bruce Fernald
FCO	Maj James Strength
EWO	Capt Adrian Wells
FEM	Sgt Tom Grimes
TV	MSgt Walter Watley Sr
IR	Sgt James Dombrosky
AG	TSgt Richard Kelly
AG	TSgt Billy Harcus
AG	TSgt Steve Gardinier
AG	TSgt Larry Johnson
AG	SSgt Jeffrey Choplin
IO	Sgt Jerry Allen

SITUATION REPORT: AUGUST 1990

In late July 1990, the President of Iraq, Saddam Hussein, ordered his Army to mass along Iraq's border with Kuwait. Citing an ages old territorial claim, he directed his military to seize the neighboring country of Kuwait. The Iraqi Army crossed into Kuwait on August 2, 1990 and in a matter of hours, Kuwaiti security forces were defeated. The Iraqi Army occupation of Kuwait City sent shock waves throughout the region. On August 3, the United Nations Security Council passed Resolution 660 demanding a full withdrawal, but Saddam refused to comply.

Throughout the western world, Iraq's invasion of Kuwait was seen as an incremental step to seize Saudi Arabian oil fields and processing facilities bordering Kuwait. If Hussein seized Saudi Arabia, he could manipulate a large percentage of the world's crude oil supply. If that were to happen, a worldwide crisis would quickly evolve, as Saudi Arabia supplied vast quantities of crude oil to European Allies of the United States. At a minimum, an Iraqi invasion of Saudi Arabia would wreak havoc on the European economy.

Recognizing the risk to Saudi Arabia, President of the United States, George H.W. Bush, offered military forces to help defend Saudi Arabia. Initially, Saudi Arabia's King Fahd resisted any notion of foreign military forces on the sacred land of the Kingdom. Not until King Fahd received an alarming intelligence briefing detailing the capability of Saddam Hussein's Army did he recognize the danger he faced.

> "The King agreed once the USG offered US force deployments after a scary intel briefing. I was in the meeting between King Fahd, SecState Baker, SecDef Cheney, CJCS GEN Powell, GEN Schwarzkopf, Lt Gen Horner, et al as a member of LTG Yeosock, CG, ARCENT and 3d Army's staff." **Lieutenant Colonel (Ret.) Michael Taylor,** US Army Special Forces[41]

After King Fahd agreed to allow US military forces to enter Saudi Arabia, the Commander of United States Central Command (CENTCOM), General Norman Schwarzkopf, ordered a mass troop deployment to Saudi Arabia under the code name Operation *Desert Shield*. To facilitate a quick response, Central Command Air Forces (CENTAF) commander Lt Gen Charles "Chuck" Horner, directed a complex air transportation bridge to fly mass numbers of U.S. troops into Saudi Arabia. By August 20, twenty thousand

---

41 LTC, Michael E. Taylor, US Army Special Forces, was Advisor to 7th Battalion, 2d Brigade, Saudi Arabian National Guard, Office of the Program Manager, Saudi Arabian National Guard Modernization Program (OPM-SANG). Mar 2015.

troops were in place in Saudi Arabia. In the following weeks, thousands more troops deployed to Saudi Arabia.

Over time, Operation *Desert Shield* rivaled the scale and scope of a World War-III scenario between NATO and the Soviet Union. Coalition and Iraqi Armies were massing on both sides of the border in a tremendous show of force of conventional military power.

Unlike SOF-centric military operations that occurred in Grenada and Panama in the 1980s, SOF was expected to play a minor role during Operation *Desert Shield*. Commanding the SOF contingent for CENTCOM was Commander, Special Operations Command Central Command (SOCCCENT), U.S. Army Colonel Jesse Johnson. By mid-August, Hurlburt's 1st Special Operations Wing (1 SOW) was directed to prepare for deployment while an Advanced Echelon (ADVON) team flew to Riyadh to search for a SOF operating base.

Finding a suitable facility to operate from was challenging since there were no previous site surveys or operations plans for basing in Saudi Arabia. Eventually, the ADVON team settled on King Fahd International Airport (KFIA), located near Dammam, about 170 miles from the Kuwaiti border. Since the airport was still under construction, facilities were crude, but the runways, taxiways, and parking areas were complete. From that point on, KFIA became the destination for 1 SOW AC-130, MC-130 and MH-53 aircraft. Aircraft began to deploy in late August 1990.

COMMAND AND CONTROL (C2)

Not long after arrival at KFIA, Air Force Special Operations Command Central (AFSOCCENT) commander Col George Gray III, discovered his AC-130 squadron had been taken away from him and assigned to CENTAF commander Lt Gen Horner.

This seemingly odd arrangement resulted from a long-standing conflicted history between SOF and conventional forces Command and Control (C2). Though divisions between SOF and conventional forces were often needed for Operational Security (OPSEC) reasons, they also fostered an environment of mistrust. Gen Schwarzkopf had dealt with C2 issues in Grenada and Lt Gen Horner dealt with C2 issues in Panama. Because of past experiences, both Gen Schwarzkopf and Lt Gen Horner wanted absolute control over all "warfighters" in theater.

> "They (SOCCENT) also are concerned that they will be ignored or misused by the 'big Army,' a concern that is often justified. I had discussed these attitudes with General Schwarzkopf in February of 1990 because of the lessons I had learned from previous joint exercises." **Gen (Ret.) Charles "Chuck" Horner**[42]

When Lt Gen Horner pulled the AC-130 away from SOCCENT control, Col Johnson felt it was an infringement on special operations assets under his command. When Col

42 Letter from Gen (Ret.) Charles "Chuck" Horner, to Author, Jan 2015.

Johnson attended the component commander meeting in Riyadh, he requested AC-130s be pulled back to SOCCENT, but Lt Gen Horner flatly rejected his request. Horner clearly felt his unity of command would be infringed if his staff did not control all strike aircraft. The situation was mitigated somewhat after Col Johnson asked Lt Gen Horner what would happen when he needed the gunships to support SOF; Horner said, "Not a problem, Jesse. If something comes up, just ask, and I'll give you everything you need."[43]

Col Johnson and Col Gray remained skeptical regarding Lt Gen Horner's promise, but Horner won the battle for operational control of the AC-130. Shortly thereafter, the 16 SOS sent four company grade officers to the Tactical Air Control Center (TACC) at Riyadh to assist mission planning efforts.

THREAT ASSESSMENT

Iraqi Integrated Air Defense System (IADS):

This system was considered one of the most formidable air defense systems in the Middle East. The IADS was capable and modern, consisting of European and Soviet Anti-Aircraft Artillery (AAA) guns and radar/infrared-guided Surface-to-Air Missiles (SAMS). The IADS was centrally led by the Air Defense Operations Center (ADOC) in Baghdad and managed by Sector Operations Centers (SOC) in specific regions. It was equipped with redundant Command

43 Email from Lt Col (Ret.) Randy Durham, to Author, Mar 26, 2014.

and Control features and connected by the French-built "Kari" Command and Control system set up according to fundamental Soviet doctrine. The IADS threat to low-altitude, slow-flying aircraft such as the AC-130 was high.

Mobile Surface to Air Missile Systems (SAMS): Another dimension of radar-guided threats were mobile SAMs. These systems were considered wild cards since they could travel long distances undetected and pop up without warning. The AC-130 was equipped with limited Electronic Counter Measure (ECM) jamming capabilities against certain threat radars.

> "Having served as the 1st SOW, Weapons and Tactics Officer, I was well aware of the capabilities or lack thereof, of the AC-130 against radar guided SAMs, particularly later generation mobile SAMs such as the SA-6 and the SA-8. The cliché expression used to instruct student AC-130 aircrew members on the importance of avoiding such radar guided SAMs systems was, 'They fly; we die.'" **Maj Jack Flanders.**[44]

Infrared Guided Missiles

By 1990, technology and proliferation of MANPADS ushered in in a new dimension of threat weapon capabilities with modern SA-14 and SA-16 missiles. These systems were equipped with cooled IR seekers and extended range up to 14k ft. AGL. Because of the portability of these mis-

44 Letter from Maj (Ret.) Jack Flanders to Author, Mar 2015.

siles, AC-130 crews expected them to be found anywhere Iraqi forces were located. There were incremental Infrared Countermeasure (IRCM) improvements made to the AC-130H during the 1980s, but offensive and defensive tactics remained fundamentally identical to those used twenty years earlier in Vietnam.

> AAA Guns: The Iraqi Army employed numerous optical and radar directed AAA guns ranging from 14.5mm through 100mm. AC-130 crews were trained to evade traced-optical AAA, but untraced-radar directed AAA was a serious threat to the AC-130.

> Fighter Aircraft: The Iraqi Air Force was equipped with modern fighter aircraft including the Mirage F1, SU-25, MIG-23 and MIG-29. They were also equipped with Mi-24, Mi-8 and Mi-17 helicopters. All Iraqi fighters presented serious threats to AC-130 operations unless either they were escorted by Coalition fighters, or the fighter threat was suppressed or eliminated.

AC-130 Limiting Factors

To mitigate threat levels of MANPADS and optical AAA, TACC mission planners mandated operational altitude over contested airspace as fourteen thousand ft. AGL and above. Unfortunately, this altitude was problematic for the AC-130H operations. Though the AC-130 could climb as high as eighteen thousand ft. to operate, performance was poor, accuracy suffered, temperatures dropped to subzero, and crews required use of supplemental oxygen.[45] Because of high operational altitudes, 20mm guns were ineffective and both 40mm and 105mm guns were only effective on soft targets such as personnel, light vehicles, and non-hardened facilities.

The Iraqi Army was equipped with modern Russian-designed armored vehicles including BTR-60, BMP-1, T62 and T-72 Tanks, but the AC-130 had little capability to destroy heavy armor.

Fighter and AC-130 communities were polar opposites. CENTAF fighter crews were well prepared for a large-scale conventional war. They had their own graduate-level training course (the USAF Fighter Weapons School) at Nellis AFB, but AC-130 crews were not represented in their curriculum, and fighters were not connected to the joint SOF community. On the opposite end of the spectrum, AC-130 crews were deeply connected to the joint SOF community and had little knowledge of conventional fighter and bomber tactics. The result was a level of misunderstanding between the two communities concerning knowledge of each other's true capabilities.

There was an attempt to form AC-130 and A-10 hunter-killer teams, but after a few trial missions, plans were dropped.

---

45 Crews were required to breathe supplemental oxygen anytime altitudes exceeded 10K ft. MSL. If a crew was required (or able) to climb above 18K ft. MSL, they were required to pre-breathe 100 percent oxygen for thirty minutes beforehand.

> "During Desert Shield we flew a handful of sorties consisting of a single AC-130 teamed with two A-10s on its wing. My personal experience flying these sorties resulted in a validation of the tactic, albeit not suitable for the upcoming battle environment. Firstly, the radar signature of an AC-130 with two A-10s on its wing could paint a target larger than a C-5. Secondly, our role was that of a spotter for the A-10 – basically a forward air controller giving the A-10 better, if any, night time capability. This tactic provided too narrow of an employment envelope, i.e., against a few hardened targets. All other expected assigned targets could be dispatched more efficiently and quicker by the AC-130 itself. And finally, the participating A-10 pilots justifiably expressed concerns over being tactically exposed at our operating altitudes and firing orbits."
> **Maj (Ret.) Phillipe LeBrun**

Considering all factors, AC-130 mission planners regarded ABGD as the only viable mission for the AC-130 until enemy threat weapons were interdicted to an acceptable level. Once Iraqi threat weapons were eliminated or reduced to an acceptable level, AC-130s would be needed to support SOCCENT ground forces as they advanced into Kuwait.

CHAPTER FIVE

OPERATIONS *DESERT SHIELD* AND *DESERT STORM*, 1990–1991

Spectre crews and maintainers based at King Fahd International Airport, Saudi Arabia endured high heat and periodic dust storms for the duration of Operation Desert Shield. (Credit: CMSgt (Ret.) Mike Longe)

On September 8, 1990, 16 SOS crews and maintainers stepped into a harsh, desolate, and scorching desert environment. The heat was oppressive, almost intolerable, routinely exceeding 120 degrees in the middle of the day. Escape from the heat was impossible, prompting crew chiefs and specialists to restrict their work schedule to nighttime hours. During the day, maintainers slept in the airport parking garage on cots and pallets of supplies. Most aircrew were holed up in the abandoned Manufacturing and Building Company (MABCO) compound about four miles from the runway. The walled compound was equipped with sixteen modular trailers fitted with window air conditioners that ran constantly to keep overall room temperature down to about 85 degrees. After a few days, Tent, Extendable, Modular, Personnel (TEMPER) shelters were delivered to the MABCO compound for maintainers and the support staff. Each TEMPER shelter was equipped with air conditioning that ran constantly, day and night.

Through the month of September, aircraft, crews, maintainers and support personnel trickled into KFIA. Eventually, the 1 SOW overtook most buildings in the MABCO compound, putting two to four crewmen to a room. Over time, the entire compound was filled with tents, support equipment, and a field clinic staffed with flight surgeons, medical technicians and dentists.

Water was an important commodity. It was easy to become dehydrated in the dry climate and several who forgot to drink were rehydrated through the insertion of saline intravenous injections that were administered by medical technicians.

Transportation at KFIA was limited, so a small group of gunners found a parking lot of abandoned vehicles and managed to get about a half dozen of them in working order. Crews used this odd collection of vehicles for transportation to and from the aircraft and MABCO compound.

Maintainers were negatively impacted by both heat and dust. Temperature inside an aircraft could be as high as 150 degrees during the day and persistent dust clouds caused serious problems for parked aircraft. Crew chiefs covered the front windows of aircraft with sheets and tarps to prevent solar heating from melting plastic items in the cockpit. Dust clung to everything, especially items covered in oil. Specialists manufactured long sleeves from a rubberized fabric material to place over the 20mm gun barrels to protect them from dust accumulation. Because of clinging dust, crew chiefs needed to wipe down flap tracks and jack screws and re-lube them every day. Engine compressor washes that were normally done every 45 days at Hurlburt needed to be done weekly.[1] Aircraft maintenance superintendent Chief MSgt Dennis "Chief 'O'" Olmstead essentially rewrote the book on how to maintain the aircraft in this new environment.

Since KFIA was still under construction, there was only one dining facility, which was equipped to feed several hundred people per day. Every day, a line of hungry people formed along all four sides inside of the building and extended out the main entrance. People stood in line for upwards of an hour waiting for an open spot at a table. Though the heat and smell of hundreds of sweaty people crammed into a small building was irritating, most thought it was worth the wait. Between the dining facility and Meals Ready to Eat (MRE), 1 SOW personnel were adequately fed.

The daily threat of lethal chemical poisoning hung over everyone's heads since Saddam Hussein was known to have

---

1 Email from TSgt (Ret.) Steve Feldmier to Author, 2014.

used chemical weapons in the past, and KFIA was in range of Iraqi SCUD missiles. Chemical warfare training drills occurred on a regular basis. All personnel were issued nerve agent antidote, anti-malaria tablets, three atropine auto-injectors, and three 2-PAM chloride auto-injectors. Personnel were also directed to take Pyridostigmine tablets to develop Soman nerve agent resistance. Thankfully, chemical warfare drills were short in duration since rapid heat buildup inside Mission Oriented Protective Posture (MOPP) gear caused excessive perspiration and rapid dehydration.

A "hurry up and wait" aspect took its toll on crewmen and maintainers, but they made special efforts to fight boredom with busywork. By late September, 1 SOW personnel had filled thousands of sandbags, strung razor wire on top of the compound walls and built bunkers from 40-foot shipping containers that could be used as emergency bomb shelters. Several squadrons of USAF A-10s arrived at KFIA and the US Army had set up a Patriot missile system between MABCO and the runway to counter the SCUD threat. When the US Army's 82nd Airborne Division arrived, they set up a giant Bedouin-type tent city north of the MABCO compound.

While everyone endured harsh Saudi Arabian environmental conditions through the month of September, they made the most of what they had. Aircrews acclimated themselves for night missions by sleeping during the day and staying awake all night. Popular pastimes included reading, playing poker or "gunners' rules" blackjack. As time wore on, boredom set in and long discussions ensued with many prophesying on events yet to come. Boring days turned into boring weeks with little entertainment.

Flying operations and proficiency training was difficult. There was no escaping the heat, and even at ten thousand ft. altitude, air flow through an AC-130H felt like it was coming out of a convection oven.

Not all the down-time was without drama. When a pilot of an AH-64 Apache was testing the fire-control system of an AH-64 Apache, he accidentally launched a live AGM-114 Hellfire missile into the makeshift bomb dump near the end of KFIA runway. The missile detonated on a pallet of bomb fuzes and it appeared KFIA was under attack. Luckily the explosion and fire were localized and there were no injuries. Word of the accident spread quickly and squelched all notions an attack was underway.

AC-130 live fire proficiency training was conducted on the nearby Saudi Air Force OED-43 Half Moon Bay range. The range allowed AC-130 crews to maintain training currency during weeks of uncertainty. The range also supported training of ground forces, who would call on the AC-130 for fire support once ground combat began.

The 16 SOS also conducted bilateral training with the US Army 5th Special Forces Group, USAF combat controllers, US Navy SEALs, and USMC Air Naval Gunfire Liaison (ANGLICO) personnel. Classes were scheduled and teams traveled to KFIA to attend sessions in the afternoon, then proceed to OED-43 after dark to practice calls for fire with gunship crews.

In October, Lt Col Billy Napier passed command of the 16 SOS to Lt Col Donn Kegel. Shortly afterward, Napier returned to Hurlburt and Kegel attended a planning conference in Riyadh.

> "Within two days of my assuming command, General Horner gave me verbal tasking at a commander's conference of his concept of operations for gunships. His primary mission was air base defense. We dedicated many sorties and developed detailed mission folders for this task. This tasking drove squadron training and mission planning efforts." **Col (Ret.) Donn Kegel**

By November, squadron leadership realized crewmen were losing proficiency at a steady rate. Since crews were unable to maintain perishable special qualifications because of limited training opportunities at KFIA, they needed to return to CONUS to train. To remedy the issue, Col Gray directed a limited crew rotation to and from Hurlburt to refresh noncurrent crews and enable fresh crews to be deployed to KFIA. Maintainers however, were not included in the rotations. The situation resulted in a bone of contention that would fester in the background for the duration of the deployment.[2]

Toward the end of November, boredom and complacency continued to be major hurdles, but morale improved as the outside temperature dropped. Crews spent less time holed up in their rooms and more time outdoors in an area between the MABCO trailers on makeshift benches and packing pallets. A rudimentary gym was put together in a

2 Email from TSgt (Ret.) Steven Feldmier, to Author, March 2014.

TEMPER tent behind one of the trailers. The Thanksgiving holiday came and went without much fanfare. Senior NCOs led the traditional serving of the Thanksgiving meal with turkey loaf and most of the fixings.

By early December, several enterprising crewmen scrounged enough supplies to build a 400 square foot wooden "Hooch" between two trailers. Constructed from whatever they could find laying around the airport or TAC compound, the structure was a welcome gathering place. Though it was solidly built, it resembled a shoddy redneck hunting cabin deep in the Alabama woods. Christened with the name "This Old Hooch" (a satirical name based on a television show), it quickly became the gathering place for all crewmen, especially after television, video tapes, and computer games were brought in. The KFIA Fire Department however, did not share the same enthusiasm as crewmen concerning "this Old Hooch" since they deemed it to be a fire hazard. Fortunately, after substantial negotiations and begging for forgiveness, the Fire Chief let it stand. It served as a CQ and recreation room for the duration of the war.

By mid-December, Iraq had been given an ultimatum to withdraw from Kuwait before January 15, 1991 or face a full-scale war. It seemed the ABGD mission that brought AC-130s to Saudi Arabia was about to morph into something more. Because of this change in posture, Maj Jack Flanders was sent to a planning conference to discuss potential gunship operations. The conference revealed numerous fighter and bomber mission plans, but few AC-130 plans.

As Christmas approached, morale calls and mail from home was heavy, especially for those who had been on station since September. On Christmas Day, Bob Hope and an entourage of USO entertainers and sports celebrities put on a show at KFIA. This was the last bit of fun for many who prepared themselves for a large-scale conventional war against Iraq.

In early January 1991, the 16 SOS was thrown a figurative curveball when Lt Gen Horner and his staff directed AC-130 gunships to support a pop-up situation in Mogadishu, Somalia. Their mission was to support Operation *Eastern Exit*, a noncombatant Evacuation Operation (NEO) of the US Embassy in Mogadishu.[3]

The Mogadishu International airport had been rendered unusable by fighting between warring clans, so neighboring Mombasa, Kenya was selected for temporary AC-130 operations. The US Navy maintained a small P-3 Orion detachment at Mombasa airport, which would be used to coordinate gunship operations into Somalia. An initial mission planning threat assessment discovered a known SA-2 missile site at Mogadishu. Intelligence analysts indicated the site was poorly maintained and most likely out of service. It was unknown if modern MANPADS existed, but older SA-7 systems were suspected. Lt Col Kegel commanded the deployment which included Capt Don Timpson and Maj Jack Flanders' crews and gunships *Grave Digger* and *Ghostrider.* Both aircraft flew missions from Mombasa into neighboring Somalia until diplomats and embassy personnel were evacuated. On January 7, 1991, the mission was complete and the aircraft returned to KFIA.[4]

---

3 Author Interview of Gen (Ret.) Chuck Horner, Feb 2015.

4 Letter to Author from Col (Ret.) Donn Kegel, Feb 2015.

> "Under a tight timeline, long distance, very little intelligence of threats near the Embassy, and minimal logistics support, the entire operation ran seamlessly. The squadron was the only USAF asset overhead to protect the USMC and Embassy personnel on the ground with the successful evacuation of 260 noncombatants to include 30 nationalities." **Col (Ret.) Donn Kegel**

By the second week of January, combat action in the Kuwait Theater of Operations was inevitable, but AC-130 crews were left in the dark regarding the roles and missions they were expected to perform. Lt Gen Horner and his TACC staff levied classification rules prohibiting anyone but the 16 SOS Squadron Commander and Operations Officer to view the Air Tasking Order (ATO). This was disturbing to AC-130 crews accustomed to working classified compartmentalized projects for USSOCOM. Not only were crews insulted, they wondered what the TACC had to hide. Fortunately, 16 SOS leadership took it upon themselves to violate the order by allowing aircraft commanders and Intelligence officers to view the ATO.

> "As we approached within 2 or 3 days before Day 1 of the Air Campaign, we were called to the WOC and given a copy of the ATO to study. The ATO actually described interdiction missions that we were well behind the power curve on planning. So, the rush was on belatedly to start mission planning and that went well until

> Intel found out that we had gained access to the ATO. The ATO, it seems, was still not considered 'releasable' to aircrews. But somehow Intel and Ops huddled up in a back room and decided to allow us to continue mission planning."
> **Maj (Ret.) Jack Flanders**

The ATO surprised aircraft commanders since there were no ABGD missions listed. Instead, gunship crews were tasked to fly interdiction missions along the Saudi-Iraq border. Expecting heavy tasking in the coming weeks, Lt Col Kegel requested his Operations Officer, Lt Col Ray Kinkaid, be sent to the TACC to add more power to the gunship TACC planning staff. Lt Col Waylett was then recalled to theater to assume the responsibility of 16 SOS Operations Officer.[5]

Just before the beginning of the air war, the last two gunship crews who had been on station since early September were replaced by Maj Paul Weaver and Capt Bill Preaskorn's crews. Maj Weaver's crew arrived on *Wicked Wanda* (69-6575) while *Predator* (69-6576) was sent back to CONUS for depot maintenance.

At about the same time, two AC-130H gunships, including the first Special Operations Force Improvement (SOFI) gunship *Night Stalker* deployed from Hurlburt to England as part of a USSOCOM deployment package in support of Operation *Desert Storm*. These aircraft remained under operational control of USSOCOM and were untouchable by CENTAF.

---

5 Letter to Author from Maj (Ret.) Jack Flanders, Mar 2015.

OPERATION *DESERT STORM*

Saddam Hussein proclaimed his army would fight the "mother of all battles" against the thirty-five nation coalition. Though Iraq had the fifth largest army in the world, the coalition was capable of defeating them with the right military equipment, training and strategy. Hussein's strategy was brute force, conventional armored tactics, and exhibitions of bravado to create fear and angst among his enemies. He was savvy to the effect of public perceptions and felt support for the war would stop when thousands of coalition soldiers were sent home in body bags. To inflict as many casualties as possible, Hussein was eager to face the coalition head-on in brutal ground combat, much like he did during his war with Iran. For this reason, Gen Schwarzkopf ordered a two phased attack to prevent large-scale ground combat until the large Iraqi Army was cut down to a more manageable size. The coalition's first phase was a bombing campaign commanded by Lt Gen Horner, referred to as the air war. During this phase, ground forces would remain south of the Kuwait/Iraq border until the air war had decimated Saddam's defense system, command and control infrastructure and a high percentage of Iraqi troops. The second phase would begin only after successful completion of the air war. A lot of faith was riding on Lt Gen Horner's TACC and their plans to systematically take down Iraq in a month long bombing campaign. This large and complex operation involving thousands of aircraft under CENTCOM's command meant the four AC-130s at KFIA were barely a dot on the TACC's horizon of capabilities.

Operation *Desert Storm* began on January 17, 1991 during a rare condition of cloud cover and moderate to heavy rainfall. Excessive dry heat of the previous months was replaced with a cold, wet, and slurry mess. For the first time, crews actually looked forward to putting on their chemical warfare ensemble for warmth.

Activity was high as scores of fighters overflew the airport on their way to bomb targets in Iraq.[6] With exception of Capt Preaskorn's crew who flew airborne alert, two more crews remained on ground alert all night.

Desert Storm AC-130H Aircraft Commanders (6)
Maj Jack Flanders
Maj Paul Weaver
Capt Bill Preaskorn
Capt Philippe LeBrun
Capt Don Timpson
Capt Paul Havel
Desert Storm Aircraft
69-6567 *Ghostrider*
69-6570 *Bad Company*
69-6572 *Grave Digger*
69-6575 *Wicked Wanda*

The first night of coalition airstrikes hit Iraqi IADS and C2 nodes hard. In return, Hussein ordered his Army to

6 History of the 1st Special Operations Wing, Hurlburt Field Florida 1 Jan-31 Dec 1991, Volume V, supporting Documents SD116.

launch SCUD missiles into Israel. In doing so, Hussein knew King Fahd would be in a precarious situation if Israel retaliated since Saudi Arabia would be perceived by other Arab nations as supporting Israel, a common enemy.

During the early morning hours of January 18, the Iraqi Army launched SCUDs from western Iraq into Israeli cities Tel Aviv and Haifa. Israeli Prime Minister Yitzhak Shamir began to take steps to retaliate, but President Bush pleaded for restraint. Fortunately, a US promise to eliminate the SCUD threat to Israel succeeded in holding off Israeli Retaliation. The same day, General Schwarzkopf directed Lt Gen Horner to locate and destroy Iraqi SCUD storage areas and launch positions. Iraq was known to have five permanent launch sites that could be targeted by bombers, but they had an unknown number of mobile Transporter Erector Launcher (TEL) systems which could be located just about anywhere.

On the night of January 18, three AC-130 missions were scheduled to target early-warning radar sites along the Saudi-Iraq border. Since a threat assessment by Intelligence analysts indicated an absence of radar threats, conditions were favorable for AC-130 operations.[7]

> "The targets considered valid by squadron leadership were Western Iraq-Saudi border early warning radar sites after careful consideration of intelligence and enemy reaction to gunship

7 Letter from Col (Ret.) Donn Kegel, to Author, Feb 23, 2015.

> flights along the border via intelligence gathering assets. We placed well qualified aircrew members in charge of preparing detailed mission folders for these targets under tight operational security." **Col (Ret.) Donn Kegel**

Aircraft commanders of the first AC-130 missions planned to cross into Iraq were Maj Jack Flanders (Ghost 01), Maj Paul Weaver (Ghost 02), and Capt Paul Havel (Ghost 04). Maj Weaver's mission was originally planned with A-10 escorts, but the attack aircraft cancelled before scheduled mission time because of weather.[8]

After takeoff and before reaching planned working areas, ABCCC diverted all aircraft to search for SCUD missile launch sites in Iraq. At one point in their mission, Ghost 02's EWO Capt Dixon Walters announced they were being tracked by SAM radar off the left wing, prompting Maj Weaver exit the area. After an entire night hunting for SCUDs all three crews landed at KFIA without finding any targets or seeing the ground because of the heavy undercast.[9]

SCUD hunting was a high priority for CENTAF but TACC mission planners found themselves in a predicament. The Iraqis chose to hide SCUDs in the daytime and launch at night and there were few aircraft under TACC command capable of locating and striking targets at night. The principal nighttime fighter was the F-117, but it was critical to

---

8 History of the 1st Special Operations Wing, Hurlburt Field Florida 1 Jan-31 Dec 1991, Volume V, supporting Documents SD117.

9 Letter from Col (Ret.) Donn Kegel, to Author, Mar 2014.

the bombing effort of Baghdad and could not be diverted for SCUD hunting. The only other aircraft with nighttime targeting capability were a few F-16 and F-15E fighters equipped with the Low Altitude Navigation Infrared for Night (LANTIRN) pod, the F-111 equipped with the Pave Tack pod and the AC-130. Because of the criticality of the SCUD hunting mission, CENTAF Deputy Commander of Operations Maj Gen John Corder directed all night capable aircraft to participate in the SCUD hunting effort. Considering the search area involved and the capabilities of their sensors, AC-130 crews viewed SCUD hunting as a find a needle-in-a-haystack task set forth in a vast sea of nothingness.

On the night of January 19, three AC-130s were tasked to perform interdiction missions into Iraq. When crews arrived, two were scrubbed for weather, leaving Ghost 04 (*Grave Digger*) as the sole gunship mission.

Commanded by Capt Philippe LeBrun, the crew of Ghost 04 received their pre-mission briefing with a surprise. Their mission was not near the border as expected, but was 140NM north of the border near the Euphrates River. Though the target area was outside of the Iraqi IADS, there were known AAA, mobile SAMs, and Iraqi MIGs in the area. The crew was confident they could navigate around known AAA and SAM sites, but they would be sitting ducks for Iraqi MIGs unless they were escorted by coalition fighters. Once the TACC promised a fighter Combat Air Patrol (CAP), Capt LeBrun accepted the mission.

> "I was tasked to lead mission planning for myself and two other AC-130s that would put one AC-130 well into central Iraq (140 miles north of the border). I assigned the deepest penetration to my crew. The other two missions to western Iraq would eventually be scrubbed/slid by one day. The Sq CC did ask my thoughts of such a deep mission. After considerable planning using provided intelligence reports and support of fighter CAP, I concluded that the mission was doable. Part of my consideration was that my assigned mission must be crucial and critical for such tasking of an AC-130." **Maj (Ret.) Philippe LeBrun**

Ghost 04 took off on time and headed for the border. Shortly after crossing into Iraq, they began detecting search radar activity, but navigated a course to keep out of launch range. Arriving overhead their assigned target area at 9,500 feet, heavy cloud cover below hindered their ability to acquire their primary target. Periodically, a break in the cloud layer revealed traffic and a railroad station, but the cloud deck below made target acquisition difficult.

While Ghost 04 maintained an orbit waiting for the weather to clear, AWACS announced an Iraqi helicopter was flying towards Ghost 04 and was likely hostile. While Capt LeBrun rolled out of orbit to evade the helicopter, AWACS called four fighters about forty miles away and closing fast. Believing they were being pursued by Iraqi MIGs and possibly an attack helicopter, Ghost 04's co-pilot, Lt Kevin Fox requested fighter support. AWACS advised Ghost 04 fighter support was not available, then announced a fast-moving aircraft was forty miles north and heading directly towards them.[10] Capt LeBrun performed a descending break towards the fighter at a ninety degree angle of bank, through the cloud deck until reaching an altitude of five hundred ft. AGL. The fighter made several turns towards them but left without penetrating the cloud deck. Unwilling to wait for another interceptor to arrive, Ghost 04 returned to KFIA in the middle of a SCUD alert.

During debrief, Capt LeBrun voiced his concern that he accepted a risky mission because a fighter CAP was promised, but no coalition fighter support arrived. Had it not been for the cloud deck, Ghost 04 would have been easy pickings for Iraqi MIGs. In response, Lt Col Kegel contacted the CENTAF/ADO, Col James Crigger, to discuss the situation. In the end, Col Crigger agreed the CAP needed to be much closer to AC-130 operations to be effective.[11] Nevertheless, LeBrun regarded the TACC's promise to support gunship operations as nothing more than lip service.

On January 20, three AC-130s were scheduled to fly interdiction missions to the same early warning sites they were unable to strike two days earlier. Weather was still a problem and Ghost 01's mission was cancelled before takeoff because of cloud cover in their target area. Capt Timpson's

---

10 Mission report of Capt Philippe LeBrun, Jan 1991 given to Author, 2014.

11 History of the 1st Special Operations Wing, Hurlburt Field Florida 1 Jan-31 Dec 1991, Volume V, supporting Documents SD117.

crew (Ghost 03) briefed and took off, but was diverted en route to their target to search for SCUDs. After more than four hours of uneventful searching, they returned to KFIA.

The same night, Ghost 02, commanded by Maj Flanders flew to Wadi al' Khirr Airfield, a suspected SCUD launch area. As Ghost 02 neared their target area, EWO Capt Bob Harlin announced they were being painted by MIG-29s who had apparently just taken off from Mudaysis Airfield, about 60 miles northwest. Fortunately, AWACS altered Ghost 02's heading while F-15 Eagles pursued the MIGs.

Arriving over Wadi al' Khirr, Maj Flanders rolled into search orbit. Sensor operators located an Early Warning (EW) radar site equipped with Flat Face and Squat Eye radars north of a runway on a bluff overlooking a wadi.[12] Maj Flanders established a firing orbit and their fire control computer malfunctioned after firing only a few rounds. Iraqis returned fire with 23mm, 37mm, and 57mm AAA. Maj Flanders noted most fire fell short, but copilot Lt Stoner observed tracerless 57mm airbursts above their altitude at about 11,000 ft. It was obvious Ghost 02 had the full attention of Iraqi AAA gunners, but fire was inaccurate and widely scattered. Sensing little threat to the aircraft, Maj Flanders elected to remain over target while the FCO attempted to remedy the fire control computer issue. After firing and re-tweaking three times, and spending almost thirty minutes over the target, Ghost 02 succeeded in damaging the radars. Afterward, Ghost 02 was directed to continue searching for

12 Mission synopsis from TSgt (Ret.) Ron Clark, given to Author, April 2014.

SCUDs, while periodically passing over areas of heavy barrage fire. When low on fuel and without locating a SCUD, Ghost 02 returned to KFIA.

Between missions, AC-130 crewmen were technically off duty, but had to remain prepared for SCUD attacks at all times. Most spent their off-duty time near a barrel fire outside *This Old Hooch*, telling stories and speculating on what their next mission had in store for them.

Crewmen gathered around the "Rumor Fire" outside "This Old Hooch."
L-R SMSgt Gary Thompson, MSgt Bob Heflin, SSgt Mark Schmauss, CMSgt Jack Hollyfield, SSgt John Blessinger, SSgt Clay Watson. (Credit: James May)

Rumors told when huddled around the burn barrel were both sometimes true and sometimes exaggerated. Because of this, the burn barrel was named the Rumor Fire and sometimes Liar Fire. Nevertheless, it was the gathering place for all crewmen during their off duty hours for the duration of the deployment.

By the evening of January 21, mission planners began tasking AC-130s as they did fighters. Each aircraft was assigned a 30x30 nautical mile "kill box" in which they were cleared to fire on any target deemed to be of military value. On this night, both crews were tasked to hunt SCUDs and the weather was clear. Ghost 02, commanded by Capt LeBrun took off first in *Grave Digger*, then proceeded to their target area in south central Iraq. Within their assigned kill box was an Iraqi command and control center, which was expected to be protected with AAA. About an hour later, Ghost 03 commanded by Capt Preaskorn took off in *Bad Company*, en route to their target area.

Once Ghost 02 entered Iraqi airspace, their mission seemed routine as EWO 1st Lt Charles "Randy" Davis directed navigation around several threat radars while en route to target. Once arriving overhead their target, Capt LeBrun rolled into a firing orbit and the crew began firing 105mm HE into two buildings. After scoring direct hits on one of the buildings, personnel were seen running towards nearby AAA sites. Within minutes, 23mm and 37mm and 57mm AAA guns opened fire. LeBrun saw heavy, but inaccurate 23mm and 37mm AAA tracer fire and traceless 57mm projectiles exploding above their altitude.

Maintaining a firing orbit, Ghost 02 began to fire at one of the AAA sites when the tell-tale flash and luminous streak of a MANPADS was seen leaving the ground from inside their orbit. Gunner Sgt Damon Duvall called a right break about the same time flight engineer SSgt George Neds called a right break for accurate AAA. Capt LeBrun broke hard right and the right scanner dispensed flares. About nine seconds later, the missile passed behind them, self-destructing well away from the aircraft. Because of the quantity and type of threats surrounding their target, it was obvious Ghost 02 was unlikely to complete its mission, so LeBrun requested a secondary target. AWACS was quick to task Ghost 02 to a priority hammer (suspected mobile SCUD) target nearby.

When Ghost 02 arrived over their new target, they discovered Flat Face and Squat Eye Early Warning (EW) radars. Wasting no time, they opened fire on both sites. After a few minutes, AWACS announced an SA-2 missile launch about thirty-five miles from the northwest. Knowing the SA-2 was probably past its effective range, he turned the aircraft to fly away from the site to lessen probability of being tracked. Suddenly, 1st Lt Davis received a SA-8 acquisition audio, then target tracking audio and signals on both ALR-69 and ALR-46. As Davis called a break, he engaged ECM pods and began dispensing chaff.

Capt LeBrun broke hard, then began a rapid descent passing 270 knots Indicated Air Speed (KIAS) before copilot 1st Lt Fox "chopped" the throttles to flight idle. About the same time the SA-2 dropped off, Davis announced an SA-8 launch. Now, with another radar guided missile closing in fast, LeBrun descended to 3,500 ft. AGL in an attempt to break lock. After defensive maneuvers, ECM and chaff failed to defeat the missile, and with only a few seconds remaining before impact, LeBrun broke hard left at 85-degrees angle-of-bank and pulled the control yoke as far aft as it would go. Suddenly, there was a bright flash across the windscreen and the aircraft bucked as if the flight controls were unloaded. At this point, the smell of burnt explosive permeated the inside of the fuselage. Crewmen began to prepare for bail out, but LeBrun found he still had full control of the aircraft. Surprisingly, when the FE scanned gauges, all systems appeared normal. The condition on the gun deck however, was anything but normal. During defensive maneuvers, negative and zero G-conditions caused spent shell casings, live 40mm ammunition, tools, parachutes, and gunners to float over the gun deck. When LeBrun pulled out of the dive, the force of 3.5 to 4 Gs violently slammed everything and everyone to the floor.

It wasn't over yet, however. Just when the crew of Ghost 02 felt they had cheated death and won, the EWO announced they were being tracked by a SA-6 radar. Since *Grave Digger* was already at about 3,500 feet MSL, there wasn't much more altitude to lose, but Capt LeBrun had no choice other than to dive towards the desert surface to break lock. The aggressive dive, increased airspeed, and kinetic energy could have resulted in a spectacular crash onto the desert floor, but LeBrun and Fox managed to pull out at about three hundred ft. AGL. Surprisingly, the aircraft was responsive and everyone checked in with no injuries or damage. Afterward, LeBrun wisely exited the area at an altitude barely above the sand dunes. Once clear of the area, Ghost 02 climbed to ten thousand ft., dumped fuel and performed a controllability check to make sure the aircraft was safe to land.

As they neared KFIA, Capt LeBrun declared an IFE, completed a no-flaps landing, taxied to parking and shut down engines. Having survived an onslaught of AAA and radar SAMs, he remained in his seat collecting his thoughts, praying, happy to have brought his aircraft and crew back home.

The Squadron commander, Lt. Col Kegel, boarded *Grave Digger*, to discuss details of the mission. Capt LeBrun recommended Capt Preaskorn's crew be recalled immediately, but it was too late, they had already crossed the border into Iraq.

> "Lt Davis and I approached Col Gray who was seated behind his desk. We both saluted and I said, Capt LeBrun and 1st Lt Davis reporting as directed sir. Col Gray stood and returned our salutes. I told Col Gray that I had broken one of his aircraft really bad. He walked from behind his desk and shook my hand and placed his left hand on my shoulder and said a heartfelt welcome back." **Capt Phillipe LeBrun**

Meanwhile, crew chiefs SSgt Steve Feldmier and SSgt Robert Knoll inspected *Grave Digger.* The over-G event had popped rows of rivets along the wing and all four engines were over-torqued. All four propellers had to be changed, which used up the entire supply of spares in the theater. Nobody could tell exactly how many Gs the aircraft experienced since the cockpit G-Meter was pegged at five. Incidentally, the underside of the fuselage showed signs of blast damage with chipped paint and scratches behind the

APN-59 radome. It appeared as if Ghost 03 had flown into a cloud of fragments from the warhead's proximity burst.

Col Gray called the CENTAF/DO Maj Gen Corder to request abort of Capt Preaskorn's mission. Surprisingly, Corder refused to recall Ghost 03.[13] Meanwhile, Capt Preaskorn had already crossed the border at a point about one hundred miles west of the hornet's nest kicked up by Ghost 02.

All was fine until about fifty miles into Iraq when Ghost 03 encountered a wall of Iraqi air defenses. Their first indication of trouble was an SA-6 acquisition radar at their 6 o'clock position that quickly handed over to a Target Tracking Radar (TTR) that locked on to the aircraft. Capt Preaskorn immediately began violent evasive maneuvers while descending rapidly to evade the SAM's engagement envelope. At the same time, Ghost 03's EWO, 1st Lt Rick Masters applied electronic countermeasures and began dispensing chaff. While trying to shake the SA-6, an SA-8 radar began tracking them as well. Masters checked jamming pods to ensure both SAMs were being countered and noticed a failure in each pod. Fortunately, a combination of partially-effective jamming, use of chaff, and a lot of luck, the gunship crew was able to prevent launch of either SAM.

Preaskorn's ordeal was far from over since Ghost 03 was flying directly into a heavy AAA barrage. By this time, all chaff had been expended and the jamming pods were partially capable. With no options available, Capt Preaskorn

---

13 Email from B Gen (Ret.) George Gray III, to Author, April 2014.

was forced to reverse course and charge past the same mobile SAM sites that he had just defeated, as they made their way back to the Saudi border. Preaskorn knew he had to descend to a dangerously low altitude to defeat tracking radars with ground clutter, so he dropped to one hundred feet AGL and pushed the throttles as far forward as they would go.

With little starlight or visual points, Ghost 03 skimmed across the sand dunes at a speed nearing 300 knots. While both pilots scanned ahead for obstacles, flight engineer TSgt Alan Garrett, did the same on night vision goggles and IR sensor operator TSgt Glenn Lemay trained his IR ball forward, also watching for obstacles.

Once Ghost 03 crossed the border, Navigator Capt John "Nasty" Nicastri announced a return to Saudi airspace. As Preaskorn began to climb to nine thousand ft. crewmen breathed a sigh of relief…they made it out without a scratch.

Checking in with AWACS for an alternate mission, Ghost 03 was diverted to Riyadh for a base security emergency. Upon arrival, they discovered there was no actual security plan to work with the AC-130 or personnel trained in radio communications to coordinate with. Desperate to resolve the reported issue, Lt Col Kinkaid was approached by the TACC/DO to take matters into his own hands.

> "I was approached by the DO and asked to work with the Security Forces in a 'calls for fire' capacity. I went with Security personnel to what I believe was a parking garage with a view of the street in front of the building…after contact

> with the aircraft was established the call went out that the 'THREAT' no longer existed. It turned out that it had been a 'rent a cop' playing with his weapon and it discharged. I followed up with the Security folks to see why they didn't have the team that had worked the ABGD plan with the gunship folks. I was told that all the cops with that knowledge had forward deployed and that none of them were in position at the bases they had experience with...kind of negated a large effort/application of the gunship role"
> **Lt Col (Ret.) Ray Kinkaid**

Ghost 03 was released to return to KFIA while Lt Col Kinkaid was advised the personnel previously trained for ABGD with the AC-130 during Desert Shield were no longer in place. At that point, it was obvious AC-130 employment for ABGD was no longer a valid mission.

The nearly fatal missions of January 21 were an awakening experience for AC-130 crews. In one night, the 16 SOS had inflicted minimum damage on Iraqi targets and almost lost two of the four AC-130s deployed and twenty-eight *Spectre* crewmen. One aircraft needed depot-level repairs, so it was effectively out of the fight. While it was painfully obvious to AC-130 crews they could not operate effectively in the current threat environment in Iraq, political pressure to eliminate the SCUD threat to Israel came straight out of President Bush's Oval Office in Washington D.C. and "NO" was not an acceptable answer regarding SCUD hunting missions. Lt Gen Horner was in a pinch to eliminate the SCUD threat. Since there were few aircraft capable of night operations under his command, political pressure to eliminate the SCUDs threat kept AC-130s in the hunt regardless of a high probability of aircraft and crew loss.

Powerless to do anything about it, AC-130 crewmen knew their luck would run out soon if they continued to be sent into a mobile radar SAM environment. Complicating the issue was the observation that current intelligence was typically a day or two behind. Confirmed threats listed on the maps may no longer be valid while areas indicated to be clear of threats could be teeming with radar SAMs which might not be detected until it was too late.

> "It was particularly troublesome for me to listen to the 1st SOW's own Intel and Ops briefers make the fine distinctions over "CONFIRMED" and "POSSIBLE" when briefing the threat permissibility in the AC-130 operating areas. The grim reality was that since SA-6/SA-8 systems were mobile and there was very little likelihood of ever having such a system identified as CONFIRMED for more than a few minutes."
> **Maj (Ret.) Jack Flanders**

> "This intelligence method of reporting threats was a key issue for aircrews and me as the squadron commander. It was an awkward method used by the TACC planning cell(s), intelligence community, and airborne command and control

> platforms and placed gunships at a greater risk."
> **Col (Ret.) Donn Kegel**

Another aggravating factor was the fact that AC-130 crews were promised a fighter CAP that wasn't there when needed badly. Without fighter support, crews found themselves alone, in the middle of Iraq with nothing but their wits, training, and luck to prevent them from being blown out of the sky.

Tactics mandated by the TACC were questionable. The kill-box tactic that worked well for high altitude/high speed fighters did not work well for low altitude/low speed AC-130s. Even if a lone gunship located an Iraqi Motorized Rifle Division in a kill box, their capability to find, fix, track, target, and engage multiple targets before being shot down was dubious at best. In that case, the situation could be viewed as a who found whom dilemma with the deck stacked against the gunship.

All things considered, morale could not have been lower. The overwhelming theme shared by a majority of crewmen was they were being sent on suicide missions for no reason other than political appeasement, and nobody in the chain of command could stop it. There was no shortage of allegations and finger pointing, so Lt Col Kegel directed an emergency Commanders Call to allow crews to voice their concerns. Col Gray was present and recognized something needed to be done quickly.

> "The SCUD hunt placed gunships into the scenario over the objections of many. The efforts of

Ray Kinkaid and me to cancel missions, decline missions of high risk, monitor airborne tasking, and keeping Col Gray informed are significant activities that changed rapidly each night, almost each hour. Col Gray and I had no control over airborne tasking to aircrews and found changes to mission tasking occurring up to take off time based on the TACC assessment of previous Allied aircraft mission progress and their own intelligence assessment. War is chaotic and never static. Mission effectiveness clarity and enemy response is going to create confusion and much uncertainty." **Col (Ret.) Donn Kegel**

Col Gray contacted Maj Gen Corder to discuss the situation and the potential to lose all gunship capability to radar SAMs leaving no capability for the ground war. Aside from aircraft loss, there was potential for up to 56 casualties. Corder agreed with Gray and granted him the authority to approve or disapprove AC-130 missions. Furthermore, if crews were redirected by the TACC or AWACS in-flight, they were instructed to contact Gray on SATCOM for a "sanity check" before accepting the tasking.

"I told Maj Gen Corder we were doing everything in our power to support Gen. Schwarzkopf's campaign plan but sending AC-130s on suicide missions won`t help. He agreed and told me that from now on I would be the final approval authority on all gunship missions." **Brig Gen (Ret.) George Gray III**

Meanwhile at the TACC, Lt Col Kinkaid had his own problems to deal with. Questionable gunship missions were being added to the ATO without coordinating with the TACC AC-130 planning staff. One mission plan sent an AC-130 directly over Baghdad, which would have almost certainly resulted in aircraft and crew loss before reaching their target. Fortunately, Lt Col Kinkaid scrubbed that mission before it was tasked in the ATO.

The SCUD-hunting effort also increased friction between the TACC staff and AC-130 planning staff at Riyadh. An unsavory situation came to a boil when a fighter planner pouring a cup of coffee in the TACC kitchen made a wisecrack about AC-130 crews running away from threats like cowards. Overhearing the comment, Lt Col Kinkaid jumped up, cornered the fighter planner and "discussed" the situation in an epic one-on-one counseling session. Noting the commotion, Maj Gen Corder intervened to keep the two from launching into a full-fledged fist fight.

Corder wanted answers and Kinkaid was happy to oblige. Rather than defending AC-130 capabilities and limitations, he requested all fighters adopt AC-130 tactics and limitations. Curious to where he was going with his demands, Corder and the fighter planner listened as Kinkaid demanded all fighters approach their target under 10,000 ft. AGL, slow to 180 knots, then orbit the target two or three times before engaging. If they were not shot down during that time, they were prohibited from using afterburner to escape a threat and could only descend to break lock of any radar threat. The fighter planner replied "that would be suicide!" Kinkaid fired back verbally "well, considering the maximum performance of an AC-130, that's exactly what you are tasking the gunships to do!" After Lt Col Kinkaid finished his impromptu instruction in gunship tactics and vulnerabilities, the learning curve of the entire non-gunship TACC staff increased and, it appeared they got it. Though it appeared the agreement between Maj Gen Corder and Col Gray resulted in sane rules of engagement, enthusiasm was short-lived.

The very next night, January 22, Maj Flanders' crew was alerted for a SCUD-hunting mission. It was an unusual tasking since the crew was ordered to go directly to their aircraft without mission planning and prepare to take off. Instructions were that they would receive an intelligence and operations briefing while strapping into their seats. This "Secret Squirrel" situation did not set well with Flanders and his crew who demanded to see details of the mission plan, but only the aircraft commander was allowed to view it.

When Maj Flanders analyzed the mission plan, he discovered they were being sent to a cluster of airfields called H-3, close to the Jordanian border and more than 750 miles from KFIA. The H-3 complex was one of Iraq's primary air bases which was equipped with concrete aircraft shelters, 23mm, 37mm, 57mm and 100mm AAA, and SA-2, Roland and Crotale radar SAMs. Furthermore, MIG fighter/interceptor aircraft could respond within 15 minutes. The site was the closest Iraqi base to Israel and was suspected of hiding SCUDs. Flanders crew was tasked to fly to H-3, escorted by two F-15E Strike Eagles identified as Mazda Flight. The basic mission plan was to locate and destroy an 85-vehicle convoy near H-3. F-15Es were to go in first and drop ordnance to suppress Iraqi air defenses, then the AC-130 was to come in solo to clean up what was left.[14]

Maj Flanders believed the mission to be absolute suicide. He surmised the AC-130 would be easy pickings for Iraqi air defense systems and viewed the potential for a successful AC-130 mission as being zero percent.

Thinking the mission was an erroneous tasking, Maj Flanders took his concerns to Lt Col Kegel who called the TACC to refuse the mission. Surprisingly, the agreement between Maj Gen Corder and Col Gray made only hours earlier was trumped by a higher command authority that caused Corder to refuse cancelling the mission. The TACC staff advised Col Gray of the order to proceed.

> "As the Aircraft Commander, it was my duty to inform the unit commander as to whether or not I could successfully reach the target, successfully destroy the target and lastly, but somewhat important to me, successfully recover the aircraft and crew after destroying the target. In my assessment the answer to all three propositions was NO – the mission was not doable. I concede that it is the commander's prerogative, after

14 Mission synopsis from TSgt (Ret.) Ron Clark given to Author, April 2014.

> hearing the aircraft commander's assessment, to conduct risk management by considering the value of the target when weighed against the risks, even great risks, and decide to launch the mission anyway. That is essentially what happened. Lt Col Kegel and Col Gray agreed with my assessment of the mission, but confided that their hands were tied due to the high-level source of the mission tasking." **Maj (Ret.) Jack Flanders**

Having received his orders, Maj Flanders had no choice other than to accept the mission and return to his crew for a mission brief. His crew listened attentively as Flanders laid out the situation. After considerable wrath had been vented, the crew accepted their duty and launched on the mission under the call sign Ghost 01.

Meanwhile at the TACC, Lieutenant Col Kinkaid reviewed the tasked mission and noticed it had recently appeared in the ATO without indication of origin. He determined the mission was poorly laid out, and it appeared to be a political tasking that arrived from parts unknown. He calculated the distance to the working area and available hours of darkness. Since it would be near sunrise before Ghost 01 arrived in their working area, he was confident the mission would cancel before Flanders crew began their attack.

After their first aerial refueling, Ghost 01 did not have confirmation of a final target location and weather started to move in. After a three-hour flight, they arrived at their designated hold point, waiting for the F-15s to arrive, but they were a no-show. When Ghost 01 queried AWACS, they did not know where the fighters were, nor were they aware of any gunship plan. It turned out Lt Col Kinkaid's predictions were correct and the poorly-planned mission fell apart before Ghost 01 entered the target area.

When Col Gray discovered the error, he recalled Ghost 01 over SATCOM and the entire crew breathed a sigh of relief as they turned back towards KFIA.

> "We headed northwest to the H-3 Airfield Complex after tweaking our guns at the range. When we finally got to the area, there was a cloud deck below us at 9K'. We orbited south of the target area, waiting for the 'cleared hot' call to go in and engage what was left of the convoy. We waited and waited and waited, orbiting all the time. This was the quietest I had ever seen or heard on a Gunship. There was usually a lot of banter...kidding and joking and all the things we used to do to keep spirits up in difficult situations. There was none of that aboard Ghost 01 that night. Finally, not long before sunrise, we were recalled home, without having to go into the 'Hornets' nest." **TSgt (Ret.) Ron Clark**

Ghost 01's mission ended with an uneventful landing at KFIA, followed by a very eventful debrief. Maj Flanders vented his frustrations to all levels of leadership, and everyone agreed the crazy and suicidal tasking needed to end before a gunship and crew were lost flying missions they were not equipped to perform.

Col Gray was disturbed the TACC continued to task AC-130s to fly missions with low probability of success and high probability of aircraft loss. Since he was getting stonewalled by Maj Gen Corder, he wrote a personal letter to Lt Gen Horner explaining the situation and potential consequences if tasking into radar SAM areas continued.

> DEPARTMENT OF THE AIR FORCE [15]
> SPECIAL OPERATIONS
> COMMAND (AFSOCCENT)
> APO NEW YORK 09855
>
> Dear Gen Horner
>
> As we enter day seven of the air campaign, I need to elevate my concerns regarding AC-130 employment to you personally. Two nights ago, we almost lost Ghost 02 when he was engaged simultaneously by a SA-6 and SA-8 while on an armed recce mission looking for SCUDS and EW/CGI sites. The evasive maneuvers required to defeat this threat overstressed the aircraft. Following four prop changes and an FCIF, we will request approval for a one-time flight to Rhein Main Germany for heavy maintenance. Ghost 03 was on a similar mission later that

15 Col George Gray III letter sent to Lt Gen Chuck Horner on Jan 23, 1991 given to Author by Brig Gen (Ret.) Gray, in 2014.

evening. Based on intelligence reports of mobile SAM movement into the area during the preceding two days of bad weather and the experience of Ghost 02, I requested the TACC abort the mission. This was denied. Ghost 03 was also engaged by SA-6 and SA-8. Superior airmanship is all that brought these aircraft back. Last night, I monitored the planned SCUD search package composed of two F-15E and one AC-130. When the gunship arrived at its orbit point south of the target, they checked in with AWACS who wanted to know what they were doing there and if they had a mission number. When AWACS queried the TACC, they were told the AC-130 was to follow MAZDA flight (2 F-15E) into the target area providing no SAM threats had been detected. AWACS then advised the TACC that MAZDA flight had departed the area over an hour ago and were unaware of any threats in the target area. I then called the TACC directors to find out what was going on. He called me back a few minutes later and told me the gunship had RTB an hour ago. Rather than discuss the mission further, I called the gunship which was still orbiting, waiting for clearance, to terminate his mission and RTB.

Sir, this time the second consecutive night the gunship aircraft in this campaign has been committed with poor results. You and your staff have put together a brilliant, fast moving air campaign with 21st century weapons and tactics. The 20th century gunship isn't fitting into this phase of the scenario very well. My gunship crews are extremely concerned—not because they are afraid of combat, but because they know they can't survive in a SAM environment orbiting at ten thousand feet. Their EW equipment is not a penetration aid, it's a last-ditch survival tool. To be absolutely honest, they have lost trust and confidence in the ability of the TACC and CENTAF to employ this resource with a reasonable degree of risk.

Sir, I cannot fault the TACC for the problems we have encountered at this early stage of the air campaign. They have far too many other priorities and resources to worry about. The problem is simply one of focus. The TACC is trying to manage a fast-paced high-tech war. From my perspective their priorities are right on target and are doing a superb job. At this point, the gunship only detracts from their performance. We believe the AC-130 has a viable role in this war, however, this weapons system requires more planning and real time TLC in this high threat environment than the TACC should be asked to devote to its employment.

> Sir, we are behind you all the way but I need your help to save this unit. They are a great bunch of guys but are simply not trained or equipped to fly in a SAM environment.
>
> George A. Gray III, Col, USAF
> Commander

Thankfully, Col Gray's letter caught the attention of Lt Gen Horner who agreed to stand down AC-130 missions until specific rules of engagement were established.

> "On the afternoon of 23 Jan, the WOC received a call from the TACC which discussed a debrief item from Lt Gen Horner who basically said to stop the emotional appeals. He said he did not want to get anyone killed, but the SCUD hunting mission is political and must fly. He instructed AC-130 missions to go no further than 10 miles across the border, quickly destroy any target, and egress back to Saudi. Once back in friendly territory, request a new kill zone and repeat the sequence until bingo fuel is reached." History of the 1st Special Operations Wing [16]

Satisfied missions into radar SAM areas were off the table, crews began flying airborne alert missions on January 23 from a holding point ten miles south of the Iraq/Saudi

16 History of the 1st Special Operations Wing, Hurlburt Field Florida 1 Jan-31 Dec 1991, Volume V, supporting Documents SD117.

border. New Rules Of Engagement (ROE) allowed AC-130 crews to analyze threat potential real-time with onboard threat warning receivers instead of relying on days-old intelligence reports. Crews flew under the new ROEs for the next six days without being tasked to cross the border.

In late January, *Grave Digger* was flown to Germany for depot-level repairs, leaving *Ghostrider*, *Wicked Wanda*, and *Bad Company* as the only AC-130s in theater. At the same time, Saddam Hussein believed an incursion into Saudi Arabia would be the catalyst he needed to start a ground war to inflict heavy casualties on the coalition much like his Army did to Iran years earlier. To facilitate his plan, the Iraqi Army set their sights on the small, out-of-the-way and lightly-defended Saudi Arabian border town of Khafji. Located on the coastal highway near the shoreline of the Persian Gulf, Saddam Hussein viewed Khafji as a golden opportunity to capture American and Saudi prisoners to use as propaganda tools.

Much earlier in the *Desert Shield* campaign, eight Observation Posts (OP) were established along the Saudi border north and west of Khafji to observe Iraqi movements and collect intelligence of activity. These lightly-armed positions were manned by small teams from Marine Force Reconnaissance, Air Naval Gunfire Liaison Company, Army Special Forces, and Navy SEALs. A small SANG security force, supported by USMC artillery was located south of the town of Khafji.

About ten miles from Khafji city limits, approximately sixty thousand Iraqi Army troops, including 1st and 5th

Mechanized Division and 3rd Armored Division forces occupying an area north of the Saudi border known as the Al Wafra Forest. The town was centered on a large man-made agricultural oasis of fruit trees, vegetables, livestock and palm groves.[17] The area surrounding the Al Wafra Forest was nothing more than barren desert; however, regular vehicle-borne patrols emerged from the forest to keep an eye on coalition forces. There were almost daily exchanges of cross border fire between the US Marine Corps and Iraqi artillery including 9K52 Luna M, Free Rocket Over Ground-7 (FROG-7) rockets.

> "Residents of Khafji had not abandoned the city after Iraq invaded Kuwait. A few left after the invasion, but the majority stayed and the city remained occupied until several days after the air campaign began. In response to coalition air attacks, the Iraqis began retaliating by firing Soviet-made FROG 7 (free rocket over ground) rockets into Saudi Arabia. FROGs are notoriously inaccurate, but, after several days of relatively harmless launches, one FROG hit an Aramco oil refinery in Khafji. The oil storage facility burned in an impressive blaze of fire and dense black smoke for days. The civilian populace panicked and fled south at that time, leaving the city totally abandoned in 'no man's

---

17 Air Force Studies and Analyses Agency, "'Battle of Khafji,' Air Power Effectiveness in the Desert," *Small Wars Journal* 1 (U) (July 1996): 1—171.

land' between the front lines of the two opposing forces." **Lt Col (Ret.) Michael Taylor**

Since the beginning of *Desert Storm*, coalition forces centered on Khafji have been harassed by Iraqi artillery and FROG-7s. Available fire support included a small element of Marine AV-8 Harriers and AH-1 Cobra gunships as well as LAV-25-AT lightly armored vehicles. On-call alert aircraft included USMC FA-18 fighters, USAF A-10 and F-16 fighters. A sand berm about 15 ft. high was constructed directly in front of the OPs to prevent Iraqi armor from conducting a frontal assault. The city limits of Khafji were patrolled by the SANG in lightly armored V-150 scout cars.

On January 29, Marine reconnaissance and USAF JSTARS aircraft detected hundreds of Iraqi vehicles emerging from the Al Wafra Forest. Within a short period of time, Iraqi armored vehicles and troops began crossing the Saudi border en-masse.[18] Within a short period, all eight OPs were overrun as Iraqi armored vehicles and troops continued to cross the border into Khafji, overrunning Marine positions.

The ground situation was intense. In the chaos, two Marine LAV-25-ATs were hit by friendly fire during the withdrawal at OP-4 (one hit by another LAV-25-AT and the other by a Maverick missile fired by an A-10), resulting in the deaths of 11 Marines.

There was limited air support available to stop the large-scale incursion. All told, Marine AH-1, AV-8, and F/A-18

18 Ibid, Appendix N.

and USAF A-10 and F-16 fighters engaged armored vehicles until they expended all ordnance, but the number of targets was overwhelming. As the battle continued, Iraqi forces continued to pour into Saudi Arabia and it was evident the battle was much more than a temporary incursion.

In just a few hours' time, the low-key town of Khafji had become the focal point of Iraqi aggression into Saudi Arabia. Saddam's move caught Gen Schwarzkopf and Lt Gen Horner by surprise and neither were made aware of the event until Iraqi forces occupied the town of Khafji.

Once Lt Gen Horner realized the activity at Khafji was escalating into a major battle, he commanded air strikes destined for Iraq to be directed to Khafji. Soon, dozens of fighters arrived at hold points near Khafji to be called in by the Direct Air Support Center (DASC), who controlled Marine FACs flying in OV-10s over the battle area. As the night wore on, scores of fighters attacked hundreds of Iraqi vehicles near the border and northward into the Al Wafra Forest.

Just after midnight, Ghost 02 commanded by Capt Paul Havel took off on *Wicked Wanda* for a routine airborne alert mission. About two and half hours into their mission, they were redirected to Khafji for an emergency CAS mission for what was being reported as a pinned down SEAL Team. Since Khafji was almost directly on the border and fell within current AC-130 ROEs, Ghost 02 headed directly towards Khafji.

Arriving on station at 0305 hours, Ghost 02 contacted ABCCC who passed them to a Marine OV-10 FAC overhead the city. Fighters were attacking armored vehicles to the west and AAA barrage fire was heavy in areas. The FAC tasked Ghost 02 to search and destroy any and all Iraqi targets they could find north of Khafji along the coastal Highway.

> "...the first thing I saw looking out of the cockpit is I'm seeing all kinds of artillery flares all over the place. I saw the OV-10 dispensing decoy flares, and saw AAA on the north side of town, going in all directions. It wasn't really aimed. It was all just spray or pray barrage type fire. The first thing he said, Hey, I need your big gun. I need you to take out any targets north of town, and you're cleared in hot. So we went in."
> **Capt Paul Havel**[19]

Once overhead their working area, sensor operators located eight Iraqi BRDMs directly on the coastal highway. Just as they rolled in on the vehicles a 23mm AAA gun opened fire on them. Wanting to eliminate the threat before firing on the vehicles, Capt Havel directed his crew to take out the AAA gun. Once Capt Havel established a firing orbit on the gun, the crew attempted to fire a 105mm HE round, but the gun failed to fire. Further attempts to fire the gun failed and it was obvious the fire-control computer was malfunctioning. Ghost 02's FCO, Maj Kevin "Moose" Johnson, was in the process of rebooting the computer when a MANPADS launch was seen by IO TSgt Ken Wood, who immediately identified the threat, called a defensive maneu-

19 Ibid.

ver and dispensed flares. Havel broke left aggressively, but the missile kept coming. TSgt Wood dispensed a second set of flares, but again, the missile kept coming. Now, more than ten seconds after launch, TSgt Wood launched a third set of flares about the same time the missile self-destructed near the tail of *Wicked Wanda*.

> "...the missile went and took the flares. It went off right underneath the tail of the airplane. I was standing holding a 105 round out when we were engaged...we pulled negative G's, which cause you to lose body weight, your body goes weightless...When the missile went off it was like daylight in the back of the airplane. And I remember our Loadmaster, TSgt Wood, fell into the scanner's bubble that's back there."
> **TSgt William Alex,** gunner[20]

Capt Havel decided to withdraw over the Persian Gulf rather than risk a second MANPADS engagement while working on the malfunctioning fire-control system. By the time Ghost 02's fire control system was working properly, Marine artillery was active at Khafji, so they remained in holding. Once cleared back to the target area, TSgt Rick Silvis located another 23mm AAA gun. This time, the 105mm gun fired on their first attempt, but the shot was a wide miss. Subsequent shots missed also. While TSgt Silvis began to compensate each shot manually to correct error,

20 Ibid, Appendix G.

each round impacted closer to the AAA gun. Once the Iraqi gun crew determined they were being targeted, they ran from the site towards a bunker but were hit by one of Ghost 02's inaccurate 105mm rounds.

It was obvious Ghost 02's fire control system was not working properly since it took twenty rounds to score a direct hit on the gun. Shifting to the 40mm gun, results were not much better when firing on two BRDMs, but they did manage to set one on fire. After more than four hours wrestling with a malfunctioning fire control system, Ghost 02 departed the area for refueling. After aerial refueling offshore, they returned to KFIA, rearmed, and had the fire control computer replaced. Just before daybreak, Ghost 02 returned to their hold point, but were not tasked. After four hours of holding, they returned to KFIA.[21]

Daylight revealed the devastation at Khafji. Destroyed and abandoned Iraqi armored vehicles and dead Iraqi soldiers littered the area north of the city. Most of the Iraqi armored force had retreated to positions north of the border, but a sizable Iraqi force occupied Khafji. Coalition forces had withdrawn to positions south of Khafji, but two Marine reconnaissance teams were trapped in the city limits and were in constant danger of capture.

The battle affected CENTCOM and Kingdom leadership in different ways. Gen Schwarzkopf considered the situation a minor inconvenience that would be soon rectified, but King Fahd was incensed that Iraq occupied sacred

---

21 Ibid, Maj Paul Havel interview in Appendix G.

Saudi Arabian soil. Because of this, Saudi General Khaled bin Sultan bin Saud advised Gen Schwarzkopf he was under direct pressure from King Fahd to expel Iraqis from Khafji at once. It was clear Saudi national pride and honor was at stake as Sultan Adi al-Mutairi wanted to lead the attack on the Iraqis himself.[22]

> "Gen Schwarzkopf said, 'Khafji is of no tactical or strategic value. Let them keep it.' But to the Saudis, this was sovereign territory and their border needed to be restored. The Saudis not only led the counterattack, they provided the only ground troop units in the battle of Khafji."
> **Lt Col (Ret.) Michael Taylor**

Throughout the day on January 30, some Iraqis fought, while others surrendered without resistance. Meanwhile, a substantial Iraqi combat reserve in the Al Wafra Forest was expected to cross the border after sunset to reinforce their presence in Saudi Arabia.

At nightfall on January 30, Maj Flander's crew (Spirit 01) reported for duty, received tasking and were briefed by 1 SOW Intelligence analysts of the situation north of the border, but neglected to tell them Khafji was occupied by the Iraqi Army. After takeoff, Spirit 01 climbed to ten thousand feet, tweaked their guns and reported to a designated hold point south of the border, directly north of Khafji.

---

22 Paul W. Westermeyer, "US Marines in the Battle of Khafji," Marines, 2008, https://www.marines.mil/Portals/1/Publications/U.S.%20Marines%20in%20Battle%20Al-Khafji%20%20PCN%20106000400_1.pdf.

Within a minute, they began taking AAA fire and detected an SA-8 missile launch indication, coming from the south. Maj Flanders performed a defensive maneuver, but the SA-8 launch was a false alarm. At that point they became aware Khafji was occupied by the Iraqis. Shortly afterward, the Marine Direct Air Support Center (DASC) requested Spirit 01 perform armed reconnaissance of the coastal highway north of the border.

> "We turned down tasking from Wingnut (Marine DASC). Target was 30 APC at 2855N 4748E. This was within a SA-2 Ring and 25NM north of the Kuwait border We were then tasked by ABCCC and validated by Bullfrog (TACC) for Armed Recce along the east coast road from A 100 North to A 85 (from Khafji to 8 NM north of the border). We restricted this to 5NM north of the border due to a SA-2 threat ring and mobile SA-6s. At this point, we were cleared to engage any targets north of the border."
> **Maj Jack Flanders**[23]

There was no shortage of targets as Spirit 01 searched for targets near the border. Hundreds of derelict vehicles were on the coastal highway. SSgt Clay Watson, Spirit 01s LLLTV sensor operator, noted some appeared to be destroyed, but most looked as if they were abandoned. The first vehicle

23 Mission report of Maj Jack Flanders etracted from AFSOC history archives, 2014.

Spirit 01 targeted was an Iraqi BRDM traveling south near the Bard'Halq desalination plant. SSgt Watson engaged the BRDM with a single round of 40mm, causing it to run off the road and run into a chain link fence. For several hours, Spirit 01 engaged targets including a Racal battlefield surveillance radar and communications site, BMP-1 and 2 armored personnel carriers, and tanks. Later in the mission, TSgt Ron Clark, Spirit 01's IR sensor operator, engaged two moving tanks. After scoring a direct hit on the lead tank, it stopped abruptly causing the second to run into the first. Spirit 01 continued to fire at both tanks until exposed fuel barrels on the rear of the first tank burst into flames, engulfing both in burning fuel.

As the night wore on, Iraqis fired artillery flares to highlight the blacked out gunship causing Maj Flanders to move to a different location. After almost four hours of near constant engagements, Spirit 01 observed thousands of rounds of AAA barrage fire ranging from 14.5mm to 100mm, but received no hits. When an illumination flare ignited at their altitude in the center of their orbit, Flanders realized Iraqis were about to zero in on them. In light of this, Maj Flanders decided to call it a night.

> "As we rolled in on the target, a flare ignited in the middle of the orbit at our exact altitude, illuminating the entire cockpit as if it were daylight. I looked at Chas Stoner, the copilot, and said 'Our work here is done; let's go home.' It was clear to me that the Iraqis were now able

> to anticipate our tactics and to neutralize them with accurately placed illumination flares, not to mention the barrage of AAA that would surely follow." **Maj (Ret.) Jack Flanders**

About the time Spirit 01 returned to KFIA, Capt Timpson's crew (Spirit 02) arrived at their designated hold point over the Persian Gulf. Within minutes of arrival, they were directed to the same general working area Spirit 01 had recently worked. Spirit 02 headed for Khafji, established a firing orbit just north of the border. Sensor operators discovered a "target rich" environment, but focused on what appeared to be a berm in the vehicle staging area.

> "The vehicles we shot, there was a bermed up area north of the border, and there were probably about 24, 25 vehicles actually parked in there. It was more or less a truck park, and apparently, they thought they were hiding because they were in this bermed up area, but it was actually a trap for them, and we had them in this enclosed area and we just pounded them. Before we left, they were all burning. They never really had a chance to run." **TSgt (Ret.) Ron Johnson,** sensor operator

Spirit 02 destroyed or damaged the vehicles and set off several large secondary explosions. As Spirit 01 discovered earlier, Iraqi AAA was getting heavier and more accurate as the night progressed.

While Spirit 02 was dodging AAA fire north of Khafji, Maj Paul Weaver and his crew were on ground alert at KFIA. At about 2230 hours, gunship maintenance crews finished repairing the malfunctioning fire control system on *Ghostrider*, then called it in as crew ready. Maj Weaver's crew was alerted and directed to functional check the fire control system on the Saudi OED-43 range.

Just before 0200, under the call sign Spirit 03, Maj Weaver's crew started engines. By 0216, they were airborne and on their way to the range. At some point, they found the fire control system was functional and all else was in working order. Considering the ongoing situation and Khafji, Maj Weaver requested to be placed on airborne alert instead of ground alert. Lt Col Kegel, approved his request on the condition Spirit 03 was to relieve Spirit 02 when their mission was complete.

Iraqi resistance north of the border grew stronger as the night progressed. At about 0400, Capt Timpson determined the escalating threat level made conditions unworkable, so Spirit 02 pulled off target and headed towards a holding area over the Persian Gulf. Spirit 02 was offered targets in heavily contested areas, which they declined to accept because of heavy AAA. While in holding, Spirit 02 contacted Spirit 03 via SATCOM to discuss the situation.

By 0434, Spirit 02 and 03 were in holding over the Persian Gulf, but no workable target areas were available. At that point, Spirit 03 had about two hours of fuel remaining, while Spirit 02 had about one-half hour. Capt Timpson advised Maj Weaver he was returning to base and recommended Spirit 03 do the same. While Timpson's crew set course for KFIA, Maj Weaver decided Spirit 03 would remain in holding in the event a workable target area became available.

> "We heard Spirit 03 on Blacklist frequency report holding at A099. We called 03...and passed that we encountered heavy AAA from 04810E and recommended he not fly further east along the border than that and fully explained the threats. We informed Blacklist that we had 30 minutes play time. Blacklist offered us 17 trucks at 2831N 4814E, we refused due to the AAA threat we had just left. They offered FROGs at 2834N 4820E which we also had to decline due to the same AAA. We left the area RTB."
> **Capt Don Timpson**[24]

Meanwhile, at KFIA, Lt Col Kegel and Capt Brian Cutts transmitted a SATCOM radio call ordering both Spirit 02 and Spirit 03 to land at KFIA no later than 0600. Spirit 02 was already on course for KFIA, but Spirit 03 did not receive the order.[25]

By 0540, activity north of the border remained heavy, but the ground situation in the Khafji city limits appeared quiet. Spirit 03 remained in holding for almost an hour and a

24 Mission report of Capt Don Timpson, extracted from AFSOC history archives, 2014.

25 According to LT Col Donn Kegel in his Jan 1991 interview, he believed Spirit 03 may have missed the call because of a "SATCOM hole" where reception was poor.

half while Marine artillery was active. When artillery operations ended, Spirit 03 received tasking from a Marine OV-10 FAC flying at fourteen thousand feet over the target area (call sign Peach 75.) Though Spirit 03 had only about thirty minutes of fuel remaining, Maj Weaver agreed to search the coastal highway on the Saudi side of the border for Iraqi vehicles and troops.

Maj Weaver established an orbit at 10,000 ft. altitude near the Saudi border post as sensor operators searched for targets. Within a minute, LLLTV sensor operator SMSgt Paul Buege detected a column of vehicles traveling south. When Spirit 03 attempted to engage the lead vehicle, their first 105mm shot was outside both sensor operators' field of view and not seen by either the pilot nor IO. The fire control computer had once again failed, so FCO Capt Art Galvan began troubleshooting procedures.

While Spirit 03 orbited the target area unable to fire, Peach 75 redirected them to the Saudi customs inspection checkpoint: a large, pillared concrete structure the Iraqis were using for cover. Maj Weaver established a firing orbit over the structure about the same time Capt Galvan was ready to re-tweak the fire control system. While both sensor operators tracked the center of the target building, the fire control system pulled both sensors off target. With an inoperable fire control computer and unreliable HUD symbology, Maj Weaver descended to nine thousand ft., then asked Peach 75 spot shots to talk them onto target.

Spirit 03's primary target on January 31, 1991; the Saudi border post north of Khafji. (Credit: Author)

Suddenly, EWO, Capt Dixon Walters, received a SAM radar warning which he determined was a false alarm. Remaining overhead the border post, but still unable to see shot impacts, Major Weaver directed gunners SSgt Harrison, TSgt Hodges and TSgt Oelschlager to load the 40mm gun with Misch Metal to better see shot impacts. After firing a few rounds, sensor operators detected shot impacts and Capt Galvan re-tweaked the gun. From that point on, Spirit 03 achieved direct hits on the border post building with both 40mm and 105mm guns.

During this time, Blacklist, Peach 75 and Ox Team (Marine ANGLICO) agreed to clear Spirit 03 to fire on all buildings on the Saudi side of the checkpoint. While Spirit 03 continued to engage targets, the right scanner, MSgt Jim

May called inaccurate AAA and advised the IO, SSgt Mark Schmauss, to watch the site.

By 0614, sunrise occurred at ground level and Spirit 03 was low on fuel. Meanwhile, at KFIA, Lt Col Kegel and Col Gray were informed by AWACS that Spirit 03 was still on station engaging targets. Lt Col Kegel was concerned Spirit 03 had not pulled off target at 0600 as directed. Knowing SATCOM coverage was spotty in that area, he contacted Lt Col Kinkaid to relay the order through the AWACS controlling the Khafji area. At 0619, the AWACS (call sign Ponca) successfully transmitted the recall order to Spirit 03. Copilot 1st Lt Thomas "TC" Bland announced the order over the main interphone system, but Maj Weaver continued engaging targets.

Two minutes after the recall order was received, Spirit 03 remained over target, engaging buildings near the border post. Still under control of Peach 75, Maj Weaver asked Navigator Capt William Grimm to advise Peach 75 they would be off target in ten minutes, but Grimm advised him they only had enough fuel for two more minutes. Maj Weaver continued firing on targets for another minute, then requested an initial heading to a refueling track.

By this time, Peach 75 was low on fuel also. As he departed, the FAC advised Spirit 03 to search for a suspected FROG-7 near the water tanks of the Bard'Halq desalination plant. Capt Grimm advised Peach 75 they only had enough fuel for a quick look, then had to depart. Sensor operators found two vehicles stopped in the middle of the road. Both sensor operators and the FCO determined the vehicles were not likely FROG-7s. Maj Weaver directed SSgt Blessinger to track and engage the vehicles, but there wasn't enough time to do so since Spirit 03 was below the Nav's calculated bingo fuel level. Further complicating the situation was the fact it was nearly ten minutes after sunrise at ground level and the rising sun was hindering vision.

Grimm advised AWACS they were returning to KFIA, then advised Maj Weaver they did not have enough fuel to remain on station. Maj Weaver still wanted to engage the target SSgt Blessinger was tracking, but once crewmen voiced their concerns over the main interphone system, Weaver decided it was time to depart. Because of low fuel state, Grimm calculated the shortest possible route to KFIA, then advised Weaver of a 210 degree roll out heading. Two seconds later, a muffled crack was heard coming from the left wing.[26] Both pilots began emergency procedures while flight engineer SSgt Damon Kanuha, announced a fire warning on number one engine. Immediately after the fire warning, Kanuha looked out the cockpit windows to see a fire engulfing the left wing between #1 and #2 engines. Realizing the the aircraft was mortally wounded, he announced over main interphone, "boys, we are going down." The raging fire weakened the wing's structure, then, merely fifteen seconds after being hit, two-thirds of *Ghostrider's* left wing broke off. The aircraft immediately rolled left, slowed into a stall, and tumbled end over end, almost straight down at a high rate of speed. During Spirit 03s descent, Capt Grimm

---

26 Two loud metallic snapping sounds are detected on the recovered Cockpit voice recorder indicating wing failure.

and 1st Lt Bland radioed "mayday" calls that were detected by AWACS. Exactly thirty seconds after being hit, Spirit 03 crashed into the Persian Gulf in about ten feet of water about 600 yards off shore.

By 0645hrs, *Ghostrider* was overdue as crew chiefs SSgt's Steve Feldmier and Gary Perez waited on KFIA for the gunship to arrive. When Lt Col Kegel called the TACC for an update, he was told the AWACS had detected a faint "mayday" in the Khafji area. Later, when Peach 75 was questioned, he said he saw a large fireball falling from the sky in his peripheral vision but was unsure if it was Spirit 03. The staff at TACC however, were certain it was Spirit 03.[27]

By mid-morning, the Battle of Khafji was waning as SANG forces, supported by Qatari armor, retook the town. After destroying over two hundred armored vehicles and capturing over four hundred Iraqi POWs, the Battle of Khafji was over by sundown. At that time, Iraq forces had retreated into the Al Wafra Forest.

The disappearance of Spirit 03 weighed heavily on everyone's minds. Reconnaissance aircraft photographed the area where the aircraft was last tracked by AWACS but all efforts to locate a crash site were unsuccessful. Some felt it was as if the aircraft had disappeared into thin air.

During the following days, AC-130 crews were assigned an airborne alert commitment near the Saudi border until February 4, when all crews were placed on ground alert.

---

27 Letter from Col (Ret.) Donn Kegel to Author, 2014.

By February 7, AC-130A aircrew and support personnel of the 711 SOS were in place at KFIA. After local area procedures and intelligence briefings, AC-130A crews augmented the AC-130H alert commitment.

Desert Storm AC-130A Aircraft Commanders (6)
Lt Col Larry Meunch
Lt Col Charlie Ware
Capt Mike Wilson
Capt Joe Norris
Capt Dan Ley
Capt Richard Haddad

Desert Storm AC-130A aircraft (5)
0011 "*Night Stalker*"
0014 "*Jaws of Death*"
0509 "*The Ultimate End*"
1623 "*Ghost Rider*"
1630 "*Azrael, Angel of Death*"

By the middle of February, CENTAF's bombing campaign had decimated Iraq's military capabilities in Iraq and Kuwait. Gen Schwarzkopf's next planned phase was a mass ground assault into Kuwait, supported by CAS aircraft. Commonly known as the ground war phase, most believed it would be a long, tedious process to clear buildings door-to-door in Kuwait City.

This facet renewed the divide between SOCCENT and the TACC regarding C2 of AC-130s. SOCCENT was expected to perform house clearing and capture missions, so they wanted operational control of the gunships. 1 SOW Army Special Forces Liaison Officer CW4 Vernon Ward worked with Lt Col Waylett to define special operations plans independently of the TACC. Lt Col Waylett knew another fight for C2 of the AC-130s was likely, but pressed on with detailed planning as if the TACC just didn't matter.

> "Mr. Ward was concerned that US ground forces would have to fight door-to-door to clear Iraqi forces from Kuwait City. He came to me and described what he feared would be an extremely dangerous mission. He wanted a commitment from me that he could rely on gunships to provide close air support. I said 'Mr. Ward, close air support for troops-in-contact is what we're here for. If you need us, we'll be there.'" **Lt Col (Ret.) Tom Waylett,** 16 SOS Operations Officer

The ground war began on February 24 while remnants of what was once the fifth largest Army in the world were on the run. Most Iraqi soldiers surrendered at first sight of coalition forces but those who fought were killed. The coalition met little resistance as they advanced into Kuwait. During this time, AC-130 crews remained on alert with no requests for fire support.

Two days later, as coalition forces neared Kuwait City, the Iraqi Army initiated a full- scale retreat to the northwest. Hundreds of vehicles of all types began pouring out of Kuwait City traveling towards Basra, Iraq on Highway 80 and Highway 8. While AC-130H crews remained on ground alert, three AC-130As (Ghost 10, Ghost 6, Ghost 7) were alerted to attack a large convoy of vehicles northwest of Kuwait City. The gunships joined scores of fighter and attack aircraft to systematically destroy hundreds of vehicles which was later named "The Highway of Death." The next day, a ceasefire was announced and the shooting war was over.

By March 1, an organized grid search began for Spirit 03. Some held out hope that the aircraft had crash landed and survivors would be found, but others felt the aircraft had crashed near Khafji. Col Gray directed a maximum effort aerial search near Khafji which was augmented by TSgt's Alan Garrett and Bill Alex, MSgt Bob Derby, SSgt Gene Cox, and Lt Col Donn Kegel. Initial results focused on the area west of Khafji since most believed it would have been logical for a crew to head that direction in a controlled bailout situation. Unfortunately, no sign of Spirit 03 was discovered.

On March 4 an HC-130P crew (call sign Boa 21) commanded by former AC-130 pilot Lt Col John Fuss spotted flashes of bright orange in the water about six hundred yards offshore. Fuss's crew radioed the coordinates (283168N 482748E) to a nearby CH-3 helicopter from the 71st Air Rescue Squadron (call sign Iguana 70). When the H-3 crew overflew the coordinates, they spotted what appeared to be wreckage scattered under water. Though the water was shallow at the crash site, no part of the aircraft projected above the water, so the crash site was invisible from the shoreline. Furthermore, tremendous impact forces created an underwater crater in the sand that contained a majority of the fuselage. Other parts of the aircraft fractured into small fragments that were scattered over a ¼ mile area.

> "We (71) received a call from the HC-130 that they spotted what appeared to be a 20 man life raft and that they were going to mark it with sea dye...on our first or second pass, we spotted a propeller and what appeared to be a piece of the leading edge...it was then that I spotted an I.R. shield laying upside down with a flap and jack screws right next to it." Written statement by **TSgt Alan Garrett**, Mar 1991

The next day, TSgt Garrett guided another CH-3 and several MH-53s loaded with a dive team and Zodiac inflatable boats. While Pararescuemen dove on the wreckage to search and recover remains, Garrett's scan of the beach revealed a flight jacket and a few other personal items. Once divers recovered the badly beaten Cockpit Voice Recorder (CVR), it was placed in a bucket of sea water to prevent corrosion, then sent back to the US for analysis.

Within days, the National Transportation Safety Board extracted the voice recording of the last thirty minutes of Spirit 03's mission. With this information in hand, Lt Col Bernie Frakes and Capt Rick Middleton were sent to KFIA to conduct an investigation.

Meanwhile, crews remained on alert until March 8 when all combat operations ceased. With the war officially over, Lt Col Kegel and Capt Timpson's crew returned to Hurlburt Field for a memorial ceremony for the crew of Spirit 03.

In mid-March, a Navy salvage team equipped with a crane barge was sent to Khafji to lift pieces of wreckage that could not be moved by hand. During this effort, more remains were discovered. The left wing was also discovered some distance from the main crash site and its external fuel tank appeared to have been hit by an explosive warhead. When the wing was returned to KFIA, a close inspection revealed fragments embedded in the fuel tank's explosion-resistant foam. Several fragments were removed, then sent to Missiles and Space Intelligence Center (MSIC) in Huntsville, Alabama for analysis and identification. Within a week, the warhead was confirmed as a late-model Russian MANPADS.

In mid-March, AC-130As returned to home station while the AC-130H remained at KFIA until May 27, 1991 when they returned to Hurlburt Field.

MISSION DEBRIEF

Command & Control: Command and control of AC-130 gunships was a contentious issue. A battle for control between CENTCOM and SOCCENT leadership resulted in misapplication of the AC-130.

Readiness, Training and Maintenance: Operation *Desert Shield/Storm* was the first large-scale conflict for AC-130s since Vietnam, Laos and Cambodia. Through the 1980s,

AC-130 crews and maintainers had become accustomed to short duration SOF missions such as Operations *Urgent Fury* and *Just Cause*. The nearly five-month wait for combat activities to begin undoubtedly affected combat readiness since proficiency and upgrade training was suppressed or delayed to a large degree. Maintaining crew proficiency was a high level of effort task during the entire operation. Some upgrade training was accomplished in Saudi Arabia, but the lengthy wait before combat operations began and spartan training facilities were limiting factors. To mitigate these training and proficiency issues, a crew rotation to Hurlburt was established to maintain proficiency levels.

Operating effectively in the harsh desert environment presented problems for both operations and maintenance. There were many environment-specific issues crews and maintainers faced, but a few stood out as issues that adversely affected the mission. One of the most pressing issues was reliability of the fire control system. Post deployment analysis determined most fire control issues were caused by clogging of pitot tubes by fine, talcum-powder-like dust which was most likely trapped during the hot/dry months. Though the dust didn't seem to cause a problem when dry, once the winter rains began, the dust trapped in pitot tubes was converted to a muddy mess that altered airflow and thus degraded fire control system reliability.

Tactics Techniques & Procedures: Throughout the 1980s, AC-130 tactics techniques and procedures were primarily focused on support of other SOF units in small scale special missions, contingencies and raids. *Desert Storm* was a significantly different tactical situation than what AC-130 crews were trained and equipped to perform. TACC planners tasked the AC-130 into a high-level threat environment the same way as a high-altitude, high-speed jet fighter. In effect, crews were ordered to fly interdiction missions under conditions exceeding the defensive capabilities and performance of their aircraft. Gunship crews flew these missions at great risk, facing a radar threat environment that kept them in a near-constant defensive posture, hindering their ability to locate and strike targets.

After *Desert Storm*, the USAF realized a communication and coordination gap existed between aircraft types and took steps to resolve the issue. The first step taken in 1992 was expansion of the USAF Fighter Weapons School to include all USAF aircraft. The USAF Fighter Weapons School's name was changed to the USAF Weapons School whose charter was documenting and training graduate level Air Force Tactics, Techniques and Procedures (AFTTP) for all USAF aircraft. It was a painstaking and an evolutionary process, but, in 2000, the first Air Force level 3-1 series manual was written and published by AC-130 tacticians. This manual and corresponding courseware became the standard for communication and mission planning with all other aircraft within the AFTTP system. Furthermore, the 14th Weapon Squadron was established at Hurlburt Field to represent SOF alongside all USAF weapon systems. In effect, after 2000, the AC-130 had its own "patch wearers" who were trained not only in AC-130 employment, but multi-platform combat operations. This arrangement would prove to pay huge dividends a decade later during AC-130 combat operations in Afghanistan and Iraq.

Mission Impact: AC-130 crews damaged armored vehicles, destroyed EW radar sites, AAA guns and personnel, but the entire SCUD-hunting endeavor produced mixed results. The Iraqi Army was tactically savvy from lessons learned during their long war with Iran. Saddam's forces went to great lengths to conceal mobile SCUDs including disguising them as civilian busses and fuel trucks. They also employed easily located decoys to draw fire away from nearby concealed missiles. From a tactical perspective, it's hard to say SCUD-hunting missions were resounding success. Even though AC-130 crews dedicated significant effort and assumed high risks taking on these missions, no AC-130 ever identified, engaged or destroyed a SCUD missile or launcher. From the strategic perspective, however, one could argue that there was success to some degree, but higher levels of success could have likely been accomplished more efficiently by high performance aircraft.

The Iraqi Republican Guard was well trained and used "shoot and scoot" tactics with their Mobile SAM systems. Likewise, they would not allow SCUD Transporter Erector Launchers (TEL) to remain in a static location for any length of time.

A total of 88 SCUDs were launched during the course of the war. One SCUD impacted near the KFIA runway without causing any damage, but another overflew the KFIA area and impacted on barracks nearby at Dhahran causing a high level of US casualties.

OVERALL ASSESSMENT

While it could be argued the gunship was a square peg in a round hole in a radar SAM environment, the gunship was capable and properly employed during the Battle of Khafji and on the "Highway of Death." All four AC-130 interdiction missions flown during the Battle of Khafji, encountered hostile Iraqi fire. Gunship crews remained on station as long as possible to deny unchecked Iraqi movement into the Khafji city limits. All crews operated at great risk with exceptional determination, but Spirit 03 was lost during the effort. AC-130A crews were effective on a roadway choked with vehicles in a way reminiscent of the original Ho Chi Minh Trail truck hunting mission the AC-130A *Pave Pronto* was developed for.

THE LOSS OF SPIRIT 03

This loss of aircraft and crew was a casualty of direct combat, exacerbated at many different levels by a chain of seemingly routine elements. Unfortunately, a high number of these elements accumulated during their mission which resulted in loss of aircraft and crew. During the investigation and years following, theories, opinions, and second-guessing ensued. The most prevalent being Spirit 03 was shot down solely because the rising sun revealed their position, enabling acquisition and lock-on by an Iraqi MANPADS. While that was likely a factor, the crew of Spirit 03 was well trained in defensive maneuvers and equipped with decoy flares. Neither countermeasure however, is effective if missile launch is not detected. A detailed examination of the CVR recording revealed nobody detected the inbound missile. The most logical explanation centers on the idea that Spirit 03 was flying north and scanning east into the rising sun when hit. This could explain why no threat call, defensive maneuver, or dispensing of decoy flares was made.

Though it is likely daybreak was a factor, it certainly was not the only factor to consider. Since both Capt LeBrun's crew and Capt Havel's crew were engaged by Iraqi MANPADS in complete darkness, it is evident the Iraqi Army had at least some night target acquisition capability.

Another factor was the AC-130 operational altitude of nine-thousand–ten thousand ft. AGL which put all AC-130s directly in the effective envelope of Iraqi MANPADS. Coincidentally, the wing failure event Spirit 03 experienced was almost identical in timeline and scope of the loss of Spectre 11 over An Loc, Vietnam in June of 1972. The principal differences between Spirit 03 and Spectre 11 are one was hit in the left wing and the other in the right wing: one was at sunrise and the other in complete darkness. This combat loss, like other AC-130 losses that preceded it, are sometimes rife with folklore and speculation because of a lack of credible information. Detailed analysis of the recovered CVR has captured the true context of Spirit 03's mission from the perspective of the crewmen themselves. No folklore, finger pointing, or guesswork can be more truthful than their final words.

THE CREW OF AC-130H *GHOSTRIDER* (69-6567), CALL SIGN SPIRIT 03:

Maj Paul Weaver	Aircraft Commander
Capt William Grimm	Navigator
Capt Dixon Walters	Electronic Warfare Officer
Capt Arthur Galvan	Fire-Control Officer
1st Lt Thomas C. Bland Jr. (promoted to Capt while MIA)	Copilot
SMSgt Paul Buege	Sensor Operator
MSgt James May III (promoted to SMSgt while MIA)	Gunner
TSgt Robert Hodges	Gunner
TSgt John Oelschlager	Gunner
SSgt Timothy Harrison	Gunner
SSgt John Blessinger	Sensor Operator
SSgt Mark Schmauss	Illuminator Operator
SSgt Damon Kanuha	Flight Engineer
Sgt Barry Clark	Gunner

SITUATION REPORT: 1991–1995

All AC-130s were in the CONUS by the summer of 1991. Total AC-130 inventory was nine AC-130H at Hurlburt Field, FL, and ten AC-130A at Duke Field, FL. Normal proficiency and upgrade training resumed and crews were once again flying local training missions and participating in Joint Training Exercises in on-and-off station locations. The 16 SOS main building had a large addition built onto it and the old "double wide" temporary building housing crew position offices was demolished and converted into a parking lot. Individual crew position sections were eliminated and designated flights were formed. Flights normally contained five crews and were designated as Alpha, Bravo, Charlie and Delta.

At the same time, the AC-130H Special Operations Forces Improvement (SOFI) program was in full swing, updating much needed fire control and avionics. The AC-130U program was also in development during this time period. The AC-130A fleet began to retire in 1994.

The loss of Spirit 03 added a thirteenth aircraft to the AC-130U acquisition program. AC-130U and AC-130H

SOFI modification accelerated development and test of electronic countermeasures systems. AFSOC also embarked on a missile defense system designed to detect and decoy MANPADS. The AN/AAR-44 threat warning system was installed and tested on the AC-130H, then added to AC-130U during development.

The early 1990s basing plan was to equip the 16 SOS with AC-130Us and transfer the AC-130H fleet to the Air Force Reserve at Duke Field. By 1994, mission commitments and theater war plans convinced Air Staff to retain the H-Models on active duty and stand up a separate squadron for the AC-130U. The 4th SOS, one of the original AC-47 *Spooky* squadrons, was selected for reactivation to operate the AC-130U.

From 1993–94, the 16 SOS was constantly deployed to support operations in Somalia and Bosnia-Herzegovina. A multi-nation deployment of military forces led by the United States was ordered to Haiti in September 1994 for Operation *Uphold Democracy*. AC-130A and AC-130H gunships deployed as part of the package and apparently the resulting show of force was enough to convince rebels to cease hostile activity.

By early 1994, the AC-130U program experienced significant engineering hurdles and substantial delays. The largest hurdle was the development and testing of the All Light Level Television (ALLTV) sensor. Since adjustments to the delivery schedule were not possible due to contractual obligations, the Air Force agreed to allow on-time delivery of partially mission capable aircraft. The first AC-130U

Gunship to be delivered to Hurlburt Field (89-0166) arrived on July 1, 1994 without an ALLTV system.

On May 1, 1995, the 4th SOS (*Spooky*) was reactivated on Hurlburt Field to conduct AC-130U operations. The initial cadre were primarily experienced AC-130H crew members from the 16 SOS transferred to the 4 SOS. During this transition period, all AC-130Us were assigned to the 4 SOS and all ten AC-130A gunships of the 711 SOS at Duke Field were incrementally retired.

CHAPTER SIX

UNOSOM II OPERATIONS, SOMALIA, 1993–1994

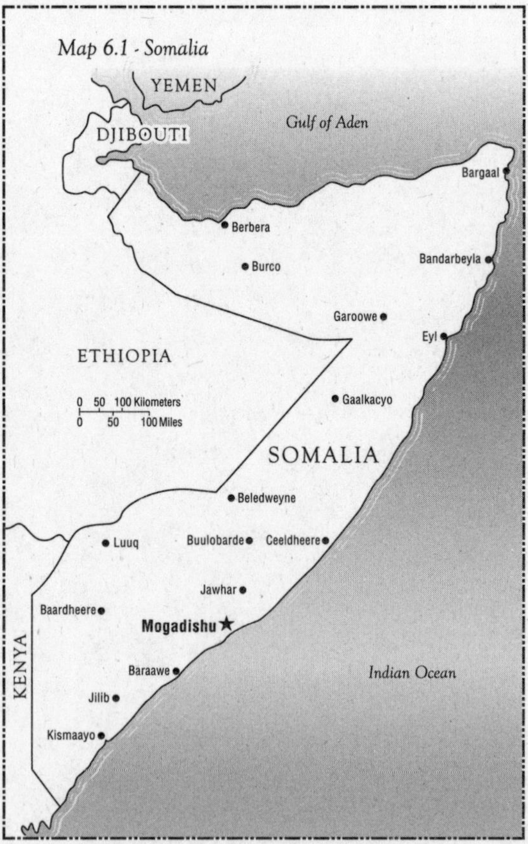

Map of Somalia (Credit: Carl Mauro II)

Somalia is located on the northeast section of the African continent in an area known as the Horn Of Africa (HOA). Somalia borders the Gulf of Aden which connects to the Red Sea and ultimately the Mediterranean Sea via Egypt's Suez Canal. Because of Somalia's proximity to this strategically important shipping and trade route, Eastern and Western Bloc powers contested for Somalia's favor during the Cold War.

Prior to World War II, Somalia was governed by tribal clans and subclans dispersed across the country, but after World War II, regions of "Somaliland" were colonized by the Italians, British, and French. During the 1950s, both Eastern and Western Bloc powers provided fragmented Somali clans with financial and military aid to maintain control of the Gulf of Aden. In 1960, Somalia gained its independence to form the Somali Republic which was led by President Abdirashid Ali Shermarke.

In 1969, after nine years of questionable activities and failed policies, President Ali Shermarke was assassinated in a coup d'état led by Somali Army Maj General Mohamed Siad Barre, who established the Socialist-based Supreme Revolutionary Council (SRC). Barre allied with the USSR who supported Somalia militarily and economically. By 1976, corruption within the SRC caused it to be disbanded and replaced by the Somali Revolutionary Socialist Party (SRSP), but Barre's failed social policies lost favor with the people of Somalia.

In 1977, Barre broke ties with the USSR, then allied with the US, UK, and France, but the economic situation in Somalia continued to decline. By 1978, Barre's rule over Somalia was challenged by tribal clan elders, prompting Barre to order the kidnapping and murder of those who opposed him. In response, tribes fought Barre's Army in a guerilla war for almost eleven years, resulting in the death of tens of thousands of Somalis.[1]

By 1989, the guerilla war in Somalia raged on, but the Cold War was drawing to a close. Since Somalia's strategic importance had faded, western financial and military support was cut. With the loss of military and economic aid, Barre's military infrastructure and capabilities declined rapidly. By late 1990, mass anti-government riots occurred in the capital city of Mogadishu as clans and subclans competed for dominance and control of the country. In January 1991, Barre's Army turned against him. After he fled the country, ungoverned chaos ensued. With no intact central government remaining, the US Embassy in Mogadishu was evacuated by the US Navy and Marine Corps supported by two AC-130H gunships redeployed from Saudi Arabia.

Throughout 1991, Somalia was a violent quagmire of lawlessness and clan warfare. Scores of Somali civilians were either killed by hostile fire or died from starvation. News reports and video footage of the crisis in Somalia highlighted the situation to the United Nations Secretary General, Boutros Boutros-Ghali. Seeking a solution to end the crisis, the UN Security Council enacted a Unified Task

---

1 Walter S. Poole, *The Effort to Save Somalia, August 1992-March 1994* (Washington, DC: Joint History Office, Office of the Chairman of the Joint Chiefs of Staff, 2005), 6.

Force (UNITAF) to coordinate humanitarian relief efforts. By late 1991, with support of the US Envoy to Somalia, Robert Oakley, international relief organizations began delivering food and medical aid. Unfortunately, transporting supplies to rural areas was problematic since unarmed supply convoys were routinely hijacked by armed rebels. To protect convoys, international aid organizations hired local tribesmen to provide security of warehouses and delivery convoys. Commonly referred to as "Technicals," tribesmen were armed with large caliber weapons mounted on small pickup trucks.[2] By 1992, a severe drought hit the area, subjecting Somalis to extreme hardship, disease and starvation.

In April 1992, the UN Secretary General met with the UN Security Council to urge increased efforts to end the civil war in Somalia. A few days later, UN Resolution 794 was passed imposing an arms embargo against Somalia and directing organized talks between warring clans. This resolution named United Nations Operation in Somalia (UNOSOM), eclipsed UNITAF. Since the UN had no troops to commit to the effort, Boutros-Ghali appealed directly to the Bush Administration for troops to be commanded by the UN in Somalia. Unwilling to place American forces in a foreign chain of command, the US Secretary of State offered up to a division of US combat troops provided they remained under US control. Thus, with approval of President George H. W. Bush, command and control of UNOSOM fell to the

2 Eventually, the title "Technical" was associated more with the armed vehicles and less with the tribesmen.

United States Central Command (CENTCOM) commanded by USMC General Joseph Hoar.

Some of the first US military to arrive were US Army Special Forces soldiers from the 5th Special Forces Group supported by USAF Combat Controllers from the 1721 Combat Control Squadron. These teams accompanied relief flights and controlled remote airfields to deliver relief supplies, gather intelligence and assess the dangers of each region. Follow-on forces included about ten thousand soldiers from the US Army 10th Mountain Division, Ft Drum NY, who coordinated security and distribution of relief supplies. As troop strength ramped up, so did attacks on peacekeepers, but restrictive Rules Of Engagement (ROE) prohibited use of lethal force unless as a last resort for self-defense.

> "The Concept of Operations was for two CCT members and two Special Forces (SF) Team members to be launched daily in support of three airfields within Somalia. We had a C-130 sitting strip alert with a Special Forces Quick Reaction Force (QRF) at Mombasa ready to send to any of the Airfields with the most hostile action that day. We worked in civilian clothes with our weapons out of sight. Things usually got interesting around 1600L when the Warlords troops would get buzzed on Khat and start commandeering/shooting up the UN food relief trucks." **MSgt (Ret.) Ronald Childress,** Combat Controller

During the early morning hours of December 9, 1992, the 1st Marine Expeditionary Force, augmented by US Navy SEALs, landed on the beach adjacent to Mogadishu International Airport under well-lit media coverage. Over the next few months, troops from France, Italy, Belgium, Morocco, Australia, Pakistan, Malaysia, and Canada provided security in individual sectors of Somalia. Referred to as UN Peacekeepers, they fanned out across the country to provide security for convoys and aid distribution centers. Because of the highly restrictive Rules of Engagement (ROE) mandated by the UN, Peacekeepers were not allowed to employ military force unless as a last resort of self-defense. Because of this, Somali clansmen considered UN Peacekeepers more of a nuisance than a threat, but nevertheless, some convoys were attacked. Eventually, because of the high level of effort and support of Peacekeepers, cities and remote villages were successfully resupplied.

By the spring of 1993, with the mass starvation epidemic under control, Somalia's most powerful Warlord, Mohammed Farah Aidid, ratcheted up anti-UN and anti-American rhetoric. Aidid easily manipulated over one million Somalis living in Mogadishu via his radio station and by organizing staged public demonstrations. Since the humanitarian crisis was resolved, the Clinton Administration had no desire to interfere with Somali political affairs. Once the Clinton Administration decided it was in the United States' best interest to withdraw US support, Boutros-Ghali feared a US withdrawal would result in a relapse of the civil war and another humanitarian crisis.

From that point on, Boutros-Ghali acted more like the leader of an international military Junta than the UN Secretary General as he pressed the United States to lead an overt military operation to disarm warring clans. In March of 1993, he convinced the UN to pass resolution 814 authorizing an aggressive military posture. Boutros-Ghali appointed US Navy Admiral Johnathan Howe as his Special Representative for Somalia and US Army Major General Thomas Montgomery as Howe's deputy. The primary goal of UNOSOM II was to disarm the two most powerful warlords in Mogadishu, Ali Mahdi and Mohammed Farah Aidid.

Mohammed Farah Aidid organized routine small-scale attacks on UN Peacekeepers with hopes the UN would withdraw from Somalia, but on June 5, 1993, SNA militiamen planned and executed a coordinated ambush of Pakistani weapon site inspectors killing twenty-four and wounding forty-four. In response, Boutros-Ghali condemned the attack and refused to withdraw UN forces. Instead, he vowed to punish Aidid with direct military action.

The emotional response to the Pakistani killings deviated from the UN Security Council's charter of peacekeeping; thus "mission creep" had begun. Nevertheless, the UN Security Council passed Resolution 837 to arrest Aidid, target his weapons storage sites and residence, negate his command and control elements, and shut down Radio Aidid.[3]

---

3 Richard W. Stewart, *The United States Army in Somalia, 1992-1994*, (Washington, DC: Government Publishing Office, 2003).

US military field commanders were concerned that disarming clans would be viewed by Somalis as an act of war by a mercenary Army. Most felt assaulting well-protected SNA enclaves with ground forces alone was foolhardy. Instead of risking casualties via ground assault, MG Montgomery directed air strikes to destroy SNA weapons and facilities prior to ground operations. Considering the precarious physical and political situation, air strikes needed to be precise. Concerns to limit collateral damage placed the AC-130 and AH-1 on top of the list.

On June 6, 1993, Gen Joseph Hoar, sent a request to the Joint Chiefs of Staff to deploy four AC-130 gunships to Djibouti-Ambouli International Airport, Djibouti, Africa. In turn, the 16 SOS was ordered to deploy within 24 hours, causing crews and maintainers to scramble to ready aircraft. Though the deployment order was received, little detailed information was provided concerning support or facilities at the deployed location.

> "When the Somalia issue was first studied by a 16 SOS plans officer, it was clear Djibouti was not a desirable bed down location. The preferred location was Mombasa, Kenya." **Maj Keith Maresca**

Deploying four AC-130s, support equipment and personnel in such a short time was challenging, especially coordinating airlift and refueling tanker support with other commands. While crews and maintainers hurried to prepare the gunships for deployment, a major security wrinkle was realized. A public 1st SOW change of command ceremony was about to occur within a stone's throw of aircraft being loaded for deployment.

> "The 1st SOW Director of Maintenance, Col Fred Gross had four AC-130 gunships towed to 'Hot Cargo' on Hurlburt Field which was about ½ mile north of the base operations parade area where the change of Command between Col Charles Holland and Col Clay Bailey was to take place at 1000. This event was to be filmed on local TV cameras and 'ops sec' didn't want the cameras filming four gunships being loaded with ammo at the same time. (It was too reminiscent of Operation Just Cause less than four years earlier)." **Col (Ret.) Jim Connors**

Moving the aircraft ½ mile from the ceremony worked well. About three hours after the ceremony, mission commander Lt Col Tom Waylett advised Lt Col Connors all aircraft were ready to go. Shortly thereafter, four fully loaded, combat ready gunships commanded by Captains Rich Forlano, Terry Crabtree, Jim Hughes and Brian Cutts took off from Hurlburt Field and set course for Djibouti. Only one overnight stop was planned for Torrejon AB, Spain since tanker support was available. Because of the distance and flying time to Djibouti, crewmen were augmented to alternate between flying and resting.

AC-130H June/July 1993 Deployment Aircraft
69-6574 *Iron Maiden*
69-6570 *Bad Company*
69-6577 *Death Angel*
69-6568 *Night Stalker*

On June 8, 16 SOS squadron commander Lt Col Jim Connors and a three hundred member support package departed via C-5 Galaxy on direct flight to Djibouti-Ambouli International Airport. After seventeen hours and three in-flight refuelings, the C-5 landed in the early morning hours of June 8. When the C-5's doors were opened, personnel were greeted with oppressive heat and dust and it was obvious little prior coordination and planning was accomplished by the US Embassy, who expected a much smaller force.

> "Upon arrival, it became apparent the available billeting, maintenance, munitions and transportation facilities were inadequate for the size of the deployments. The US Embassy in Djibouti was unaware of the operations size and had not briefed the host nation government. As a result, 1 SOW forces were scattered over three locations, had to store munitions in the open, and were prohibited by local authorities from expanding operations once the logistical tail caught up."
> **Maj Keith Maresca**

About six hours later, all four AC-130s landed at Djibouti-Ambouli International Airport.[4] The US Ambassador to Djibouti and his staff were accommodating by giving 16 SOS mission planner's easy access to the air-conditioned Embassy for initial mission planning and command and control.[5]

> Threat assessment: The SNA was equipped with small arms weapons including pistols, rifles, machine guns, RPGs, recoilless rifles, and mortars. Most of the SNA arsenal originated in the Soviet Union, but many US built weapons were in their inventory. These weapons posed no threat to the AC-130 operations unless aircraft were either on approach or on the ground at Mogadishu International Airport.
>
> Anti-Aircraft Artillery (AAA): SNA weapons included 12.7mm and 14.5mm machine guns, but they were typically optically aimed, sometimes without use of sights. These weapons were not considered a threat to the AC-130 except when on approach or parked on Mogadishu International Airport.
>
> Radar SAM systems: Planners were confident the SA-2 site in the city was inoperable and

4 Email from Col (Ret.) Frank Kuska to Author, Dec 2014.
5 E-mail from Col (Ret.) Mike Byers to Author, Dec, 2014.

unserviceable. There were known Mobile Radar SAM systems in Somalia.

Man Portable Air Defense Systems (MANPADS): The potential for MANPADS existed and had to be mitigated. Though UN aircraft operated freely bringing in supplies and equipment without being engaged, they were not a threat to the SNA and would not likely be engaged. Once AC-130s began to engage SNA targets, there was potential for retaliation via MANPADS, provided the SNA was so equipped. To counter the MANPADS threat, the AC-130 fleet was equipped with the AN/AAR-44 IR Countermeasure system that was touted as being able to detect a launch and automatically dispense flares via the ALE-40 system. The system was so new it had not been fully tested, but, if it worked, the MANPADS threat would be greatly diminished.

The SNA skill set: The average SNA militant was battle hardened after many years of civil war. They tended to operate in cells or packs and were notoriously unpredictable, but were moderately capable of large-scale coordinated attacks.

Fighting Vehicles: Somalis employed armed light commercial trucks with large crew-served machine guns. These vehicles provided rapid mobility for 12.7mm, 14.5mm, and 23mm

AAA guns used for ground to ground attacks. These vehicles were commonly referred to as "Technical Vehicles" which were favored by the SNA for speed, mobility and firepower.

Armored Vehicles: The SNA possessed nearly three hundred tanks including the US built M47 Patton and M41 Walker Bulldog, British Centurion and Soviet-built T-54-55. Armored Personnel Carriers included nearly five hundred Soviet-built BTR40/50/60 and a mixture of other APCs. Most of this equipment was determined to be in poor condition or abandoned with operational status unknown.

AC-130 MISSION PLANS

On June 10, Lt Col Connors led a joint team to Mogadishu via AC-130 to begin mission planning. At Mogadishu, AC-130 planners met with Combat Controllers and US Army Special Forces planners to build a grid overlay method to identify and predesignate targets identified by the UN staff. Targets and desired effects mandated by Boutros-Ghali, Admiral Howe, MG Montgomery, and a committee of UN personnel were rife with political constraints. It was clear the targeting committee was wholly uneducated in weapons effects and gunship capabilities.

AC-130 strikes were held to strict Rules Of Engagement (ROE) and short timelines and were not allowed to fire on any target without approval by the committee. Because of the extensive approval process, adaptation to an emergency ground situation would likely fail. Furthermore, the State Department and UN Security Council was politically sensitive to avoid injuring or killing Somali civilians who surrounded most targeted areas. For this reason, use of the AC-130s 20mm guns was forbidden because of ricochet potential, and all strikes would be done with 40mm and 105mm guns. Furthermore, all strikes would be announced via loudspeakers at least thirty minutes prior to allow Somali civilians to evacuate the target area. Because of these limitations, AC-130 planners felt tasking was overly optimistic, unrealistic, and tactically unsound, but they did their best to develop plans within the parameters of UN mandates.

Operating three AC-130s over closely spaced target areas in urban terrain was challenging. To simplify radio communications and aircraft identification, the 16 SOS was assigned the call sign Reach which would be used every day for the duration of the mission. To ensure adequate separation when in firing orbit, each crew was assigned an altitude between seven thousand to nine thousand feet AGL. Nevertheless, some target areas were so closely spaced that overlapping orbits presented risks for the lower AC-130 to receive hits from the upper gunship. To mitigate this issue, two aircraft would strike first while the third would remain in holding until called in.

> "All of these pre-planned targets were marked by laser and controlled by the two Combat Controllers and 1st SOW Liaison personnel.

> The observation point picked was the rooftop of the UN Pakistani Army Headquarters building…the tallest building overlooking the target area. Some targets were as close as 100 meters. A three-foot-high concrete wall around the roof protected personnel from shrapnel when 105mm rounds were fired." **SMSgt (Ret.) Steve Jones**

The first three strike missions were directed at Aidid's infrastructure. To collect current intelligence and get eyes-on the working area, planners were flown via helicopter over each target.

Capt Chris Mazur's crew was assigned a major SNA operations center known as the Cigarette Factory. This large, walled compound contained SNA personnel, equipment and weapons, but the crew was allowed only twenty minutes to strike numerous targets in two locations.

Capt Hughes' crew was assigned to the radio station that broadcasted Radio Aidid. This was a difficult target requiring surgical accuracy since the UN committee wanted Radio Aidid off the air, but didn't want Somali music records to be destroyed in the process. Thus, the plan identified what part of the building the records were stored and asked that area not be targeted.

Lt Col Waylett's crew was assigned a weapons storage area containing military vehicles and tanks, which most believed were abandoned and most likely unserviceable. Though the AC-130 had little capability to destroy heavy armor, a direct hit on track treads or road wheels could render tanks inoperable.

THE BEGINNING OF UNOSOM II STRIKES

On the afternoon of June 11, maintenance crews performed preflight checks on three sun-beaten aircraft as temperatures inside exceeded 130 degrees F. The aircraft were fully loaded with 40mm and 105mm ammunition and fueled at a waivered weight of 165,000 lbs. About an hour before sunset, Reach 67 (Capt Mazur), Reach 68 (Capt Hughes), and Reach 69 (Lt Col Waylett) took off on a 2.5 hour flight to Mogadishu International Airport.

It was dark by the time crews reached Mogadishu. On final approach, Reach 68 encountered problems with the newly installed AN/AAR-44 Infrared Detection set/countermeasure flare launching system.

> "We approached the Mog lights out and waited to turn on landing lights until very short final. Well, when Hughes (lead) turned them on ~200 ft., the reflection off the water was enough to kick off flares. His co-pilot, Blake Bushman, quickly announced that over interplane so the other EWOs could de-couple." **Col (Ret.) Frank Kuska**

While crews landed and taxied to the refueling area, the airport was buzzing with activity and AH-1 Cobra gunships patrolled the perimeter of the airport. While the AC-130s were being refueled, sounds of distant gunfire and the sight of an occasional large-caliber tracer skipped off the runway into the sea. During this time, helicopters equipped with loudspeakers flew over each target area broadcasting a warning to Somalis that a strike was pending.

About 30 minutes before scheduled strikes, crews took off, tweaked their fire control system/guns over international waters, then orbited offshore until it was time to proceed to their working areas. Reach 67 and Reach 68 were first to arrive over their assigned targets while Reach 69 remained in holding. Precisely on their pre planned time, both crews began firing. As soon as Reach 67 began firing on the Cigarette Factory compound, SNA militants began to scatter.

> "Too many buildings and not enough time to shoot them all. Next target, ammo storage facility, was a little tricky to find. Once we confirmed it, we put a couple of delays through the roof...about 10 seconds after the first delays went through, the Somalis came running out. I remember about 20 or so scattering in all directions." **Col (Ret.) Jon Peck,** Reach 67 Navigator

Meanwhile, the ground party, (call sign Victor 01) observed gunship strikes from the roof of the Pakistani headquarters building.

> Pakistani soldiers would come up to the roof and cheer whenever the gunship was firing. They were happy to see their dead and wounded comrades avenged. They would also bring us tea and cookies on trays while wearing white gloves. They were told many times to get down behind the wall to keep from being injured." **SMSgt (Ret.) Steve Jones,** USAF Combat Controller

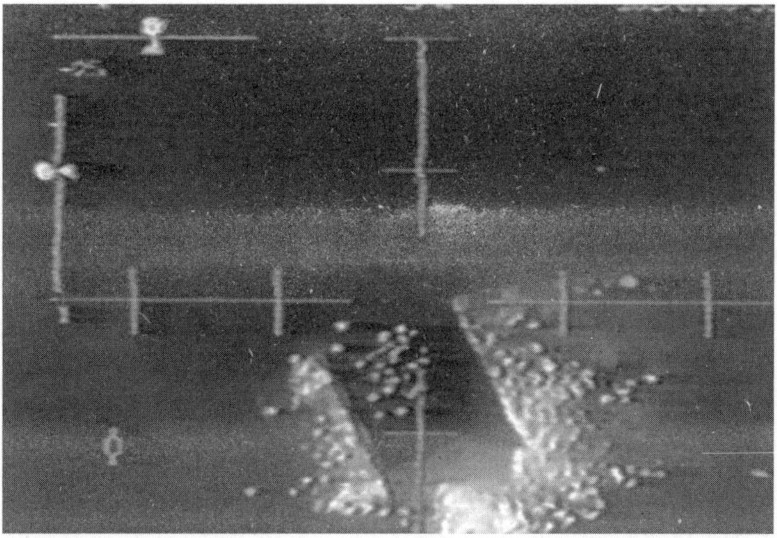

The first shot fired by Reach 67 on the Cigarette Factory. (Credit: Col (Ret.) Jon Peck)

At the radio station, Reach 68 fired their 40mm gun while a leaky hydraulic actuator hose sprayed a thin film of hydraulic oil on the floor. When it came time to fire the 105mm gun, gunners loaded the 105mm rounds with care to keep from dropping the 42-pound High Explosive round while moving on the slick floor. Reach 68 fired 96 rounds of 105mm HE during their attack, rendering heavy damage to the building and power transformers. During their mission the AN/AAR-44 system malfunctioned again and was de-coupled.

By now, 20 minutes had elapsed, so Reach 67 pulled off target to enable Reach 69 to fire on a weapons storage site. After establishing a firing orbit and attempting to fire, FCO Capt Tony Stefanik discovered his fire control computer was malfunctioning. The computer failed to reboot, so using a technique first employed in Grenada ten years earlier, gunners rigged the 105mm gun for manual lanyard firing. After firing a few rounds in this degraded mode, they scored one hit on a tank, but the inaccuracy of lanyard firing and concern for collateral damage prompted Lt Col Waylett to cease firing. When the AC-130 strike window ended, all crews returned to Djibouti.

The morning after the gunship's first attack in Mogadishu, US Ambassador to Djibouti, Charles Baquet, was called over to the President of Djibouti's office to explain what gunships were doing in his country. Apparently, the US State Department neglected to mention AC-130s were not cargo aircraft, but gunships. Surprised with the revelation, Ambassador Baquet visited Lt Col Connors in the mission planning room.

> "I gave the ambassador a general description of the gunships capabilities; told him the gunships were defending the US and UN forces in Mogadishu and would probably get tasked to do it again that night. The ambassador said OK he would handle it and gunship personnel never heard anything else about it." **Col (Ret.) Jim Connors**

On June 13, Capt Cutts crew (Reach 67) accompanied by Mission Commander Maj Keith Maresca was launched to engage a target named Atto's Garage. This was a facility known for manufacturing of "technical" vehicles which was owned by Osman Ali Atto, one of the wealthiest people in Somalia and Aidid's chief financial backer. Again, ROEs were restrictive, mandating all fire be placed within the confines of a fenced compound. After establishing a firing orbit over Atto's Garage, Cutts directed the use of 40mm HEI (Misch Metal), the least lethal round available. When the crew began firing on vehicles in the compound, exploding 40mm Misch Metal projectiles sent thousands of burning pyrophoric fragments 30 ft. into the air creating a thunderous light show. As expected, SNA personnel ran from the compound in panic while Reach 67 engaged targets. A tractor-trailer inside the compound was engaged with a 105mm HE. Nearing completion of their attack, a 40mm failure to fire malfunction occurred. After an unsuccessful attempt to fire the gun manually, Reach 67 rolled out and jettisoned the defective round in the Indian Ocean. Unable to return to the target before their pre-planned Time On Target (TOT) had expired, Reach 67 landed at Mogadishu International Airport for fuel before departing for Djibouti.

> "Following our strike on Atto's Garage, we landed at Mogadishu for fuel, only a couple of miles from where we had been firing. This was necessary because CENTCOM did not release any tankers to support the AC-130 missions in Somalia." **Col (Ret.) Brian Cutts**

On June 14, review of Reach 67's BDA tapes revealed less damage to Atto's Garage than what was expected. Capt Terry Crabtree's crew (Reach 67) was launched to re-strike, but with 105mm HE instead of 40mm Misch Metal. Though it was recognized that firing 105mm HE increased the risk of collateral damage, use of 105mm was considered a necessary risk.

Reach 67 took off just after dark. Arriving overhead Atto's Garage, the sound of the AC-130 caused personnel to run from the compound. Again, with restrictive ROEs in place, Reach 67 fired their first 105mm round with extreme caution, but were greeted with a surprise.

> "Exactly on our predetermined time, Capt Crabtree cleared us to engage the facility and to everyone's surprise, our first round was not on target. I immediately checked all settings since the 105mm round fell outside the compound area. After a careful quick check of the fire-control system, I recommended continuance of the engagement. The second round found dead center on the target." **Capt Russell "Sully" Sullivan,** Fire-control Officer

After carefully pounding the walled compound for about an hour, Reach 67 was sent to a weapons storage facility about a mile to the west. As they fired on the facility with 40mm and 105mm, the weather closed in. Unable to maintain a clear view of the target, Reach 67 returned to Djibouti.

There was still a long list of targets that had yet to be engaged. Furthermore, collateral damage concerns, restrictive ROEs, and short Time On Target (TOT) contributed to less damage than the AC-130 was capable of, a situation requiring a number of re-strike missions.

On June 15, *Night Stalker* was scheduled to fly a strike mission. Though not widely known, it was the only AC-130H of the original eleven produced that had not logged a combat mission.[6] Knowing this, *Night Stalker*'s crew chiefs SSgt Ben Weber and SSgt Dave Rhodes were happy to see their aircraft leading the next day's strikes.

On June 16, all four aircraft sat on the ground while waiting for the weather to clear. During this time, AC-130 planners were bombarded with changes to the plan directed by the UN Targeting Committee. One planner counted twenty-six changes or adjustments to strike plans. The situation was confusing to say the least, but planners had no option other than to adapt to the changes as they poured it.

On June 17, Aidid was in hiding, prompting Admiral Howe to offer a $20,000 bounty for his capture, which was certainly out of bounds relating to the UN charter and could aptly be described as a personal vendetta against Aidid. Later that evening, the weather was clear and a three-ship strike package was ready to launch. Leading the effort was *Night Stalker* (Reach 66) commanded by Capt Rich Forlano, accompanied by mission commander Lt Col Mike Byers. Second was *Death Angel* (Reach 67), commanded by Capt Paul Havel, and the airborne spare was *Iron Maiden*

6 AC-130E/H *Night Stalker* was a training aircraft stationed at Hurlburt during Vietnam for the duration of the war. It's first attempt to fly a combat mission was for Urgent Fury in Grenada, but after takeoff, it aborted for an engine fire. It also missed Panama and Desert Storm.

(Reach 68), commanded by Capt Don Timpson. Following the same profiles as previous missions, Reach 66 and Reach 67 took off from Djibouti and flew directly to Mogadishu International Airport where they landed for fuel. When fully fueled, Reach 66 taxied to the end of the runway for what should have been a normal heavyweight take off. When Forlano applied power, the heavy aircraft slowly accelerated down the runway until lifting off. All was normal until about 500 ft. AGL, when *Night Stalker*'s number three engine caught fire.

> "I was sitting in the scanner seat for this mission and I certainly had never seen an engine fire. First a few sparks, and then a red glow from the tailpipe. Within seconds the flame intensified and could be seen out the right paratroop door by the loadmaster, Shane Tungate. Just as I was about to hit my call switch to notify the crew of the fire, the flight engineer announced the fire over main interphone." **SSgt Greg Hlavaty,** Reach 66 gunner

Capt Forlano realized shutting an engine down on his heavy aircraft at low altitude and airspeed was a high-risk decision. Noting the burning engine was still producing power, he decided to continue gaining airspeed while climbing to a safer altitude. At the same time, TSgt Rob Withrow (FE) began dumping fuel to lighten the aircraft. Once in stable flight, the copilot shut down number three engine via fire handle which extinguished the fire and feathered its propeller.

Unable to continue their mission with three engines, Forlano declared an In Flight Emergency (IFE) and was cleared to land with an approach over the city. Realizing the aircraft would be an easy target for SNA small arms on that approach, he opted to land from the opposite end of the runway with an over water approach. Navigator Capt Mike Marra plotted a course knowing the airport's navigation aids were inoperable and they would be landing with a tail wind. About this time, the crew began configuring the aircraft for an emergency landing when they discovered the throttle lever for number four engine was jammed at the full power setting. Knowing it would be impossible to land safely with one engine stuck on full power, they kept the engine running until short final. From that point on, *Night Stalker* would be committed to land since it would not have enough power to climb for another approach.

On final approach, Capt Forlano directed number four engine shut down. Reach 66's copilot, Capt Chris Ferraraccio began shut down procedures, eventually needing to pull number four's fire handle to feather its prop. Despite the loss of both engines on the right wing and the need for heavy left rudder inputs, Forlano's approach and landing was smooth, though much faster than normal. The emergency, however, was not over since they still needed to stop and reversing two engines on the left wing would cause them to run off the runway. About half way down the runway, *Night Stalker* was still traveling over 100 knots so

Forlano applied much heavier than normal brake pressure to slow the aircraft. Not knowing if they were able to stop before running into a wall at the end of the runway, the crew braced for impact.

Reach 66 squealed to a stop just short of the runways end. The smell of burning brakes permeated the inside of the aircraft while Capt Forlano pulled off the runway onto a taxiway. Now clear of the active runway, Forlano activated alarm bells, and ordered an immediate emergency egress. The crew quickly evacuated *Night Stalker* as smoke poured from red-hot main landing gear brakes. From a distance, the crew watched the glowing brakes with hopes they would not start a fire that would ultimately destroy their aircraft. Within minutes, the overheated brakes melted fusible plugs in each tire rim, causing all four main tires to deflate. It was obvious Reach 66 wasn't going anywhere that night.

Capt Havel's crew was refueling while Reach 66 landed IFE. Less than fifteen minutes after witnessing Forlano's IFE, Reach 67 taxied past the crippled aircraft, rolled onto the runway, and took off. Reach 67 was assigned the task of re-striking Atto's Garage, residence and weapon storage areas. Because an AH-1 strike several days earlier resulted in a number of civilian deaths, ROEs had been changed requiring AC-130 crews to illuminate targets with their 2KW spotlight for five minutes prior to firing. Furthermore, they were required to coordinate attacks with a psychological operations team on the ground near the target area. If that wasn't enough, Reach 67 was directed to begin each attack by firing a single 40mm round on target, then wait five minutes for Somalis to evacuate before firing for effect. Considering the task at hand, AC-130 crews found these restrictions political and silly, but nevertheless followed the ROEs to the letter. When they arrived overhead their first target, weather was a factor and only about two thirds of their orbit unusable because of cloud cover. Regardless of the limitation, Reach 67 damaged Aidid's residence and guard house then proceeded to Atto's residence. Within an hour, they managed to destroy Atto's residence, two weapons storage caches, two roadblocks, several technical vehicles and two front-end loaders.

About an hour after Reach 66 landed IFE, Reach 68 arrived at holding from Djibouti. To make the rigid timeline, Capt Timpson's crew flew directly to Reach 66's target area. Using the same ROEs as Reach 67, the crew discovered their 2KW spotlight would not slave to the LLLTV sensor. Not wanting to abort the mission, gunners SSgt Tony Millhouse and SSgt Kevin Neperud took turns manually positioning the spotlight onto the target via "talk-on" by Timpson. Once Reach 68 was confident the target was clear of personnel, they began firing. For the next two hours, Reach 68 carefully fired dozens of 105mm rounds onto Atto's Garage and an ammunition storage area, scoring several large secondary explosions. When low on fuel and ammunition, Capt Timpson landed on Mogadishu airport, taxied next to Reach 66, then shut down.

When Timpson met with Forlano to hash out a plan of action, the sounds of Reach 67 engaging targets a few miles away with 105mm HE rang out. An inspection of *Night*

Stalker revealed a blown bleed air duct on the right wing. Since the aircraft wasn't repairable, gunners from both aircraft transferred seventy-six rounds of 105mm HE ammunition from Reach 66 to Reach 68 while refueling was in progress. After refueling was complete, Timpson's crew hurriedly started engines, taxied and took off to fire on the targets originally assigned to Reach 66. Understandably, Forlanos's crew was not happy to be stranded on the Mogadishu airport, but had no choice other than to remain in place as *Reach 68* fired on their assigned targets only a few miles away.

By the time Reach 68 began engaging targets, Reach 67 had completed their strikes. After landing and refueling, gunners trans-loaded the remaining 24 rounds of 105mm from Reach 66 onto Reach 67, then about half of Forlano's crew boarded Reach 67 for the trip back to Djibouti. The rest of Capt Forlano's crew waited next to their crippled aircraft for Capt Timpson's crew to finish their strike mission before being picked up and flown back to Djibouti. When the night was over, *Night Stalker* sat alone near the perimeter of the airport with a blown bleed air duct, all four props feathered, and four flat tires.

As soon as Capt Forlano's crew returned to Djibouti, maintainers were briefed on the condition of *Night Stalker*. Immediately afterward, gunship maintenance technicians gathered tools and parts needed and prepared for a trip to Mogadishu. Early the next morning, they flew via C-141 Starlifter directly to Mogadishu International Airport. Upon landing, they were met by three escorts who transported them to *Night Stalker*.

> "Based on debrief from the crew, we gathered tools and some parts and boarded a C-141 to Mog. We were met by three men in civilian clothes who briefed us on the dangers of the area. We were instructed not to get on top of the aircraft and to wear our flak vests at all times because of possible sniper gunfire. Due to the extreme heat/humidity and location of the aircraft damage, within five minutes we had broken the rules. Vests were off and we were on top of the aircraft. All day long Cobra helicopters were flying the perimeter and constant gunfire could be heard." **CMSgt (Ret.) Christopher Langlois**

It was a long day for the maintainers since they had already worked a full shift at Djibouti before being flown to Mogadishu. After about 14 hours of work, MSgt Chris Langlois, TSgt Ken Curry, TSgt Tom Riley, SSgt Marty Theis, SSgt Ben Weber, and Sgt Dave Rhodes completed all repairs possible, but had to wait for a new bleed air duct to be flown in from Djibouti. At the end of their long day, the team was exhausted, but the local tent city was full. Fortunately, one of the deployed medical units offered up their cots so they could get some rest. The next day, a new bleed air duct was delivered and installed. Satisfied the aircraft was repaired, Capt Cutts primary crew was flown to Mogadishu on an

Army C-12 to retrieve *Night Stalker* and the maintenance team. Fortunately, the return trip to Djibouti was uneventful.

Though Boutros-Ghali and Admiral Howe thought Aidid's hold on Mogadishu would be diminished by air strikes, they actually had an opposite effect. Aidid convinced citizens of Mogadishu that UNOSOM II forces were enemies of Somalia. He understood the power of international media and wanted UNOSOM II forces to be portrayed as cold, heartless assassins to easily duped international media representatives who were swarming all over Mogadishu. His militia used women and children as human shields, placing them on or near targeted areas with hopes they would be killed and the images of mutilated women and children would be broadcast world-wide. In an ironic twist, loudspeaker announcements and spotlight use before firing enabled staging of tragic scenes instead of preventing them. It seemed Aidid was much more in control of the political situation in Mogadishu than the UN could ever hope to be.

Once the UN Secretary General decided air strikes were not affecting Aidid as expected, he requested CENTCOM begin an aggressive ground operation to capture SNA leaders including Aidid. Gen Hoar did not agree with the recommended course of action, but was overruled by Secretary of Defense Les Aspin and the Joint Chiefs of Staff. Tasked with capturing Aidid, USSOCOM stood up a Joint Special Operations Task Force (JSOTF) planning team. The next day, 1 SOW Special Mission Planners Capt Dion Scaglione and SSgt Doug Michna reported to Ft Bragg, NC to coordinate with USSOCOM planners for Operation *Caustic*

Brimstone, a classified "snatch & grab" mission to capture Aidid. For reasons of operations security, the JSOTF chain of command had no connection to UNOSOM II or JTF-Somalia commanders. Instead, the JSOTF would receive orders and report directly to Gen Hoar only.

Mission planners hoped the Pentagon and State Department would act quickly to approve *Caustic Brimstone* while AC-130s were still in place in Somalia, but the State Department rejected the plan and reduced the scope of *Caustic Brimstone* to a small, limited deployment void of AC-130 support. USSOCOM leadership pushed back, hoping to increase the scope of the mission to include AC-130s, but the State Department refused. When mission plans were complete, planners returned to their home units.[7]

In the days following the June 17 strikes, the UN targeting committee requested more AC-130 strikes. By then, an insidious onset of political positioning stymied the entire effort since any UN country could veto a target at any point. Several times, crews took off with an approved target list only to be cancelled before reaching Mogadishu. After the 4th of July, AC-130s were released by CENTCOM and by mid-July, the last C-5 out of Djibouti departed with Lt Col John Easley's maintenance support package.

After landing on Hurlburt, crewmen and maintainers learned another deployment was already in the works, but to an entirely different continent. The next day, the first AC-130 left Hurlburt, headed for Italy to support Operation

7 E-mail from Lt Col (Ret.) Dion Scaglione to Author, June 2014.

Deny Flight missions over Bosnia and Herzegovina. A few days later, two more AC-130s and three crews were in place at San Vito dei Normanni AS, Italy, ready to begin flying missions over the war-torn region.

Meanwhile, special mission planners at Hurlburt were recalled to Ft. Bragg to resume Operation *Caustic Brimstone* planning. Getting the AC-130s back to the Horn of Africa proved to be challenging however. Because the government of Djibouti was not enamored with supporting further AC-130 operations, the State Department decided all operations were to be conducted from Mogadishu International Airport. This was a major issue since there was no C-130 support in Mogadishu and the logistic footprint exceeded capabilities of the largely non-functional airport. Furthermore, Somalis, especially the SNA, feared the AC-130 after the June attacks and were likely to attack AC-130s with small arms, RPG and Mortar fire to destroy all aircraft as they sat in the parking area. The risk of loss of four AC-130H gunships out of a world-wide fleet of nine negated operations based out of Mogadishu International Airport. AC-130 planners suggested operating from the US Navy P-3 station in Mombasa, Kenya, but their request was flatly denied. Once Gen Hoar and the Undersecretary of Defense for Policy presented the plan, they decided to exclude AC-130s from Operation *Caustic Brimstone* because they believed another AC-130 deployment would be perceived as an expansion of the US military role in the region.

> "...General Hoar, the head of the Central Command, recommended against sending the gunships. General Hoar believed that the Army helicopters in Somalia provided adequate firepower and that the dispatch of the gunships would enlarge the American military presence in the region at a time when Washington was looking to transfer the mission entirely to the United Nations, officials said. Frank G. Wisner, the Undersecretary of Defense for Policy, also recommended against sending the gunships, an official said." (Gordon 1994)

This decision was not well received by AC-130 or USSOCOM planners. With no AC-130s available, air support for the JSOTF relied solely on small arms and rocket fire from 160th SOAR AH-6 and MH-60 Defensive Armed Penetrators (DAP) helicopters. For more than a decade, AC-130 and TF-160 crews worked together as a team, and both units respected each other's contributions to the overall mission. Contrary to Gen Hoar's opinion, JTF leadership and planners believed they needed AH-6s, MH-60 DAPS and AC-130s to provide overlapping capabilities. While the topic was being debated at the USSOCOM, CENTCOM, and US State Department level, AC-130 crews participated in pre-deployment training with the Task Force in El Paso, TX.

After a live fire/dry fire rehearsal from July 12–19, 1993, the tactical mission plan was complete. The mission to capture Aidid was named Operation *Gothic Serpent* and the

JSOTF was named Task Force Ranger, commanded by MG William Garrison.[8]

When Capt Scaglione traveled to Ft. Bragg to brief *Gothic Serpent* AC-130 mission plans, he began his briefing with a well-known axiom in the gunship community: "When you don't need a gunship, almost anything will do; but, when you need a gunship, nothing else will do." He then went on to describe the scenarios in which the AC-130s would be indispensable. Capt Scaglione laid out a convincing scenario to get AC-130 support added back into the mission plan and operate from the neighboring country of Kenya. MG Garrison and USSOCOM Commander General Wayne Downing were convinced the task force needed AC-130s and armor support for Task Force Ranger, but their request was denied by the Chairman of the Joint Chiefs of Staff Gen Colin Powell, Secretary of Defense Les Aspin, and CENTCOM commander, Gen Hoar.

> "I think it's important to note that the Task Force Ranger leaders were not the ones making the call for no AC-130 support, but that Task Force leaders would have to make due with the fire support assets they had with 160th SOAR once the final deployment package was determined."
> **Lt Col (Ret.) Dion Scaglione**

On August 22, the 440 member JSOTF deployed to Mogadishu, ultimately conducting capture missions begin-

8 Email from Lt Col (Ret.) Dion Scaglione, to Author, June 2014.

ning in late August. By October, Aidid remained in hiding, but TF-Ranger captured a number of the leaders of Habar Gidir (Aidid's sub clan) including Osman Atto. On October 3, during a routine capture mission in central Mogadishu, USSOCOM Assaulters successfully apprehended several Habar Gidir lieutenants. As the mission progressed, Aidid's SNA militia shot down two helicopters over the city with small arms and RPG-7 fire. The capture mission quickly turned into a rescue mission and throughout the night, vastly outnumbered soldiers and airmen fought a pitched battle for survival. As the battle unfolded, MG Garrison sent an urgent request to "get the AC-130s here now" directly to President Clinton. President Clinton immediately ordered AC-130H gunships and armored personnel carriers to Somalia. By the time the battle ended, 18 American soldiers were dead and more than eighty were wounded. Chief Warrant Officer 3 (CW3) Michael Durant was captured and his whereabouts were unknown.[9] Nearly one thousand Somalis were dead and the city of Mogadishu was in utter chaos.

In response to the situation in Somalia, AC-130 crews at San Vito AS, Italy were alerted to redeploy immediately to Africa to support the TF-Ranger element. Operation *Deny Flight* missions were put on hold as all four AC-130s on station were being prepared to redeploy. Since Mogadishu International Airport was routinely mortared, the most logical location to deploy to was the US Navy P-3 detachment at Moi International Airport, Mombasa, Kenya, where

---

9 Mark Bowden, *Black Hawk Down* (New York, NY: Atlantic Monthly Press, 1999), 333.

AC-130s could operate for several days with whatever they brought from Italy.

The first two AC-130 gunships commanded by Capt Chris Mazur and Capt Bob Sack left San Vito on October 5. Both crews took off at maximum gross weight, fully packed with as much support equipment as possible. Each aircraft was manned with a full tactical crew, a combat load of ammunition, several crew chiefs and a security policeman. Both crews flew 14-plus hour flights directly to Mombasa. The following day, Capt Mark Demers and Capt Kevin Fox's crews departed for Mombasa, leaving only a skeleton staff at Brindisi. While en route, Fox's crew experienced an aircraft problem and had to divert to Cairo, Egypt for one day.

October 1993 Re-Deployment	
Aircraft	Aircraft Commander
69-6568 "Night Stalker"	Capt Chris Mazur
69-6576 "Hell Raiser"	Capt Robert Sack
69-6573 "Heavy Metal"	Capt Mark Demers
69-6569 "Fatal Attraction"	Capt Kevin Fox

On October 6, Gen Downing and his staff including AC-130 planner Capt Scagilone, landed at Mogadishu airport just in time for a memorial service for the 18 soldiers killed. Later that evening, a SNA mortar round impacted near the TF Ranger hangar, killing an Army SF Soldier and injuring a dozen others. With CW3 Durant missing and the city in disorganized chaos, the SNA was emboldened by their victory and further attacks were likely.

As soon as the 16 SOS arrived in Mombasa, Lt Col Connors received orders directing 24-hour surveillance coverage over Mogadishu. This was challenging since there were not enough crews on station to fill a 24-hour flying regimen. Nevertheless, crews were committed to fly at maximum effort to meet tasking. The basic mission scenario was to take off with a full load of ammunition and fuel, clear an area of international waters of the Indian Ocean, dispense MK-25 markers, then tweak all guns on the markers. When the tweak was complete, crews would fly directly to Mogadishu International Airport, land for refueling, brief with TF-Ranger, then take off to perform their tasked mission.

AC-130 missions began on October 7. Since refueling tanker support was not available, takeoff times were spaced several hours apart to overlap coverage. The first two missions were flown by Captains Sack and Mazur. Sack's crew flew to Mogadishu in the afternoon to plan with TF Ranger and fly a surveillance mission over Aidid's facilities.

> "Upon arrival at Mogadishu, we were met by Capt Scaglione and about twenty-five TF Ranger personnel. Every Ranger we met said they were extremely glad we were there. We were taken into a briefing room and handed gridded satellite photos (GRG's) of the entire city. Highlighted were the areas of interest like Aidid's residence, Atto's garage, Olympic Hotel and the two crash sites. After briefing, one of the

> Rangers wanted to take me up in a helicopter and overfly the wreckage and major points of interest. Considering the earlier fate of daylight low-level helicopter flights over Mogadishu, I surmised the GRG's would work just fine. As soon as our aircraft was refueled, we took off to fly our mission." **Lt Col (Ret.) Jerry Harris,** Fire Control Officer

It was dark when Capt Sack's crew completed their mission and headed back to Mombasa. By then, Mazur's crew landed on the blacked-out airport for refueling and to brief with TF-Ranger. Once refueled, they took off searching for mortar positions. Though finding several suspicious locations, neither crew was cleared to fire.

The next night, Sack departed for Mogadishu on *Hell Raiser*, landed for fuel and mission tasking from MG Garrison. During an earlier planning session, his staff considered a number of options to prevent additional mortar attacks, then settled on a high-intensity show of force via AC-130 to communicate to CW3 Durant the AC-130 was on station, and to send a clear message to those holding him what would happen to them if fighting continued. Once assigned tasking, Sack's crew took off, established a firing orbit centered on a road intersection near Radio Mogadishu, then opened fire with twenty rounds of 105mm HE. After firing, they remained overhead for several hours until low on fuel. Capt Mazur's crew arrived on station to relieve Capt Sack's crew and repeated the same mission profile on a road intersection near the Cigarette Factory. When they fired 105mm HE and 40mm HEI at maximum effort, SNA militia members were seen jumping out of windows and running from the compound in a panic. After the attack, Mazur's crew remained on station, monitoring activity until low on fuel, then returned to Mombasa. Though nobody realized it at the time, *Night Stalker* had fired its guns in combat for the first time.

The next morning, Aidid called for a unilateral ceasefire, but, nevertheless, AC-130 missions continued. UNOSOM II soldiers found the constant prop noise of an AC-130 gunship orbiting over Mogadishu invoked fear in SNA ranks. That factor alone was not sufficient to convince the SNA to release CW3 Durant, however. While AC-130s and Navy P-3s (often mistaken for AC-130s) rode shotgun over Mogadishu, MH-60s flew overhead the city with loudspeakers blazing in an effort to locate and rescue CW3 Durant. As a result of this activity, it was rare to find anyone wandering the streets at night, but indiscriminate firing resulting from inter-clan fighting continued within the city.

> "Stray bullets would still find their way onto the airport grounds during daylight conditions. We finished a refueling stop and requested clearance from the tower. CCT refused to let us taxi. They stated that the northeast end of the field was taking fire and they couldn't authorize us to taxi into that area. I don't recall who came up with the idea, but we explained to CCT that if we

> could get airborne, the sniping would stop. We said we were willing to take off to the north-east. This was a risky proposition as it would require us to fly at rooftop height over the city. CCT agreed and let us go. Bob determined our best course of action was to rotate at max effort takeoff speed and accelerate in ground effect. He would then start an early right turnout over the sand dunes and water in order for us to avoid flying over the city." **CMSgt (Ret.) Mike Longe,** FE

By October 13, the overall situation at night appeared relatively quiet and the most visible sign of activity was arc welding flashes coming from buildings. Welding also caused false alarms of the AN/AAR-44 threat detection system, so all crews decoupled the system to avoid depleting flares.

On October 14, CW3 Durant was released and the remains of those killed during the battle were returned. With a full ceasefire in effect, TF Ranger prepared to depart Mogadishu. On October 23, the last elements of TF Ranger left Somalia and control of all AC-130s was passed to the Joint Task Force/10th Mountain Division.[10] The Clinton Administration wanted to pull all US forces from Somalia immediately, but, once again, Boutros-Ghali pleaded for continued US support. After the UN passed Resolution 954, the Clinton Administration agreed to retain US forces in Somalia.

---

10 Email from Lt Col (Ret.) Dion Scaglione to Author, June 2014.

To cover this tasking, AC-130 support was reinforced with additional personnel and support equipment being flown in from Hurlburt to provide over watch security for 10th Mountain Division soldiers and UNOSOM II forces.

> "Rich Wallace and I were hustled out of the squadron and flew to Pope and boarded a C-5 with some folks from that area and flew nonstop (2 A/Rs) to Mogadishu. We landed in Mogadishu amidst a lot of action on the ramp and in the city. When Task Force Ranger pulled out, Rich and I moved in with the 10th Mountain and continued the LNO role working Gunship missions 24/7. We would fax target charts to the unit in Mombasa or sometimes meet the airplane in Mogadishu and give them a verbal update on the nights missions" **Col (Ret.) Steve Wiggins**

Since AC-130 missions were scheduled every night to cover a period from sundown to sunrise, all four crews surpassed 100 flying hours in the first two weeks, but missions continued with one crew exceeding 160 hours in a five-week period. Missions followed a repeatable methodology, but once tanker support arrived, crews no longer had to land at Mogadishu for fuel. Support equipment including ammunition was stored on one end of the airport runway, but everyone knew firing authorization was unlikely.

By the end of November, eight crews were operating from Mombasa, flying missions day and night. After almost sixty days of constant mission activity and overly restrictive ROEs, crews were getting burned out. Most felt their contribution was solely to satisfy JTF-Somalia and UN politicians, but the overwhelming theme shared by crews and maintainers was the mission had evolved into a quagmire of mediocrity and UN indecisiveness.

> "Droning for hours over the city with no radio chatter, coupled with chronic fatigue from revolving crew days, proved too much for even the most dedicated crew members. When the body needs to sleep, it will sleep regardless of a person's needs or desires. We had no hot water on the aircraft and some of us took to ingesting 'Sanka Shots' in a desperate effort to remain alert. We would take one Sanka Coffee packet from the MREs, pour the crystals into our mouths, followed by a swig of water. An instant caffeine high resulted but soon there would also arrive the rebound, feeling more tired than before." **CMSgt (Ret.) Mike Longe,** flight engineer

Since all missions were essentially the same with little deviation, boredom and complacency took its toll. Crews flew the exact mission profile for weeks without any sign of an end. By the end of November, political pressure made ROEs more restrictive, ridiculous, and unworkable. One night, Capt Seth Junkin's crew tracked a Technical vehicle firing its gun and requested clearance to fire, but after an hour and a half of radio traffic, they ran out of fuel without being cleared.

> "It was very frustrating, since we were not allowed to fire on the vehicle that had been firing on us off and on for nearly an hour and a half. Through all of our efforts, we tracked the vehicle until we were low on fuel, and never received clearance to fire." **SMSgt (Ret.) Wayne White,** gunner

As time passed, the overly restrictive ROEs gave crews the perception their only contribution was providing constant noise over Mogadishu. From a ground perspective, soldiers felt the AC-130 was a "security blanket," but, at the same time, the SNA was aware they would not likely be fired upon because of the overly restrictive politically-driven ROEs.

During off days, crews spent their time in Kenyan hotels as if they were tourists stuck in one place for months on end without the chance to escape. The traditional "post-flight beer" became more of a ritual for some and hijinks and practical jokes on the waiters became commonplace. To add excitement to the routine blandness of the mission, some crews started "buzzing" the beach in front of the hotel at low altitude on their outbound leg of a mission. After a gunship crew challenged a C-5 crew to buzz the hotel, an "aluminum overcast of screaming engines" amused crewmen but terrorized unsuspecting tourists. After that, the practice of buzzing abruptly ended.

As the weeks passed, crews and maintainers accepted their fate and settled in for the long haul. Thanksgiving and

Christmas meals were catered nicely, but the backdrop of a seemingly endless and meaningless mission weighed heavily on morale. Everyone looked forward to January 1, 1994 when the AC-130 mission was supposed to end; but, in late December, The UN Security Council managed to extend the AC-130 deployment to March 31, 1994. This was another letdown for crews and maintainers, but both airborne and ground alert missions continued into March with virtually no deviation.

At 1703 hours on March 14, 1994, Capt John "JP" Palen's crew boarded *Hell Raiser* (call sign Jockey 14) for a routine 8.5 hour mission. After successfully tweaking their 40mm gun over the Indian Ocean, they began tweaking their 105mm gun. After firing five shots, a direct hit extinguished one of two MK-25 markers the crew was targeting. While IR sensor operator TSgt Bobby Daniel shifted to the remaining marker, copilot Capt Kevin Thompson directed another marker to be launched. Once launched, gunners called the gun ready and armed. All seemed to be normal, but when the 105mm gun fired, a loud explosion rang out, number one propeller literally flew off its engine, and the entire left wing was on fire.

Capt Palen ordered a crew check in and there were no injuries, but *Hell Raiser* was in bad shape. The aircraft was filled with smoke and burning fuel seeped into the fuselage, which was extinguished by gunners. Palen and Thompson maintained control of the aircraft while navigator Capt Dave Mehlhop plotted a course to a nearby airport in Malindi, Kenya. While *Hell Raiser* headed towards the airport, Flight engineer TSgt Steve Anderson was concerned that the number two engine was on fire and could stop with an unfeathered prop at any moment. If this were to happen, excess drag on the left wing would likely cause control issues, a stall, and crash, so Thompson pulled the engine's fire handle to shut down the engine. With number two prop feathered, TSgt Anderson began to dump fuel to lighten the aircraft. Unfortunately, with two engines out, the heavily loaded gunship no longer had enough power to remain airborne. Palen and Thompson struggled to control the aircraft while it descended at a rate of fifteen hundred–two thousand feet per minute.

Capt Palen realized he was not going to make it to the airport and directed his crew to bail out. Crewmen scrambled to the back of the aircraft to don emergency equipment and parachutes. As soon as MSgt Roy Duncan opened the right paratroop door, four crewmen bailed out.

> "I stepped up to the door, looked back to see my fellow crew members standing in line, just before I closed my eyes I saw the right wing raise up. That was the moment I forced myself out the door and struck the side of the aircraft and began to spin/twist. I threw my arms and legs out, stabilized myself, pulled the ripcord and watched the parachute unravel between my legs. 'Wham,' opening shock and I was under a full canopy. I turned my head to the right and was surprised at how close I was to the aircraft. I

> could hear the engines roaring and could see the huge white flame burning on the left side of the gunship. That is a sight I will never, ever forget!! I watched as another gunner exited the aircraft and felt a sense of relief thinking that everyone was going to get out. Then, before I knew it, I was about to land in the Indian Ocean. I inflated my life-preserver units as I hit the water, released my parachute and there I was, all alone floating miles off-shore without a life raft just hanging in my LPUs." **MSgt (Ret.) Dave Ceurvels**

When it was too low to bail out, MSgt Duncan closed the right paratroop door and advised other crewmen to brace for impact.

Now dangerously close to the water's surface and descending rapidly, Capt Palen spotted a large rock near the beach, directly in his flight path. After altering his course to avoid hitting the rock, the aircraft contacted water at a speed in excess of 160 knots. During a series of hard impacts that followed, the fuselage and cockpit separated, causing a wall of water to rush into the fuselage. A jet of water blasted through the fuselage ripping the booth, guns, ammunition from the floor of the aircraft. When the wall of water hit the cargo door, it ripped if from its hinges. From that point on, contents of the fuselage, including some crewmen were ejected from the back of the fuselage in a debris line about 1,800 ft. long. When *Hell Raiser* came to rest, the cockpit section had turned 180 degrees, with the nose pointing towards the broken fuselage. The wreckage quickly sank in about 15 ft. of water. Both pilots and the flight engineer escaped from the submerged cockpit, but seven crewmen didn't survive the crash. Furthermore, three of the gunners who bailed out were recovered by local fishermen, but SSgt Bill Eyler was not found.[11]

A search and rescue mission continued for three days and an accident investigation team was sent from Hurlburt to Mombasa. AC-130 operations were curtailed and a memorial service was held for those lost in the crash. Fifteen days later, the AC-130 mission in Somalia ended—all aircraft and personnel returned to Hurlburt.

On January 27, 1995, the 16 SOS was tasked to deploy to Somalia once again to support Operation *United Shield*, USCINCCENT Combined Joint Task Force, Phase IV. It was feared the warring clans would pose security risks for withdrawing forces, especially at the Mogadishu airport. The operation was primarily a USMC controlled Non-Combatant Evacuation Operation (NEO). A package of four AC-130H gunships, two KC-135 tankers, 409 personnel consisting of eleven aircrews and maintainers and support personnel began to arrive in Mombasa, Kenya on 1 February. The gunships were tasked to provide nighttime support and USMC AV-8 Harriers and AH-1 Cobras were tasked to provide daytime support. The AC-130H was tasked by JCS because of their capabilities to limit collateral damage in the urban environment of Mogadishu.

11 SSgt William Eyler was the first to bail out, but was never found, even after several days of searching.

Apparently, AC-130 capabilities were viewed with skepticism by the JTF command staff in charge of the operation who were not convinced AC-130H gunships were as accurate as claimed. 16 SOS Liaison Officer Maj Bob Morrow arranged a demonstration for the JTF staff from the USS Belleau Wood: an amphibious assault ship. The demonstration involved the Navy crew placing several wooden crates with a flare affixed to one of them on the water surface. Afterward, the ship backed off a safe distance as an AC-130 crew orbited the target. Once cleared to fire, their first shot demolished the crates and their second shot extinguished the flare. The Marines were impressed with the truth in advertising of AC-130 capabilities. However, the probability AC-130s would be cleared to fire was remote.

> "Prior to operations beginning, MGen Zinni met with the local warlords. He said that if they kept things quiet, he would keep the gunship offshore. If they made trouble, he would bring the gunships overhead and they would lose face among their people. This worked pretty well. About halfway through the deployment, he allowed us to come close to the shore—'Just make sure your wings are not over land.' This allowed our sensor operators, navs, and FCOs to get a lay of the land in the event they ever got a CFF mission."
> **Col (Ret.) Frank Kuska**

AC-130 guns remained silent for the duration of the deployment. Crews flew 43 missions in 25 days, logging 404.1 flight hours, before returning to Hurlburt Field.

In March of 1995, AC-130s again deployed to Mogadishu airport for a seventy-two hour period during the final evacuation of Somalia, concluding the efforts of four deployments in three years.

MISSION DEBRIEF

AC-130 crews performed well during the June–July 1993 strikes, which caught the SNA by surprise. Unfortunately, AC-130 mission tasking during the UNOSOM II effort was dubious at best. The UN targeting committee, led by MG Montgomery, was inexperienced with AC-130 weapons effects and tactics, resulting in unrealistic expectations and damage levels. The psychological effect of AC-130 strikes waned quickly after restrictive ROEs mandated advanced announcements of pending strikes. This aspect gave SNA militants time to evacuate targeted areas alongside Somali civilians. After June air strikes did not result in capture of Aidid or affect the SNA as much as Boutros-Ghali expected, mission creep resulted in a full-fledged military action. Fundamentally, the mission in Somalia failed because politicians tasked the US military to perform a military task, then "tied their hands" for fear the US would appear to be an aggressor to the rest of the world.

AC-130 EXCLUSION FROM THE JSOTF

The political decision to eliminate AC-130 support for TF-Ranger had tragic consequences in terms of the loss of American lives and contributed to the failure of the overall mission. Though sending the AC-130s after the October 3 battle was purely a knee-jerk political reaction by the Clinton Administration, the gunships appear to have made a psychological impact on Aidid as he called for a cease fire the next day after AC-130 crews performed violent shows of force on October 8.

> "In disclosing his request for the AC-130's, General Garrison said the use of the gunships might have had an important psychological effect on the Somalis. 'The Somalis were petrified of the AC-130,' General Garrison told the Senate committee. But he also argued that the failure to send them did not deprive his force of the firepower it needed since it had helicopters. But Larry Joyce, who stunned the panel into silence with a moving eulogy for his son, a Ranger who was slain in the battle, rejected that argument. Mr. Joyce, who served two combat tours in Vietnam, told the panel the gunships would have been a potent weapon. Without them, Mr. Joyce said, Army helicopters were forced to hover at 75 feet to direct their fire, making them vulnerable targets." (Gordon 1994)

While it is true 160 SOAR AH-6 and MH-60 DAP helicopters performed magnificently while supporting TF Ranger, teaming them with AC-130s would have provided ground commanders with a greater range of well proven lethal options. Furthermore, AC-130s could keep eyes on target constantly for hours at a time without the need for run-in headings or gaps in fire support coverage for refueling and rearming.

Prior to Operation *Gothic Serpent*, AC-130s were an integral element of every JSOTF during joint exercises and real-world operations. These operations exemplified the fact that Special Operations personnel were proficient and skilled in directing AC-130 during convoy escort missions. This, coupled with the overhead "birds-eye" view, lethal and sustained fire support would have made a big difference for TF-Ranger.

> "The Gunships would clearly have made a difference in the execution of the 3 Oct mission. With that said, there were limitations on incorporating them into the fight. Gun runs by little birds were conducted sometimes within 10 feet of friendlies; remarkable fire support. So where the combat was most personal the Gunships would not decisively change the outcome. But for other sites, say crash site two with Durant's crew and Gordon and Shughart, the AC's could have established a wider perimeter and possi-

bly altered the ultimate outcome. We owe it to future operators to ensure we provide the most versatile platform under extreme conditions such as those we experienced in Mogadishu, in so many cases that platform remains the venerable AC-130." **Lt Col Dan Schilling,** USAF CCT, Task Force Ranger

POST OCTOBER 1993 MISSION ACTIVITY

After TF Ranger left Mogadishu, crews continued to perform long-duration missions with no clear-cut mission objective in a seemingly endless loop of dubious tasking. This overwhelming "tying of hands" manifested a level of complacency, disinterest, and cognitive dissonance that culminated with the loss of an aircraft and eight crewmen. In the end, the 16 SOS paid an enormous price during UNOSOM II, but the overall situation in Somalia did not change. After US forces pulled out of Somalia, the situation continued to deteriorate. By March of 1995, all UN efforts in Somalia ended as if no UN involvement had ever happened. Most believe the UN mission in Somalia has gone down in history as being a giant UN failure.

THE LOSS OF *HELL RAISER* (JOCKEY 14)

AFSOC commander Maj Gen Bruce Fister temporarily suspended all AC-130H operations and directed an Accident Investigation Board (AIB) headed by Lt Col Jim Lawrence. The AIB traveled to Malindi Kenya to begin their investigation. It was obvious a 105mm gun explosion caused the crash, but the cause of the explosion was unknown, and there were no living witnesses who were working the gun at the time of the explosion. Much of the wreckage was pulled from the Indian Ocean and transported to Hurlburt Field for analysis.

During the course of the investigation, a well-known shortcut procedure of dispensing MK-25 markers though the 105mm gun tube was suspected as being the cause of the accident. Within six months, Air Force Research Labs had duplicated the explosion twice during ground testing, proving the explosion was caused by a high-speed in-bore collision between a live HE round and a MK-25 marker. With the cause of the explosion determined, all other physical aspects of the accident fell into place. It was clear the crew of Jockey 14 was unaware the MK-25 failed to fall from the bore. In response, procedures and policies were formally established to prevent potential for a similar accident in the future.

Crewmen lost on March 14, 1994,

Capt David J. Mehlhop	Navigator
Capt Anthony Stefanik	Fire-control Officer
Capt Mark A. Quam	Electronic Warfare Officer
MSgt Roy S. Duncan	Loadmaster
TSgt Robert L. Daniel	Sensor Operator
SSgt William C. Eyler	Sensor Operator
SSgt Brian P. Barnes	Aerial Gunner
SSgt Mike E. Moser	Aerial Gunner

CHAPTER SEVEN

OPERATIONS *DENY FLIGHT* AND *DELIBERATE FORCE*, 1993–1995

Bosnia and Herzegovina (Credit: Carl Mauro II)

The Balkans have a turbulent and bloody history of warfare and foreign domination. At the end of World War-1, the Kingdom of Serbs, Croats, and Slovenes was established in 1918. The new political system included formerly independent kingdoms of Serbia and Montenegro and parts of the former Austria-Hungary. The result was a population of multiple ethnic and religious groups, lacking national identity and goals. The new country was named Yugoslavia in 1929. During World War-II, the Germans invaded Yugoslavia and western powers supported royalist guerillas known as Chetniks, who fought the Germans and communist partisans. After the Chetniks realized their people were being decimated by the Nazis, they ended combat operations against the Germans. Western powers then turned their support to the Russian communists, who eventually drove the Axis forces out of Serbia and Yugoslavia by 1945. At the end of World War-II, Josip Broz, also known as "Tito," leader of the Yugoslav partisans, was considered a national hero. In 1946, he became prime minister of the communist state renamed the Federal People's Republic of Yugoslavia. Tito ruled with an iron fist, and renamed the country the Socialist Federal Republic of Yugoslavia, and declared himself "President for Life" in April of 1963. The country was faced with economic hardships until 1980 when Tito died. The country remained in economic turmoil as the cold war ended. In 1990, elections were held in the republics of Yugoslavia. The ethnic tensions suppressed by Tito resurfaced with Slovenian and Croatian voters wanting more autonomy and those in Serbia and Montenegro favoring national unity. As a result, Serbs in Croatia did not want to be a minority in a sovereign Croatia and began demonstrations and civil disobedience. Tensions continued to increase and on June 25 1991, both Slovenia and Croatia declared independence from Yugoslavia. In the fall of 1991, Serbs living in Croatia established the Republic of Serbian Krajina within the borders of Croatia and began a campaign of slaughter they called "ethnic cleansing" accompanied by a full-scale civil war.[1]

By January of 1992, a ceasefire was declared by Croatian and Serbian presidents and three United Nations Protected Areas (UNPA) were established in Croatian areas controlled by Serbs. On February 21, 1992, the United Nations Security Council adopted Resolution 743 which established a Protection Force (UNPROFOR) commanded by General Philippe Morillon to provide safe havens in UNPA enclaves. Fighting in Croatia spilled into Bosnia-Herzegovina in 1992 and the scope of peacekeeping operations was expanded to include six security zones with UNPROFOR forces authorized to use force to defend them.[2]

On July 14, 1993, the National Command Authority through the Joint Chiefs of Staff gave an executive order to deploy aircraft to support United Nations Security Council Resolution (UNSCR) 836. The overall operation fell under the command of NATO's 5th Allied Tactical Air

1 Dr. Harold E. Raugh, Jr., *Operation Joint Endeavor, V Corps in Bosnia-Herzegovina 1995-1996, An Oral History* (Ft. Leavenworth, KS: Combat Studies Institute press, 2010).

2 Ibid.

Force (5 ATAF) which provided for the use of Close Air Support (CAS) assets to protect UNPROFOR in Bosnia-Herzegovina. A Combined Air Operations Center (CAOC) was established at Vicenza, Italy to control the hundreds of fighter aircraft and helicopters from the US, UK, France, Italy, the Netherlands, Spain, Turkey, and the multinational NATO airborne early warning force. The mission, named Operation *Deny Flight*, sought to prevent attacks between the warring factions by enforcing no-fly zones to prevent attacks on the designated safe areas.

Initially, two AC-130H gunships from Hurlburt were tasked to support *Deny Flight*, but within a few days the request was upgraded to four. Coincidentally, while planning for the deployment, a four ship combat deployment to Djibouti had just returned to Hurlburt. When 16 SOS commander Lt Col Jim Connors met squadron Operations Officer Lt Col Mike Byers on the flight line, he first welcomed him back home, then immediately directed him to get ready for another deployment, but this time to Europe.

BOSNIA AND HERZEGOVINA THREAT ASSESSMENT

> AAA guns: Optical and radar directed guns ranging from 14.5mm through 60mm were known to be in the area.
>
> Surface to Air Missile systems: SAMs present in the region included SA-2 Guideline, SA-6 Gainful, SA-9 Gaskin and an unknown number

of IR MANPADS including SA-7b Strela and SA-14 Gremlin. The Bosnian Serb Army operated a capable, but somewhat spotty Integrated Air Defense System (IADS), which was a significant concern for low and slow AC-130 crews. Lessons learned during *Desert Storm* were applied by gunship crews to develop effective defensive tactics, coupled with the recently installed AN/AAR-44 threat detection and IR countermeasures system. Nevertheless, Electronic Countermeasure systems capable of successfully jamming the myriad of enemy threat weapon radars in the operating area had not yet been procured. AC-130H Gunships initially deployed with ALQ-119 Electronic Countermeasure (ECM) pods which provided limited capabilities against radar threat systems in Bosnia-Herzegovina. Tactics to counter the multi-aspect cooled seekers of SA-14 and SA-16 were also developed and validated post *Desert Storm*. The new tactic was instituted in lieu of the Vietnam era tactics to defeat older IR threats such as the SA-7. In all cases, AC-130 survivability potential in the threat environment was directly proportional to operational altitude, which routinely exceeded ten thousand feet AGL.

<u>Fighter Interceptors/Helicopters</u>: MIG fighters were known to operate in the area and coalition Air Forces were authorized to shoot them down

on sight to enforce the established no-fly zone. MIG CAPs were well established, therefore the Fighter/Interceptor threat to AC-130 operations was determined to be minimal. Helicopters were allowed to fly to distribute humanitarian supplies. Both sides easily defied the no-fly mandate with relative impunity by covertly arming helicopters, sometimes painting red crosses on them to disguise them as medical aircraft.

Aircraft 6573 refueling over the Atlantic Ocean en route to Brindisi, Italy, 1993. (Credit: USAF photo)

Mission commander Lt Col Mike Byers led the deployment, which involved about 250 personnel. Aircraft Commanders Maj John "Marcus" Hicks, Maj Charles "Greg" McMillan, Capt Bob Sack and Capt Jim Bowe flew AC-130H gunships *Heavy Metal*, *Ghostrider*, *Night Stalker* and *Fatal Attraction* across the Atlantic Ocean to Brindisi, Italy. Beginning on July 17, AC-130s arrived on an Italian

Air Force airfield on the outskirts of Brindisi, to begin operations. Upon arrival, a maintenance control center, munitions storage area and operations facilities were established. Because of an alert commitment, aircraft remained loaded (including flares and chaff) in the parking area on the ramp. During initial operations, maintainers adopted two stray dogs they named Shadow and Guido who became squadron mascots.

Since lodging was scarce on the Italian base, crews and maintainers were billeted about seven miles away on a fledgling Air Force Space Command satellite tracking site at San Vito dei Normanni Air Station. Travel to and from San Vito was by bus.

> "When we got to San Vito, a Joint Special Operations Task Force (JSOTF) was in place. They were tasked and focused on the combat rescue and recovery for Deny Flight. Our mission tasking and tactical control came from NATO's 5 Allied Tactical Air Force (5 ATAF) Vicenza, IT, through the Air Tasking Order published daily by the 5 ATAF Combined Air Operations Center. There was the normal two-way education process between the ATO developers and us, but overall, we enjoyed a professional and courteous relationship." **Col (Ret.) Mike Byers,** Mission Commander

Since San Vito was scheduled to close, it was diminished when crews arrived. The BX and Commissary were still in operation but scaled back and slated to close within months. Crews first to arrive were billeted in a three-story barracks building with officers on the third floor, enlisted on the second and Special Forces and SEALs on the first. Maintainers set up a tent city in the parking lot near Space Commands' "Elephant Cage" antenna array.

> AC-130 Tasking: Mission objective for AC-130 crews was to provide on-call CAS but the actual mission tasking followed more along the lines of Armed Reconnaissance. A CAS request was known as "Blue Sword" tasking, so crews flew missions fully loaded, armed and ready to fire at all times. NATO rules of engagement however, hindered the ability of crews to react tactically.
>
> The fires network was complicated. NATO rules of engagement singled out the AC-130 as the only fixed-wing CAS asset that could be controlled by Joint Fires Officers (JFOs) situated throughout Bosnia Herzegovina. Because JFOs represented multiple nationalities and levels of training, some were far from competent in terminal air control procedures. Since the ROEs permitted practically anyone able to authenticate via tactical radio to call for fire, gunship crews had to be especially alert to ensure valid targeting.[3]

3 Email from Lt Col (Ret.) Harry Clawson to Author, June 26, 2013.

> Missions were lengthy and crews flew between 120 to 140 nautical miles to Bosnia. Sorties averaged 10–12 per week. Primary items of interest were artillery sites and vehicle convoys. Targeted areas included Sarajevo and Gorazde. Crews flew missions fully loaded, armed and ready to fire.

OPERATION *DENY FLIGHT* OPERATIONS

Lt Col Byers was Mission Commander while Maj Brian Bergdahl served as Operations Officer. The first missions were routine armed reconnaissance events with little activity noted, but several crews drew sporadic and inaccurate AAA fire. To mitigate threats, operational altitude was increased above ten thousand AGL in known radar threat areas.

A common nighttime tactic used by Bosnian Serbs was to shine bright spotlights into the air to harass strike aircraft, perhaps with hope that they would coax them into bombing or shooting civilian targets to exploit a position to force NATO command leadership to either restrict the Rules of Engagement in their favor, or perhaps cause a withdrawal of strike aircraft altogether.

NATO command leadership regarded the most important aspect of AC-130 capabilities as video recording of current intelligence. Henceforth, AC-130 video tapes were forwarded directly to National Command Authorities in Washington D.C., complete with recordings of the usual "salty language" of *Spectre* crews. After more than a few unsavory comments made it all the way to President Clinton, a no-cuss mandate was levied on crews.[4]

In early August, Lt Gen Ashy, AIRSOUTH commander, along with the 5 ATAF commander and his entourage, accompanied Capt McMillan's crew on an aerial tour of downtown Sarajevo. While sensor operators demonstrated nighttime capabilities of the AC-130, flight engineer MSgt Mike Longe noticed a problem.

> "Oil quantity is dropping pretty fast as we turn towards Brindisi and given the AC-130's three-engine performance, I recommend not shutting the engine down until we absolutely have to... meaning no more oil pressure. The entourage had no idea why we were heading for home. In their minds, it is a four-engine airplane. What's so bad about losing one?" **CMSgt (Ret.) Mike Longe**

When oil quantity dipped below zero, MSgt Longe directed the copilot to feather #3. Eventually, Capt McMillan made an uneventful three engine landing at Brindisi. Though the mission was cut short, General Ashy and his entourage left with a satisfactory understanding of AC-130s systems and limitations.

On August 14, 1993, a crew commanded by Capt Jim Bowe flew *Night Stalker* on a routine armed reconnaissance mission over Bosnia and Herzegovina. The electronic environment was "noisy" from multiple sources, includ-

4 Email from Col (Ret.) Mike Byers to Author, Oct 2015.

ing US and allied ships. Bowe's crew was somewhat on edge considering the electronic threat level beneath them. About 40 miles off the coast of Croatia, EWO Capt Steve McNaughton directed the pilot to take a "hard left turn." Though the threat seemed out of place, Bowe began performing an aggressive maneuver to mitigate the threat. A short time later, McNaughton discovered the threat warning was actually coming from their own ECM pods.[5] About a half hour later, when they entered Bosnia-Herzegovina, McNaughton detected a SA-6 search radar.

> "Shortly after passing into B-H, we hear a very calm EWO voice over the intercom saying 'break left, break left, radar SAM.' Pat Madden and I looked at each other thinking 'why is the EWO calling a practice break while we are in country?' About the same time, Pat saw a SA-6 warning on the AN/ALR-69 and it soaked in the EWO was calling an actual break. We performed a left descending break from about 14,000 AGL, heading for a valley and attempting to put terrain between us and the threat." **Lt Col (Ret.) Jim Bowe,** pilot

Capt Bowe performed a descending/jinking maneuver while wearing night vision goggles. At the same time, the EWO provided jamming and the IO dispensed chaff. Bowe eventually broke lock as *Night Stalker* dropped to two hun-

5 It was later discovered that only one pod should be used at a time since they would fight against one another if both were active simultaneously.

dred ft. AGL. They then navigated toward their planned Split corridor low-level route. After re-entering Bosnia-Herzegovina at low level, Bowe climbed to ten thousand ft. AGL to proceed with their mission.

Later in their mission, the crew spotted headlights of a small pickup truck on their left side. While sensor operators tracked the truck a MANPADS launch was detected. Decoy flares were launched, but the missile seemed to be locked onto them. A second set of decoy flares was launched, but had no effect either. The navigator also fired a decoy flare from his overhead flare gun mount, but the missile kept coming. About the time missile impact was inevitable, it detonated with a bright flash several hundred feet from the gunship. The only casualty was FCO Capt Rich Wallace who was hit by a fire extinguisher that fell out of its mount.

Capt Bowe exited the area, then landed uneventfully. Debrief was interesting since a British Battalion (BRITBAT) Detachment in Split suggested the crew was mistaken and what they saw was not MANPADS, but instead fireworks being launched during a wedding ceremony. The crew found that assessment amusing since they were about thirty miles from the area where the wedding ceremony had taken place and were not aware of any fireworks capable of that range or altitude. This incident became to be known as "the wedding party." Strangely enough, the newly-installed AN/AAR-44 IR threat detector system did not detect a missile launch. Sensor operators however, recorded the missile plume and smoke trail in flight on the gunship's BDA recorder. Analysis of the video tape revealed the missile was likely an SA-14.

Bowe's crew was indeed fortunate that night since the gunship's altitude was at the missile's maximum range, and the missile's self-destruct feature turned out to be the only thing that prevented it from being hit.[6]

After the wedding party incident, operational altitudes were increased with some crews flying on the edge of AC-130 performance capabilities. The operational ceiling was set at seventeen thousand MSL. Climbing to altitude over the Adriatic was routine, but slow. The conditions at altitude were cold and taxing on the crew since they wore oxygen masks for four or five hours at a time.[7]

> "Gunners and Loadmasters had cold weather flight jackets, long johns, and wool socks, but those items only provided minimum protection from the cold we encountered. I recall Maj Bergdahl working very hard to get the backenders more cold weather gear. One day we showed up for a mission and found a pile of cold weather gear in the middle of the mission planning room. It was like a gift from heaven."
> **CMSgt (Ret.) Bill Turner,** gunner

During these four-plus hour missions, the entire aircraft would become cold soaked. After landing in warm weather at Brindisi, the entire aircraft would become wet with condensation.

6 Email from Col (Ret.) Mike Byers, Oct 2015.

7 Some crews climbed to as high as twenty-three thousand ft MSL to mitigate threats in high terrain.

> "It was cold at altitude, we were near 18,000 feet every night, and landing back at Brindisi the inside of the airplane would condensate to the point it seemed like it was raining inside." **MSgt (Ret.) Bryan McMahan,** gunner

The extreme environmental conditions at altitude made for difficult airborne alert missions since it took such a long time to climb to altitude and fly to their target area. Though crews were alerted regularly, by the time they were at altitude ready to respond, they were no longer needed. Crews named alerts "Taco Bell" missions (run to the border) which usually ended with crews ordered to return to Brindisi as soon as they arrived on station. Since it was common to be recalled to the same target, crews routinely stayed on station for 45 minutes to an hour on airborne alert before returning to Brindisi. Eventually AC-130s were placed on ground alert.

> "Many times, we would detect artillery duels beneath us while we orbited. It became fairly routine for both sides to eventually stop firing at each other and begin firing at us. This was another good reason to maintain a high operational ceiling" **CMSgt (Ret.) Doug Gosch,** gunner

Just as crews and maintainers began to stabilize operations in San Vito in early October 1993, an urgent situation in Somalia occurred. All four aircraft and personnel were re-deployed to Mombasa, Kenya to support Task Force Ranger in Mogadishu, Somalia. Amazingly, AC-130s were not removed from the *Deny Flight* commitment as two gunships and crews were placed on constant alert on Hurlburt to support *Deny Flight*. The Hurlburt alert commitment continued until January 1994 when two AC-130s returned to Italy while more crews and aircraft continued operations in Somalia. Overall, the nine aircraft squadron was heavily loaded and spread thin with operational tasking and was maintaining AC-130s at Hurlburt, Mombasa and Brindisi simultaneously.

Gunners working the 40mm gun at high-altitude, on supplemental oxygen.
(Credit: MSgt (Ret.) Wes Fields)

The winter months in Europe were excruciatingly cold for crews which were compounded by high operational altitudes to mitigate the threat of MANPADS and

SA-6 SAMs. Winter operations at altitude were brutal. Temperatures inside the aircraft were sub-zero, causing an extremely uncomfortable environment with an increased risk of frostbite. Some crews worried about the operation of the 105mm gun in temperatures that caused the hydraulic fluid of the recoil cylinder to thicken, which put extreme stress on the aircraft. The constant internal airflow of the AC-130H that was tolerated in Southeast Asia, Grenada, Panama, and Kuwait had become unmanageable during the winter months in Bosnia and Herzegovina. A flight surgeon at San Vito measured the temperature near the aft guns was -40F.[8] There was no practical work-around solution to stop the bitter cold at higher altitudes. Generally, heat ducts blasting high-temperature bleed air dissipated so fast there was no heat within a foot or so on either side of the duct. Recognizing the problem, maintainers did whatever they could to replumb the ductwork, and 16 SOS leadership took it on their own to bypass regulations to purchase electric socks and special cold weather gear from a sporting goods catalog.

> "The environmental challenges faced by the crews were intense. The cold was remarkable--it was almost like going back to B-17 days. The standard issue cold weather gear simply was not adequate. We also ran into a little red tape... some in the AF felt any gear worn on an aircraft had to be tested and fire proof. After making the

---

8 Email from MSgt (Ret.) Brad Sims to Author, 2015.

calculation that the chance of frostbite was much greater than catching on fire, I told the squadron to get whatever they needed from wherever they needed to keep warm." **Col (Ret.) Mike Byers**

The arrival of spring and summer months were wholeheartedly welcomed by crews. Though cold temperatures were still encountered at high altitude, they were nowhere near as severe as during the Winter months.

NATO's *Deny Flight* aircraft drew first blood on February 28, 1994, when two pairs of USAF F-16 fighters shot down four Yugoslav Air Force Super Galeb light attack aircraft on a bombing mission against Bosnian government forces.[9] Throughout the remainder of 1994, AC-130H crews continued *Deny Flight* missions over Bosnia and Herzegovina. By December 31, former US President Jimmy Carter negotiated a four-month cease fire between the BSA and the Bosnian-Croat federation forces. During this period, both sides replenished supplies and weapons, while AC-130 gunships remained on station in Brindisi.

On May 1, 1995, the Croatian Army launched an invasion of Serb-held Western Slavonia. Economic sanctions began to hurt Serbia so much that Slobodan Milosevic decided to stop sending aid across the border to the Bosnian Serbs.

On August 29, 1995, *Night Stalker* (69-6568) was hours away from being returned to Hurlburt about the same time Operation *Deliberate Force* began. Once tasking was

9 Col Robert Owen, *Deliberate Force: A Case Study in Effective Air Campaigning* (Maxwell Airforce Base, AL: Air University Press, 2000), 21.

received, *Night Stalker* was the first AC-130 to launch. In the early morning hours of August 30, Capt Tolbert's crew fired the first shots of the campaign on artillery sites surrounding Sarajevo, scoring 6568's first combat kills since it was built.[10] The same night, Major Wise's crew launched but did not fire due to conflicting Rules Of Engagement.

The crew of Ghost 31 after firing the first shots of Operation Deliberate Force and achieving the first combat kills of aircraft 6568. (Credit: MSgt (Ret.) Ed Nissen)

Coinciding with strikes on August 30, a French Mirage 2000 aircraft (call sign Ebro 33) was shot down. Both of the pilots successfully ejected and a massive rescue effort was underway. An AC-130H commanded by Major Wise escorted MH-53 crews as they searched for survivors.

10 69-6568 previously logged combat time in June of 1993 and conducted suppressive fires in Somalia in October of 1993, but this mission was "first blood" for the aircraft.

Unfortunately, low-lying fog prevented locating survivors and one MH-53 was hit by AK-47 fire in the process.

The second night, Major Wise's crew launched and fired on more artillery sites. Capt Tolbert's crew continued the search for the pilots of Ebro 33, contending with poor weather conditions. Their mission ended without locating survivors.

> "We (Tolbert's crew) were looking for Ebro 33 the following night on 6575, complete with an inebriated French Para on board to 'help' us in case we found the crew. On the first two nights of the Bosnia Air War, it was us and Jim Wise's crew." **MSgt (Ret.) Ed Nissen,** Loadmaster

Weather was better on the third night as Capt Leo Cissell's crew searched the objective area for 30 minutes but found no trace of the survivors. On the withdrawal, MH-53 helicopters drew sporadic small arms fire, received multiple hits, and two crewmen were wounded. Cissell's crew suppressed hostile forces with gunfire, then escorted the rescue force as they withdrew from the area.

> "On the last night, as we escorted the helo(s) out they received indirect fire and we returned 40mm fire in the direction of the point of origin to suppress the threat." **Lt Col (Ret.) Tommy Montgomery,** Fire-control Officer

By the fourth day of the campaign, more gunship crews were added to the fight, including crews commanded by

Captains Jim Marsh, Chris Ferraraccio, and Greg Langas. Crews continued to fire on artillery sites and Electronic Warfare sites. The combination of high operational altitude and troublesome fire control systems made precise firing difficult.

> "We hit an EW radar site near Mostar. An SA-16 launch sent us home after about firing 75 105s and 30-something 40s. It took us forever to hit the building." **MSgt (Ret.) Jim Gary,** Gunner

Operation *Deliberate Force* ended on September 20, 1995. During that operation, AC-130 crews flew a total of 32 sorties. Crews fired on multiple artillery emplacements and radar sites around Sarajevo with mixed results. Ultimately, the Dayton Peace Accords resulted in an end to the violence in Bosnia and Herzegovia by establishing territorial divisions among the ethnic groups.

MISSION DEBRIEF

The AC-130's role during Operation *Deny Flight* was Close Air Support, but because of overly complicated NATO rules of engagement, little CAS was accomplished. The enemy threat weapon arsenal within Bosnia and Herzegovina forced AC-130 crews to fly at high altitude to mitigate threats. During these missions, crews and aircraft routinely met physical limits, especially in the winter months. Though the AC-130 added some level of value to the overall mission by video recording findings for Intelligence analysis, their primary mission of CAS was not fully implemented.

EPILOGUE

Following the end of the war in Vietnam, Laos, and Cambodia in 1975, the AC-130 program languished until 1983 during Operation *Urgent Fury*. Cited as being a valuable SOF asset in support of Special Operations ground and naval forces, the AC-130 found more kinship with the US Army and Navy than the USAF. Only after the United States Special Operations Command (USSOCOM) was established in 1987, did the AC-130 program receive high-level support. In turn, USSOCOM tasking sealed the AC-130's fate as USSOCOM's heavy firepower, dedicated to supporting USSOCOM surface forces. In concert with other USSOCOM elements, classification procedures masked a large swath of AC-130 operations. Now, decades later, the declassified story of the AC-130 gunship has been told, but the story of *Spectre* continues to build under a cloak of darkness, even today.

EVENT CHRONOLOGY

1976

Jan 8: Two AC-130H participated in Exercise *Jack Frost* in Alaska

Jan 14: One AC-130H searched for a tugboat which was three days overdue in the Mississippi River, but with negative results.

Jan 25: One AC-130H participated in Search and Rescue Training with HH-53 helicopters from Hill AFB.

Mar 8: One AC-130 Flew to Howard AFB, Panama to demonstrate capabilities to leadership of US Southern Command.

May 4–25: Two AC-130H participated in Exercise *Solid Shield*.

Aug 25: Two AC-130H participate in Joint Training at Howard Air Force Base, Panama.

Aug 28: Four AC-130H were placed on alert for Korean augmentation in response to an incident on the Korean DMZ.

Aug 5–8: Six AC-130H participated in Exercise *Brave Shield Xv*.

Oct 31: One AC-130H participated in a SAR mission for a boat missing in the Gulf of Mexico.

1977

Jan 11–Feb 3: Two AC-130H participated in Exercise *Jack Frost* in Alaska.

May 2–17: Two AC-130H participated in Exercise *Solid Shield* at Ft Bragg, NC.

Jul 26–Aug 5: Two AC-130H deploy to Alaska for quick reaction *Black Lighting* tasking.

Aug 22–30: Two AC-130H participated in Exercise *Blue Flag 77-3* on the Eglin Reservation.

Aug 29: One AC-130 responded to a SAR request for a Marine F-4 that had crashed in the Gulf of Mexico and a rescue helicopter that had ditched in the same area. The Gunship acted as on-scene command post, provided illumination and used its visual sensors. Unfortunately, the search was fruitless.

Sep 12: One AC-130H deployed to George AFB, CA for quick reaction Exercise *Rapid Retriever*.

Oct 11–Nov 11: Three AC-130H participated in Exercise *Bold Eagle* on the Eglin Reservation.

Nov 25–Dec 19: AC-130H participated in Exercise *Red Flag* at Nellis AFB, NV.

1978

Jan 14–Feb 2: Two AC-130H participated in Exercise *Empire Glacier* 78 in the Northeast U.S.

Mar 7–17: Two AC-130H participated in Exercise *Team Spirit* in Korea.

May 3–26: Two AC-130H participated in Exercise *Solid Shield 78*.

May 22–26: Six AC-130H participated in Exercise *Sea Spectre* to test rapid response capabilities.

Nov 16–Oct 3: Three AC-130H participated in Exercise *Gallant Eagle* on the Eglin Reservation.

Nov 8–10: One AC-130H deployed to McChord AFB, WA to support the U.S. Army 9th Infantry Division with live-fire on Yakima Firing Range.

Nov 13–Dec 4: Two AC-130H deployed to Howard AFB, Panama to support a US Southern Command exercise.

1979

Jan 10–Feb 15: Two AC-130H participated in Exercise *Jack Frost* in Alaska.

Jul 8: Two AC-130H deployed to Howard AFB, Panama and placed on alert for a developing situation in Managua, Nicaragua. The mission did not materialize.

Aug 3: One AC-130H deployed to Ft Campbell, KY for a dry-fire simulation mission. This was a one day round-trip mission.

Aug 8: One AC-130H successfully airdropped a Zodiac inflatable boat into Hurlburt lake. This was a first for any AC-130.

Oct 12–28: Four AC-130H participate in Exercise *Bold Eagle* on the Eglin Reservation.

Nov 13–15: Four AC-130H set a world record nonstop flight from Hurlburt Field to Andersen AFB, Guam.

Nov 13–Mar 3 (80): AC-130 crews deploy to Guam, setting world record C-130 nonstop flight.

1980

Jan 1–3 Mar: Four AC-130H were deployed to Guam to train for Operation *Rice Bowl.*

Mar 14: All Hurlburt C-130s temporarily relocated to Duke Field while Hurlburt runway was repaired.

April 4: Contract awarded to install air refueling capabilities to five more AC-130H.

April 24–25: Four AC-130H deployed to Wadi Kena Egypt for Operation *Eagle Claw.*

May 3–19: Two AC-130H participated in Exercise *Solid Shield*

July: AC-130H participates in Operation *Honey Badger* in southwestern U.S.

1981

Feb 14–24: Two AC-130H participated in Exercise *Blackhawk Iv* in Panama. While on a training mission, gunships participated in a SAR mission in Ecuador searching for a downed Army Helicopter. Eight sorties in bad weather and difficult terrain failed to locate the helicopter.

Mar 11–18: Two AC-130H participated in Exercise *Team Spirit* in Korea.

Aug 7–11: Two AC-130H participated in Exercise *Ocean Venture.*

Sep 13–26: Two AC-130H participated in Exercise *Marvel Exodus.*

Oct 13–19: Three AC-130H participated in Exercise *Bold Eagle* on the Eglin Reservation.

Nov 2: One AC-130H diverted from a training mission to search for an F-15 that had crashed into the Gulf of Mexico. The search ended without success.

Nov 24: Three AC-130H deployed to Virginia to search for downed F-4 pilot lost in the Atlantic Ocean. Search results were negative.

1982

Jan 30–Feb 7: Two AC-130H participated in Exercise *Vagabond Warrior* in Hawaii.

Feb 10–19: Two AC-130H participated in Exercise *Kindle Liberty 82* in Panama.

Feb 13–Apr 26: Two AC-130H participated in Exercise *Team Spirit* in Korea.

Mar 8: Two AC-130H participated in joint forces capabilities demonstration in Charleston, SC.

Apr 26–May 17: Two AC-130H participated in Exercise *Ocean Venture 82* in the Caribbean.

Jul 17–26: One AC-130H deployed in the United Kingdom in support of Exercise *Trail Mace Iii.*

Oct 14: One AC-130H participated in a SAR mission at Colorado Springs, CO.

1983

Feb 4–5: Two AC-130H participated in Exercise *Prairie Runner* at Patrick AFB, FL.

Mar 1: Four AC-130H begin Operation *Bield Kirk*, based at Howard Air Force Base Panama.

Jul 19–17: One AC-130H participated in *Granite Scar 1*, a test of a defensive countermeasures system.

Aug 13–29: Two AC-130H participated in Exercise *Bright Star* at Cairo West Egypt.

Aug 22–Sep 23: Seven AC-130H participated in *Granite Scar 2* testing at Eglin AFB.

Oct 22–Nov 24: Six AC-130H participated in Operation *Urgent Fury*, Grenada.

1984

Jan 1–Dec 31: AC-130H continues Operation *Bield Kirk/ Blue Flame*.

Jun 4–13: Three AC-130H participated in Exercise *Eight Falcons* at Hunter Army Airfield, Savannah, GA.

Oct 24: One AC-130H illuminated Bob Hope's entrance and opening remarks during a benefit show in Fort Walton Beach.

Nov 13–17: Two AC-130H deploy to Pope AFB, NC for joint training.

1985

Jan 1–Dec 31: Two AC-130H continue Operation *Blue Flame* over El Salvador.

Jan 22: Two AC-130H deploy to Alaska to participate in Exercise *Brim Frost*.

Oct: Three AC-130H gunships were deployed to Aviano, Italy for a classified mission. After more than a week sitting alert in Aviano, the mission cancelled and gunships re-deployed to Hurlburt.

Nov: 16 SOS participated in a Special Mission Operational Test and Evaluation Center (SMOTEC) test of multiple types of 105mm ammunition.

Nov 11–16: One AC-130H participated in ECM tactics development at China Lake, CA.

Dec 2–10: Four AC-130H participated in Exercise *Purple Duck*, an operational readiness exercise at Biggs Army Airfield, El Paso, TX.

1986

Jan 15–21: One AC-130H supported Army SOF training at Ft Bragg, NC.

Jan 29–31: One AC-130H performed a firepower demonstration for US Army personnel at Ft Sill, OK who contributed to the SMOTEC 105mm ammunition evaluation/test. The demonstration concluded the evaluation.

Mar 10–Apr 1: Two AC-130H deployed to Korea to participate in *Exercise Team Spirit.*

Apr 22–24: One AC-130H participated in Exercise *Hammer Of Justice* at Redstone, AL.

Apr 22–May 12: Two AC-130H deployed to Roosevelt Roads, PR to participate in Exercise *Ocean Venture 86.*

Nov 30: One AC-130H and crew participated in defensive tactics training at China Lake, CA.

1987

AC-130A and AC-130H gunships begin participating in Operation *Elaborate Maze* in Panama.

Mar 13–15: One AC-130H participated in a dry fire demonstration, ECM testing and a static display for key Air Force Systems Command personnel at Wright-Patterson AFB, OH.

Mar 18–22: The 16 SOS provided both live and dry-fire CAS training support at Yuma Marine Air Station, AZ.

Mar 20–Apr 14: Two AC-130H and three crews participated in Exercise *Team Spirit 87* in Korea.

Mar 25–Apr 7: Three AC-130H and crews flew nine sorties in the Hurlburt area to support AC-130/A-10 tactics development.

Apr 5–10: Three AC-130H and crews participated in joint CAS training with the 82nd Airborne Division at Ft Bragg, NC.

Jul 31–Aug 9: The 16 SOS began low level-training at St Joseph MO and Davis Monthan AFB, AZ.

Aug 3–7: 16 SOS conducted a firepower demonstration for the US Army 2nd Armored Division.

Aug 15–28: The 16 SOS participated in joint interoperability training with the Navy at San Diego.

Oct 30–Nov 9: Two AC-130H and three crews deployed to Volk Field, WI, for an operational readiness exercise.

Nov 1–7: One AC-130H supported Army CAS training at Vieques Island, PR.

Dec 6–9: One AC-130H supported the US Army 10th Mountain Division during training at Little Rock AFB, Arkansas.

1988

AC-130A and AC-130H participated in Operation *Nimrod Dancer* in Panama

Jan 9–23: Two AC-130H participated in joint readiness training.

Mar 24: Two AC-130H, three crews and forty maintainers deployed to Korea for Exercise *Team Spirit 88*.

Jul 2: 16 SOS participates in Exercise *Gallant Eagle*.

Oct 13–16 Nov: Two AC-130H, crews and maintainers participated in Exercise *Foal Eagle 88*.

Nov 14–18: One AC-130H and crew and 25 maintainers conducted bi-lateral training at Roosevelt Roads, PR.

1989

Jan 9–13: One AC-130H performed an air drop test at Ft Bragg, NC.

Apr 8: An AC-130H on a local training mission was diverted to intercept a suspected drug smuggling aircraft. It was successfully located, tracked and provided valuable information to the US Customs Service.

Apr 24–28: Two AC-130H participated in a capabilities exercise.

Jun 22: An AC-130H on a local training mission was diverted to assist in search for a downed civilian aircraft. The mission was unsuccessful.

Sep 24: One AC-130H participated in CAS training for US Army Rangers at Ft Bragg, NC.

Oct 12–15: One AC-130H conducted a hot refueling/rearming test at Ft Campbell, KY.

Oct 31–Nov 9: Two AC-130H deployed to Korea to participate in Exercise *Foal Eagle*.

Nov 22–27: Two AC-130H fly close formation while firing to allow a USAF photo crew to film and photograph the gunships in flight.

Dec 5–14: 16 SOS crews participated in formation air refueling training as well as a full-scale training mission for Operation *Blue Spoon*, the overthrow of the Noriega regime in Panama.

Dec 18: Two AC-130H crews deploy to Panama to support Army SOF operators during *Acid Gambit.*

Dec 19–20: Seven AC-130H and two AC-130A participated in Operation *Just Cause*.

1990

Jan 3: Operation *Just Cause* ends and Operation *Promote Liberty* begins.

Aug 30: Five AC-130H gunships, crews and maintainers deploy to Saudi Arabia for Operation *Desert Shield*.

Sep 8: AC-130H gunships begin to arrive at King Fahd International airport, Saudi Arabia.

Dec 21: The AC-130U, the newest model gunship made its first flight from Rockwell International's Palmdale, California facilities to Edwards Air Force Base.

1991

Jan 3–7: Two AC-130H participated in Operation *Eastern Exit*, Somalia.

Jan 18: First AC-130H missions flown during Operation *Desert Storm.*

Jan 31: AC-130H #69-6567, call sign Spirit 03, shot down during the Battle of Khafji.

Feb 7: Five AC-130A are in place at KFIA, Saudi Arabia.

Feb 26: First AC-130A cross border mission into Iraq.

Mar: Five AC-130A return to Duke Field, FL from KFIA, Saudi Arabia.

May 27: The last two AC-130H gunships return to Hurlburt from KFIA, Saudi Arabia.

Apr 2: First flight of AC-130U, tail number 0511 at Palmdale, CA.

Aug 13: First AC-130U live-fire (40mm, 105mm).

Oct 1: 1 SOW transferred from Air Mobility Command (formerly MAC) to AFSOC.

Gunship maintenance personnel were consolidated within the 16 SOS, making it the largest squadron in the USAF.

Dec 12: First AC-130U 25mm live-fire.

1992

Jan 15–24: AC-130A deploys to western US for counter-drug efforts of JTF-6.

Jan 31: Building 91029 on Hurlburt Field was dedicated as The Spirit Building in honor of fourteen crewmen lost during Operation *Desert Storm.*

Apr 2: Initial flight of first production AC-130U.

Apr 22: AC-130U sets gunship altitude record of 31,100 feet (pressurized).

Jul 30: Last Pave Spectre aircraft flown before SOFI modification.

Aug 22: Hurlburt converts to the USAF Objective Wing concept. flight line maintenance personnel are assigned to the 16SOS making it one of the largest squadrons in the USAF.

Oct 1: Ownership of Hurlburt Field officially transferred from Air Mobility Command (AMC) to AFSOC.

Oct 28–Nov 12: Two AC-130H participate in Exercise *Foal Eagle.*

Dec 11–20: AC-130A deploys to western US for counter-drug efforts of JTF-6.

1993

June 7: Four AC-130H deploy to Djibouti, Africa to strike targets in Mogadishu, Somalia then return in early July.

July 17: The first of four AC-130H gunships arrive in Italy to participate in Operation *Deny Flight.*

Four AC-130H re-deployed from Italy to Mombasa, Kenya to support operations in Mogadishu, Somalia.

Loadmaster SrA Kristin Kelley became the first female crew member assigned to a gunship squadron.

1994

Jan: Two AC-130H return to Brindisi, Italy to support the Operation *Deny Flight* mission in Bosnia-Herzegovina.

Mar 14: AC-130H gunship 69-6576 experiences a 105mm gun explosion and crashes into the Indian Ocean near Malindi, Kenya. Eight crewmen were lost.

Mar 31: AC-130s return to Hurlburt from Somalia.

July 1: First AC-130U (166) delivered to Hurlburt Field.

Sep: AC-130A and AC-130H gunships deploy to support Operation *Uphold Democracy*.

Oct 19: AC-130A 56-0509 becomes the first of ten to retire.

Nov 14: Formal roll out of the first AC-130U occurs at Hurlburt.

1995

Feb 1: 16 SOS deploys to Mombasa, Kenya for Operation *United Shield*.

May 1: 4th Special Operations Squadron activated at Hurlburt Field.

Aug 29: Aircraft 69-6568 scores first personnel kill in Bosnia-Herzegovina

Sep 10: AC-130A 53-3129 "The First Lady" is the last AC-130A to retire.

Sep 20: Ceasefire declared in Bosnia Herzegovina.

ACKNOWLEDGMENTS

The author is especially indebted to the following individuals who shared their recollections, expertise and effort to ensure an accurate and truthful story was told. Most reviewed numerous manuscript drafts to ensure the highest level of comprehensive AC-130 history was captured.

A

CMSgt Jerry Andersen, USAF (Ret.)

Mr. William Alexander

B

Col Michael Byers, USAF (Ret.)

Col Gerald Buckman, USAF (Ret.)

Col Richard "Rick" Bowman, USA (Ret.)

LTC Lewis "Bucky" Burruss, USA (Ret.)

Lt Col Daniel Baradon. USAF (Ret.)

Lt Col Michael Brennan, USAF (Ret.)

Maj James Bowe, USAF (Ret.)

CMSgt Don Boudreaux, USAF (Ret.)

Mr. Ray Brandes

C

Col James Connors, USAF (Ret.)

Col John Carney,
USAF (Ret.)
Maj Michael Couvillon,
USAF (Ret.)
MSG Dale Comstock,
USA (Ret.)
TSgt Ronald Clark,
USAF (Ret.)
Lt Col Dave Coombs,
USAF (Ret.)
CPL David Crowe, USMC
Mr. Jeff Clark

D

Lt Col Richard Daugherty,
USAF (Ret.)
Lt Col Randy Durham,
USAF (Ret.)
Maj Mark Demers,
USAF (Ret.)
Capt Charles "Randy"
Davis, USAF

E

LTC Henry "Ike"
Eisenbarth, USA (Ret.)
SMSgt John Eklof,
USAF (Ret.)

F

Lt Gen Bruce Fister,
USAF (Ret.)
Col Chuck Fry, USA (Ret.)
Lt Col Bernard "Bernie"
Frakes, USAF (Ret.)
Maj Jack Flanders,
USAF (Ret.)
SMSgt Eddie Fowler,
USAF (Ret.)
TSgt Steven Feldmier,
USAF (Ret.)

G

Brig Gen George Gray
III, USAF (Ret.)
Col John "Pappy"
Gallagher, USAF (Ret.)
Col Michael Guidry,
USAF (Ret.)
Lt Col Francis "Robert"
Gabreski, USAF (Ret.)
MSgt Alan Garrett
USAF (Ret.)
CMSgt Mike Gilbert
USAF (Ret.)
Mr. Tom Guercio

H

Gen Charles "Chuck" Horner, USAF (Ret.)
Lt Gen Bradley Heithold, USAF (Ret.)
Maj Gen John "Marcus" Hicks, USAF (Ret.)
Col Kevin Higgins, USA (Ret.)
Col Gary Holland, USAF (Ret.)
Col Paul Havel, USAF (Ret.)
MSG Paul Howe, USA (Ret.)
MSgt Kyle Hurst, USAF (Ret.)
SPC Chuck Holton, USA

I

CPT Wade "Ish" Ishimoto, USA (Ret.)

J

SMSgt Steven Jones, USAF (Ret.)
Dr. Robert Jordan

K

Col Donn Kegel, USAF (Ret.)
Col Frank Kuska, USAF (Ret.)
Col James Kyle, USAF (Ret.)
Lt Col Raymond Kinkaid, USAF (Ret.)
Maj Don Kemper, USAF (Ret.)
CMSgt Martin Klukas, USAF (Ret.)
Ms. Katrina Kiecker

L

Col William Lane, USAF (Ret.)
Lt Col James Lawrence, USAF (Ret.)
Maj Philippe LeBrun, USAF (Ret.)
CMSgt Michael Longe, USAF (Ret.)
CMSgt Glenn Lemay, USAF (Ret.)
CMSgt Christopher Langlois, USAF (Ret.)
CSGM Richard Lamb, USA (Ret.)

M

Col Charles "Mac" McMillan, USAF (Ret.)
Col Robert Monarch, USAF (Ret.)
Lt Col Rick Masters, USAF (Ret.)
Lt Col Tommy Montgomery, USAF (Ret.)
Maj Kenneth Moerscher, USAF (Ret.)
MSG Frank Morales, USA (Ret.)
MSgt Tony Millhouse, USAF (Ret.)
GySgt Joseph Muccia, USMC (Ret.)
SSG Darin Marcinkevicius, USA (Ret.)
SGT Donald "Joe" Miller, USA
LCpl Mike Morrison, USMC
Mr. Kurt Muse

N

CMSgt Wayne Norrad, USAF (Ret.)

P

Maj Gen Robert Patterson, USAF (Ret.)
Col William "Billy" Preaskorn, USAF (Ret.)
Col Jon Peck, USAF (Ret.)
Lt Col John Palen, USAF (Ret.)
Maj Mike Poddubny, USAF (Ret.)
SFC Emil Praslick, USA (Ret.)
SMSgt William Patterson, USAF (Ret.)
Sgt Larry Peterson, USAF

R

Col James Roper, USAF (Ret.)
Lt Col Michael Radford, USAF (Ret.)
Maj Emmett "Otis" Redding, USAF (Ret.)
Mr. Barry Rosen

S

Col David Sims, USAF (Ret.)

Lt Col James Strength, USAF (Ret.)
Lt Col Charles Stoner, USAF (Ret.)
Lt Col Dion Scaglione, USAF (Ret.)
Maj Terry Sears, USAF (Ret.)
Capt William Sims, USAF (Ret.)
MSG Patrick Savidge, USA (Ret.)
MSgt Robert "Scotty" Scott, USAF (Ret.)
MSgt David Schnoor, USAF (Ret.)
Mr. Dennis Santiago

T

Lt Col John Townsend, USAF (Ret.)
Lt Col Michael Taylor, USA (Ret.)
Lt Col Wayne Thom, USAF (Ret.)
SGT Richard Trundy, USA

V

CMSgt John Varner, USAF (Ret.)
SGM Kelly Venden, USA (Ret.)

W

Lt Gen Donny Wurster, USAF (Ret.)
Maj Gen Michael Wilson, USAF (Ret.)
Col Steven Wiggins, USAF (Ret.)
Lt Col Thomas Waylett, USAF (Ret.)
Lt Col Rich Wallace, USAF (Ret.)
CW4 Vernon Ward, USA (Ret.)
MSgt Clay Watson, USAF (Ret.)
MSgt David Wilson, USAF (Ret.)
Ms. Sarah Walter

GLOSSARY

1LT	First Lieutenant (Army)
1st Lt	First Lieutenant (Air Force)
1SG	First Sergeant (Army)
2LT	Second Lieutenant (Army)
2nd Lt	Second Lieutenant (Air Force)
A1C	Airman First Class
AAA	Anti-Aircraft Artillery
AATTC	Advanced Airlift Tactics Training Center
ABCCC	Airborne Battlefield Command and Control Center
ABGD	Air Base Ground Defense
AC	Aircraft Commander
ACC	Air Component Commander
ADO	Assistant Director of Operations
ADOC	Air Defense Operations Center
ADM	Admiral (rank)
ADVON	Advance Echelon
ADSID	Air Delivered Seismic Intrusion Detector
AFAL	Air Force Avionics Laboratory
AFMPC	Air Force Manning and Personnel Center
AFRES	Air Force Reserve
AFSOC	Air Force Special Operations Command

AFSOCCENT	Air Force Special Operations Command Central Command
AFTTP	Air Force Tactics Techniques & Procedures
AG	Aerial Gunner/Airborne Gunner
AGL	Above Ground Level
AIB	Accident Investigation Board
ALE	Air Launched Expendable
ALO	Air Liaison Officer
Amn	Airman
ANGLICO	Air Naval Gunfire Liaison Company
AP	Armor Piercing
AOC	Air Operations Center
AOR	Area Of Responsibility
APC	Armored Personnel Carrier
APDS	Armor Piercing Discarding Sabot
APFSDS	Armor Piercing Fin Stabilized Discarding Sabot
AP-I	Armor Piercing-Incendiary
ARVN	Army of the Republic of Vietnam
AR	Aerial Refueling
ARRS	Aerospace Rescue and Recovery Squadron
ASD	Aeronautical Systems Division
ATAF	Allied Tactical Air Force
ATF	Arraijan Tank Farm
ATO	Air Tasking Order
AWACS	Airborne Warning And Control System
AWADS	Adverse Weather Aerial Delivery System
BC	Black Crow (sensor)
BCU	Battery/Cooling Unit

BDA	Bomb Damage Assessment/ Battle Damage Assessment
BMC	Battle Management Center
BMNT	Begin Morning Nautical Twilight
BRITBAT	British Battalion
C2	Command and Control
C3	Command Control and Communications
CAP	Combat Air Patrol
Capt	Captain (Air Force, USMC)
CAPT	Captain (Navy)
CAOC	Combined Air Operations Center
CAS	Close Air Support
CBS	Columbia Broadcasting System
CCT	Combat Control Team
CCTS	Combat Crew Training Squadron
CENTAF	Central Command Air Force
CEP	Circular Error Probable
CIA	Central Intelligence Agency
CIDG	Civilian Irregular Defense Group
CMSgt	Chief Master Sergeant
CINCSO	Commander In Chief Southern Command
CINCPACAF	Commander In Chief Pacific Air Forces
CJTF	Combined Joint Task Force
COA	Course Of Action
COMALF	Commander Airlift Forces
CONUS	Continental United States
CP	Co-Pilot
CPT	Captain (Army)
CQ	Charge of Quarters

CROC	Combat Required Operating Capability
CRS	Component Repair Squadron
CSM	Command Sergeant Major (Army)
CTZ	Corps Tactical Zone
CVR	Cockpit Voice Recorder
CWO	Chief Warrant Officer (Army)
DAP	Defensive Armed Penetrator
DASC	Direct Air Support Center
DET	Detachment
DMZ	Demilitarized Zone
DoD	Department of Defense
DTA	Dual Target Attack
ECAS	Emergency Close Air Support
ERO	En Route Overtaking (Tanker)
EW	Early Warning/Electronic Warfare
EWO	Electronic Warfare Officer
ECM	Electronic Countermeasures
FAARP	Forward Area Arming and Refuel Point
FAC	Forward Air Controller
FCO	Fire-control Officer
FDO	Fire Direction Officer
FSO	Fire Support Officer
FE	Flight Engineer
FID	Foreign Internal Defense
FiST	Fire Support Team
FMLN	Farabundo Martí National Liberation Front
FO	Forward Observer
FPS	Feet Per Second
FROG	Free Rocket Over Ground

FSO	Fire Support Officer
G-Force	Gravitational Force
GTE	General Telephone & Electric Corporation
GLINT	Gated Laser Illuminator for Night Television
GLO	Ground Liaison Office
GSOLL	Gunship Special Operations Low Level
HE	High Explosive
HEAT	High Explosive Anti-Tank
HEP-T	High Explosive Plastic-Tracer
HE-P	High Explosive-Plugged (plugged tracer cavity)
HE-I	High Explosive-Incendiary
HE-I-P	High Explosive-Incendiary-Plugged (plugged tracer cavity)
HE-I-T	High Explosive-Incendiary-Tracer
HE-I-T-NSD	High Explosive-Incendiary-Tracer-Non Self Destroying
HoA	Horn of Africa
HUD	Head Up Display
HUMINT	Human Intelligence
IADS	Integrated Air Defense System
IFE	In Flight Emergency
IFF	Identification Friend or Foe
IMC	Instrument Meteorological Conditions
IO	Illuminator Operator
IR	Infrared (sensor/operator)
ISC	Infiltration Surveillance Center
JCS	Joint Chiefs of Staff
JFO	Joint Fires Officer

JRT	Joint Readiness Training
JSOTF	Joint Special Operations Task Force
JTF	Joint Task Force
KFIA	King Fahd International Airport
KIA	Killed In Action
KIAS	Knots Indicated Airspeed
KLA	Kosovo Liberation Army
KW	Kilowatt
LANTIRN	Low Altitude Navigation Infrared for Night
LAP	Load Assemble Pack
LAU	Launch Adapter Unit
LGB	Laser Guided Bomb
LLLTV	Low-light-level-television (sensor)
LM	Loadmaster
LNO	Liaison Officer
LP	Listening Post
LTC	Lieutenant Colonel (Army)
Lt Col	Lieutenant Colonel (Air Force)
LTD	Laser Target Designator
LTD/R	Laser Target Designator/Ranger
LTV	Ling-Temco-Vought
LWCP	Loader's Weapon Control Panel
LZ	Landing Zone
MABCO	Manufacturing and Building Company
MAC	Military Airlift Command
MAJ	Major (Army)
Maj	Major (Air Force and USMC)
Maj Gen	Major General (Air Force)
MG	Major General (Army)

MANPADS	Man Portable Air Defense System
MAU	Marine Amphibious Unit
MIA	Missing In Action
MIL	Milliradians
MK	Mark
MM	Millimeter
MOPP	Mission Oriented Protective Posture
MRE	Meal, Ready to Eat
MSgt	Master Sergeant (Air Force)
MSG	Master Sergeant (Army)
MSIC	Missile and Space Intelligence Center
MSL	Mean Seal Level
NASA	National Aeronautics and Space Administration
NATO	North Atlantic Treaty Organization
NAV	Navigator
NCA	National Command Authorities
NDA	Non-Disclosure Agreement
NEO	Non-combatant Evacuation Operation
NGO	Non-Government Organization
NI-CAD	Nickel-Cadmium
NJM	New Jewell Movement
NOD	Night Observation Device
NVG	Night Vision Goggles
OECS	Organization of Eastern Caribbean States
ODA	Operational Detachment Alpha
OL-A	Operating Location-Alpha
OL-B	Operating Location-Bravo
OP	Observation Post

OPCON	Operational Control
OPFOR	Opposing Forces
OPLAN	Operation Plan
OPORD	Operations Order
OPSEC	Operational Security
PACAF	Pacific Air Forces
PAVN	People's Army Vietnam
PCS	Permanent Change of Station
PDF	Panama Defense Force
PFC	Private First Class (Army)
PGU	Peculiar Gun Unit (ammunition for specific gun)
POL	Petroleum, Oils and Lubricants
POW	Prisoner Of War
PRA	People's Revolutionary Army
PRG	Provisional Revolutionary Government
RFG	Radio Free Grenada
RMC	Revolutionary Military Council
RNO	Results Not Observed
ROE	Rules Of Engagement
RPG	Rocket Propelled Grenade
RTB	Return To Base
RWR	Radar Warning Receiver
SAM	Surface to Air Missile
SANG	Saudi Arabian National Guard
SATCOM	Satellite communications
SAR	Search And Rescue
SAS	Special Air Service (Britain)
SEAD	Suppression of Enemy Air Defenses

SEAL	Sea, Air, Land (Navy)
SGM	Sergeant Major (Army)
Sgt	Sergeant (USAF)
SGT	Sergeant (Army)
SECAF	Secretary of the Air Force
SF	Special Forces
SFOD	Special Forces Operational Detachment
SMSgt	Senior Master Sergeant
SMOTEC	Special Mission Operational Test and Evaluation Center
SOAG	Special Operations Aviation Group
SOAR	Special Operations Aviation Regiment
SOC	Sector Operations Center (Iraq)
SOCCENT	Special Operations Command Central Command
SOCSOUTH	Special Operations Command South
SOF	Special Operations Forces
SOFI	Special Operations Forces Improvement
SOLL	Special Operations Low Level
SOS	Special Operations Squadron
SOTS	Special Operations Training Squadron
SOUTHCOM	Southern Command
SOW	Special Operations Wing
SPA	Surprise Package Aircraft
SPC	Specialist (Army)
SPO	Systems Program Office
SQUAWK	Select transponder code
SrA	Senior Airman (Air Force)
SRC	Supreme Revolutionary Council (Somalia)

SRO	Sensitive Reconnaissance Operations
SRSP	Somali Revolutionary Socialist Party
SSG	Special Situation Group
SSG	Staff Sergeant (Army)
SSgt	Staff Sergeant (Air Force)
STAMP	Standard Air-transportable Munitions Package
STS	Special Tactics Squadron
TAC	Tactical Air Command
TACAN	Tactical Air Navigation
TACC	Tactical Air Control Center
TACP	Tactical Air Control Party
TEMIG	Tactical Electromagnetic Impulse Generator
TEMPER	Tent, Extendable, Modular, Personnel
TFW	Tactical Fighter Wing
TG	Transportation Group
THREATCON	Threat Condition
TIC	Troops-in-contact
TOC	Tactical Operations Center
TOT	Time On Target
TOW	Tube-launched Optically tracked, Wire Guided (missile)
TP	Target Practice
TP-T	Target Practice-Tracer
TS	Top Secret
TTP	Tactics Techniques and Procedures
TTR	Target Tracking Radar
UARRSI	Universal Aerial Refueling Receptacle Slipway Installation

UN	United Nations
UNITAF	Unified Task Force
UNPA	United Nations Protected Area
UNPROFOR	United Nations Protection Force
UNSCR	United Nations Security Council Resolution
UTM	Universal Traverse Mercator
USA	United States Army
USAF	United States Air Force
USAFSS	United State Air Force Security Service
USCINCLANT	Commander in Chief, Atlantic
USMC	United States Marine Corps
USN	United States Navy
USO	United Services Organizations
US SOCOM	United States Special Operations Command
SOUTHCOM	Southern Command
VADM	Vice Admiral (rank)
VAQ	Visiting Airmen Quarters
VDC	Volts Direct Current
VHF	Very High Frequency
VHS	Video Home System
VNAF	Vietnamese Air Force
VR	Visual Reconnaissance (area)
WOC	Wing Operations Center
WP	White Phosphorus

REFERENCES

Afkhami, Gholam Reza. *The life and times of the Shah*. Berkeley, CA: University of California Press, 2009.

Air Force Studies and Analysis Agency. "'Battle of Khafji' Air Power Effectiveness In The Desert." *Small Wars Journal*. I (U) (July 1996):1–171.

Ballard, Jack S. *The Development and Employment of Fixed-Wing Gunships: 1962-1972*. Washington, DC: Office of Air Force History, 1982.

Bolger, Daniel P. "Special Operations and the Grenada Campaign," *The US Army War College Quarterly: Parameters* 18, no. 1 (December 1988): 49–61.

Bowden, Mark. *Black Hawk Down*. New York, NY: Atlantic Monthly Press, 1999.

Carney, John. *No Room for Error the Covert Operations of America's Special Tactics Units from Iran to Afghanistan*. New York, NY: Ballantine Books, 2002.

Clancy, Tom, Carl Stiner, and Tony Koltz. *Shadow Warriors: Inside the Special Forces*. New York, NY: Berkley Books, 2003.

Cole, Ronald. *Operation Just Cause, The Planning and Execution of Joint Operations in Panama, February 1988-January 1990*. Washington, DC: Joint History Office, Office of the Chairman of the Joint Chiefs of Staff, 1995.

Couvillon, Michael J. *Grenada Grinder: the Complete Story of AC-130H Spectre in Operation Urgent Fury*. Marietta, GA: Deeds Publishing, 2011.

Gordon, Michael R. "U.S. Officers Were Divided on Somali Raid." *The New York Times*, May 13, 1994. https://www.nytimes.com/1994/05/13/world/us-officers-were-divided-on-somali-raid.html.

Jones, Kenneth J. *The Enemy Within: Casting Out Panama's Demon*, El Dorado, Panama: Focus Publications, 1990.

Kissling, Herbert. *An Air Commando and Special operations Chronology, 1961-1991*. Hurlburt, FL: First Special Operations Wing, Air Force Special Operations Command, United States Air Force, 1991.

Kyle, James and John R. Eidson. *The Guts to Try: the Untold Story of the Iran Hostage Rescue Mission by the on-Scene Desert Commander*. New York, NY: Orion Books, 1990.

Lawrence, James D. *Airman's Odyssey: An Air Force Special Operator's Incredible Journey*. Marietta, GA: Deeds Publishing, 2013.

Lenahan, Rod. *Crippled Eagle, A historical Perspective of U.S. Special Operations 1976-1996*. Charleston, SC: Narwhal Press, 1998.

Milani, Abbas. *The Persian Sphinx: Amir Abbas Hoveyda and the Riddle of the Iranian Revolution*. Washington, DC: Mage Publishers, 2001.

Milani, Abbas. *The Shah*. New York, NY: Palgrave Macmillan, 2011.

Owen, Robert. *Deliberate Force: A Case Study in Effective Air Campaigning*. Maxwell Airforce Base, AL: Air University Press, 2000.

Pickering, Thomas R. and Paul F. Gorman "News Briefing on Intelligence Information on External Support of the Guerrillas in El Salvador." Washington, DC: Released by the Department of State and the Department of Defense, August 1984.

Raugh, Harold E. Jr. *Operation Joint Endeavor, V Corps in Bosnia-Herzegovina 1995-1996, An Oral History*. Ft. Leavenworth, KS: Combat Studies Institute press, 2010.

Reynolds, Nicholas E. *Just Cause: Marine Operations In Panama, 1988-1990*. Washington, DC: History and Museums Division, Headquarters US Marine Corps, 1996.

Risen, James. "Secrets of History: The C.I.A. in Iran—A Special Report.; How a Plot Convulsed Iran in '53 (and in '79)." *The New York Times*. The New York Times Company, 2000.

Russell, Lee E. and Albert M. Mendez. *Grenada, 1983*. London: Osprey Publishing, 1985.

Capt Sims, William F. *Somalia Diary*. San Antonio, TX: Burke Publishing Co., 1999.

Spector, Ronald H. *US Marines in Grenada 1983*. Washington, DC: History and Museums Division Headquarters, US Marine Corps, 1987.

Stewart, Richard W. *Operation Urgent Fury: The Invasion of Grenada, October 1983*. Washington, DC: US Government Printing Office, 2008. https://history.army.mil/html/books/grenada/index.html.

Stewart, Richard W. *The United States Army in Somalia, 1992-1994*. Washington, DC: Government Publishing Office, 2003. https://history.army.mil/html/books/070/70-81-1/index.html.

History of the 1st Special Operations Wing, Hurlburt Field Florida 1 Jan-31 Dec 1991, Volume V supporting Documents SD117

Walter S. Poole, *The Effort to Save Somalia, August 1992-March 1994* (Washington, DC: Joint History Office, Office of the Chairman of the Joint Chiefs of Staff, 2005), 6.

Westermeyer, Paul. "US Marines in the Battle of Khafji." Marines, 2008. https://www.marines.mil/Portals/1/Publications/U.S.%20Marines%20in%20Battle%20Al-Khafji%20%20PCN%20106000400_1.pdf.

Wilder, Elizabeth Ann. "The Graneda Revolution." The Grenada Revolution Online, 2001. https://www.thegrenadarevolutiononline.com.

Yates, Lawrence A. *The US Military Intervention in Panama: Origins, Planning and Crisis Management June 1987-December 1989*. Washington, DC: US Army Center of

Military History, 2008. https://history.army.mil/html/books/just_cause/CMH_55-1-1_Just_%20Cause_opt.pdf.

Zonis, Marvin. *Majestic Failure: The Fall of the Shah*. Chicago, IL: University of Chicago Press, 1991.

Tactical Air Command Formal Flying and Related Training Publication, student text, USAF Operational Training Course AC-130H Weapons Mechanics, Department of the Air Force

History of the Second Air Division, USAF, 1 July 1983-31 December 1983, (all extracts are unclassified), 125

INDEX